DISCARD

AFRICAN AMERICAN LAWMEN, 1867–1877

VOLUME I

The first reading of the Emancipation Proclamation before the cabinet / painted by F.B. Carpenter ; engraved by A.H. Ritchie.

AFRICAN AMERICAN LAWMEN, 1867–1877

VOLUME I

LIEVIN KAMBAMBA MBOMA

NASHVILLE, TN

FRONT COVER IMAGE:
Library of Congress Prints and Photographs Division Washington, D.C. 20540 USA
http://hdl.loc.gov/loc.pnp/pp.print
Library of Congress Control Number
98501907
No known restrictions on publication.
1 print : lithograph ; 28.6 x 37.7 cm (sheet) | Group portrait of African American legislators: Robert C. De Large, Jefferson H. Long, H.R. Revels, Benj. S. Turner, Josiah T. Walls, Joseph H. Rainy [i.e., Rainey], and R. Brown Elliot.
Original Format
photo, print, drawing
LCCN Permalink
https://lccn.loc.gov/98501907

BACK COVER IMAGE:
Title: The first reading of the Emancipation Proclamation before the cabinet / painted by F.B. Carpenter ; engraved by A.H. Ritchie.
Creator(s): Ritchie, Alexander Hay, 1822-1895, engraver
Related Names:
Carpenter, F. B. (Francis Bicknell), 1830-1900 , artist
Date Created/Published: c1866.
Medium: 1 print : mezzotint.
Summary: Print shows a reenactment of Abraham Lincoln signing the Emancipation Proclamation on July 22, 1862, painted by Francis B. Carpenter at the White House in 1864. Depicted, from left to right are: Edwin M. Stanton, Secretary of War, Salmon P. Chase, Secretary of the Treasury, President Lincoln, Gideon Welles, Secretary of the Navy, Caleb B. Smith, Secretary of the Interior, William H. Seward, Secretary of State, Montgomery Blair, Postmaster General, and Edward Bates, Attorney General. Simon Cameron and Andrew Jackson are featured as paintings.
Reproduction Number: LC-DIG-pga-02502 (digital file from original print)
LC-USZ62-2070 (b&w film copy neg.)
Rights Advisory: No known restrictions on publication.
Call Number: PGA - Ritchie (A.H.)--First reading ... (E size) [P&P]
Repository: Library of Congress Prints and Photographs Division Washington, D.C. 20540 USA http://hdl.loc.gov/loc.pnp/pp.print

Contents

Acknowledgments

Data for a book are always gathered by the researcher alone, but for the completion of this design, I received support from various people. From the beginning to the final draft of this book, I had tremendous support and constructive criticism from many professors, archivists, and librarians, including family friends. Similarly, editors also provided much guidance and counsel to help make this book possible. Without the contributions of the people listed above, I would have faced numerous challenges to complete the final draft of this manuscript. With the assistance of professors and editors, many obstacles, which would have increased the difficulties of piecing together this book, were diminished.

Among editors and proofreaders, I am grateful for Michael Kiggins, who was the senior editor for this work. As an English professor at Nashville State Community College, he devoted his time and energy line-editing this manuscript. His suggestions and guidance were quite helpful. In addition to Professor Kiggins, I credit history professor Ramona Shelton of Motlow College for line-editing the manuscript. Her contributions are worth noting. With respect to the proofreaders, I credit Kelly Siro, a librarian at the Nashville City Archives, and Megan Sheridan, a librarian at the Nashville Southeast Branch, for proofreading the manuscript. The input of these two proofreaders has also been considerable. As librarians with a background in academia, their contributions were valuable.

Of the professors who helped to guide my thoughts, I would especially like to credit the following individuals: Professors Marvin, Joel Dark, Kenneth J. Peak, Adebayo Oyebade, Pippa Galloway, and Michael Montgomery.

Professor Michael Montgomery made a significant impact upon in this work. He proofread the manuscript and gave me impeccable suggestions.

With respect to archivists, at Tennessee State Archives, Dr. Tom Kanon provided me with illuminating support, such as the analysis of data collected for the completion of the manuscript. He also read the first draft, providing salient suggestions and constructive criticism. Similarly, he shared with me his writing experience for his own book.

From the same organization, Mr. Trent Hanner, Kevin Cason, and Allison Griffey, the Reference Librarians, and Darla Brock, the Archivist at the Tennessee State Library, made important contributions during the collection of data for the completion of this book. They advised me to consult the various documents, including city directories, so I could collect credible and authoritative facts on the subject under examination. They were always there when I needed them whenever I visited the Tennessee State Archives.

I must also acknowledge Delisa Harris, a reference librarian at Fisk University, for furnishing me documentations on James Carroll Napier. In Tennessee, I am grateful to have had the help of Vanderbilt University, Fisk University, Tennessee State University, Tennessee State Archives, and the librarians of the Davidson County Archives for providing access to authoritative primary documents for this research.

In Washington, D.C., I would acknowledge the contributions I received from Valerie Haeder, Reference Librarian, Serials Division at the Library of Congress, Arlene Balkansky, Reference Specialist, Serial Government Publications Division, and Jonathan Eaker, Reference Librarian in the Prints & Photographs Division at the Library of Congress. The listed librarians rendered me unconditional support while I was conducting my research on African American lawmen in the city of Washington. Reference Librarian Jonathan Eaker assisted me with the selection of the photograph, which I used for the cover of the book.

As for other institutions of knowledge, I am grateful for the support I received from the Edmondson Pike Librarians. Additionally, I must thank Kathryn Hall for her technical support in the final draft. At the Southeast Nashville Library, I am thankful to all the librarians, especially Greg Hall, Megan Sheridan, C. Wesley, and Alma Pearson, for helping with my technical difficulties. Also, I must acknowledge the input of John Cherry, a librarian and media technician at the Southeast campus of Nashville State Community College, who assisted me in creating this manuscript.

In addition to the previously mentioned people, I am grateful to my family and those who gave me moral support while I conducted my research. I am thankful to Miah Ernest, Guy Muhire Musana, Justin Durunna, Robert Pullen, Sallue Kromah, and Luseni B. Kromah for their support, encouragement, and guidance. They were good listeners whenever I shared my research process with them.

Preface

The inclusion of African Americans in law enforcement has not been thoroughly investigated. While there are many documents relating to the inclusion of African Americans in law enforcement, the data regarding their employment in this field have always been limited. While I majored in criminal justice, little attention was paid to African American lawmen. To illustrate the dearth of this scholarship, the inclusion of African Americans as correctional officers during the period under investigation was not even discussed in assigned readings. Furthermore, previous judicial duties performed by African Americans during Reconstruction were virtually ignored. Regulator positions held by African Americans during the same period were not discussed. Moreover, the election of African Americans as mayors was not even documented. Because of these gaps, I felt compelled to investigate whether people of the African race made any contributions to law enforcement during Reconstruction.

The analysis on African American lawmen was not done in isolation. When I finished my work on *The Employment of African Americans in Law Enforcement, 1803–1865*, data revealed that African descendants were entrusted with minor law enforcement responsibilities. Likely, they were also empowered with military police duties during the Civil War. After these discoveries, I decided to explore whether African Americans served as lawmen during Reconstruction.

Upon starting this investigation, I consulted Professor Marvin Dulaney's book, titled *Black Police in America*, which helped to shape my views. From there, I decided to conduct an in-depth study on African American lawmen during Reconstruction. In addition to the work of Professor Dulaney, many police and Americans historians, from time to time, mention law enforcement positions held by African Americans in their academic works.

Just like Professor Dulaney, historian Dennis Charles Rousey collected and analyzed important data on the employment of African Americans in the police force in the city of New Orleans during Reconstruction. Similarly, Howard N. Rabinowitz documented salient records on African Americans who served as law enforcement officers after the Civil War. Moreover, Eric Anderson collected and presented these facts in his book on African American law enforcement officers in North Carolina. In Mississippi, Buford Satcher and Vernon Wharton collected and presented factual data on African Americans who served in law enforcement in the period under examination. The accounts of African American lawmen in Florida were also collected by Professor Canter Brown in 1998. In his book—*Florida's Black Public Officials, 1867–1924*—Brown documented the various law enforcement positions held by African Americans. In Virginia, Professor Luther Porter Jackson wrote an outstanding monograph on African American officeholders in that state. They served as justices of the peace, policemen, constables, and board of managers. His work contains undeniable facts on the employment of African American lawmen.

Leading American historians such as Professor Eric Foner, Richard White, and Allen C. Guelzo have also presented facts on the reconstruction of the Southern states after the Civil War. Even though these authors employ the term *reconstruction* as a national project, there is little data indicating that this phenomenon was enforced in other states which were not subject to the policies and enforcement of that project. Regardless of their approaches on the study of Reconstruction, Professor Foner's work remains prominent in American history. His work has been quoted by many scholars with concentration on the reconstruction of the Southern states. Foner documented vividly the inclusion of African Americans in American politics during Reconstruction. Likewise, he noted the shaping of the United States by the founding fathers. He stressed the re-emergence of the United States as one nation for all. Last, Professor Allen C. Guelzo has also contributed to academia with respect to the Reconstruction period.

In addition to the work of scholars, African American Reconstruction officials made major contributions on political and law enforcement literature regarding their own people. For an example, in 1888 an African American Reconstruction official named John Wallace wrote *Carpetbag Rule in Florida*. In his book, Wallace discussed law enforcement positions held by African Americans in Florida. Wallace served as a military man in the Second United States Colored Troops for two years and six months. After the war, in 1868, during the Constitutional Convention, he served as a messenger. In the same year, he was elected constable in Leon County. He was also elected twice as a member of the Texas lower house and served two terms in the Texas Senate.[1]

In Mississippi, John Roy Lynch, also an African American who served as a federal regulator, authored the book titled *The Facts of Reconstruction*. Lynch clarified many discrepancies, noting that African Americans were a dominant power in the local government in his state. He also listed law enforcement positions held by African Americans in Mississippi. He recorded important data on high-ranking African American officers in the state and federal levels.[2] Another African American author and Reconstruction official who deserves credit is Mifflin Wister Gibbs. In his book, *Shadow and Light*, Gibbs discussed the progress of his people. He listed the names of many African Americans who served at the state and federal level. Additionally, he noted positions which he held during the Reconstruction period. He is the first ever African American elected as municipal judge.[3]

Moreover, Frederick Douglass also recorded important information on law enforcement duties performed by African Americans in addition to military and political endeavors. He served as United States Marshal.[4] John Mercer Langston wrote an important book about his life, as well as his contributions in American politics. He recorded law enforcement titles which he held during his career. Moreover, he discussed his appointment as sanitary regulator in Washington, D.C.[5] William J. Simmons and Henry McNeal Turner, both Reconstruction African American religious leaders, documented valuable data on prominent African American officials. The work of these two authors remains prominent in the literature about African Americans. In their book, the names of African Americans elected or appointed officials were recorded.

In addition to the previously discussed African American Reconstruction officials, Booker T. Washington documented important facts about political and law enforcement progress made by people of African descent during the period under analysis.[6] In addition to Washington, the works of Carter G. Woodson, the founder of African History Month, were consulted from time to time. Woodson recorded data on the political, religious, and governmental duties performed by African Americans during the Reconstruction era.[7] His works published by the Association for the Study of Negro Life and History stand prominent in African political literature. W.E.B. Du Bois also wrote a well-documented book on the inclusion of African Americans as government officers during Reconstruction. Frank Lincoln Mather also made an important contribution in the literature of African Americans, acknowledging the names of African Americans who served in the government and in private industries.

Like Mather, American writers such as Charles Nordhoff (1876) and Edward King (1875) revealed major contribution data on the employment of African Americans in law enforcement in the many states they visited. The works of these two writers have been referenced by many historians. Local historians in Southern states have also recorded significant materials on the inclusion of African Americans as government officials at each level (local, county, state, and federal) during Reconstruction.

Like Nordhoff and King in Mississippi, Forrest Cooper, in *Reconstruction in Scott County*, mentioned the names of a few African Americans who performed law enforcement duties. Similarly, Julia Kendall, another Mississippi Reconstruction writer, documented the law enforcement titles African Americans held in Lafayette County. F.Z. Browne recorded pertinent information on African Americans who served as law enforcement officers in Oktibbeha County during Reconstruction. The accounts of these writers revealed authoritative information regarding law enforcement and the political and social aspects of African Americans during the period which they investigated.

In addition to the work of scholars, in the city directories of states subjected to Reconstruction policies, the names of African American lawmen were listed. In these directories, they were either identified as "colored," "Col'd," or by an asterisk. In Florida, sometimes they were recorded as Africans. As in the states under Reconstruction, in Washington, D.C., and the state of Indiana, African Americans were also identified as "colored" in the city directory. In the United States census organized by the Ancestry.com, law enforcement positions held by African Americans were also recorded. The city directories and the United States census remain the most authoritative documents where data on African American lawmen can be collected.

This current study examines the inclusion of African Americans in law enforcement in each state subjected to Reconstruction. In addition, law enforcement positions held by African Americans in states not subjected to these policies were also recorded. Contrary to the studies conducted by other writers, I explored the inclusion of African Americans in all levels of criminal justice, highlighting not just their appointment to police departments, but also their involvement in the courts and correctional systems. Furthermore, regulatory duties performed by people of the same race were investigated and recorded. This book also examines the Fourteenth Amendment enacted by the United States Congress for the enfranchisement of African Americans and their inclusion in the American body politic.

Notes

1. John Wallace, *Carpetbag Rule in Florida: The Inside Workings of the Reconstruction of Civil Government in Florida after the Close of the Civil War.* Da Costa Printing and Publishing House, 1888, p. 3. Wallace was born in North Carolina as slave. In 1862, he escaped from bondage to General Burnside. Like other African slaves, on August 14, 1863 he enlisted in the Second United States Colored Troops. He served as a soldier for two and a half years. During the Constitutional Convention of 1868, he was appointed messenger of that institution. In 1868, he was appointed as constable in Leon County, Texas. In addition to his law enforcement position, he was elected twice as member of the Texas lower house as well as member of the Senate for the same number of terms.

2. See John Roy Lynch, *The Facts of Reconstruction.* Neale Publishing Company, 1913. Lynch was a Mississippi Congressman. In 1884, he served also as Chairman of the Republican National Convention. He was appointed Fourth Auditor of the United States Treasury, p. 5.

3. Mifflin Wistar Gibbs, *Shadow and Light: An Autobiography with Reminiscences of the Last and Present Century*. W.W. Gibbs, 1902.

4. Frederick Douglass, *Life and Times of Frederick Douglass. Written by Himself, His Early Life as a Slave, His Escape from Bondage, and His Complete History to the Present Time*. Hartford, Conn.: Park Publishing, 1882.

5. John Mercer Langston, *From the Virginia Plantation to the National Capital; Or, The First and Only Negro Representative in Congress from the Old Dominion*. American Publishing Company, 1894.

6. Booker T. Washington, *The Story of the Negro: The Rise of the Race from Slavery, vol. 1*. Associated Press, 1909.

7. Carter Godwin Woodson, *The History of the Negro Church*. Associated Publishers, 1921.

Introduction

The inclusion of African Americans in law enforcement from 1867 to 1877 has been explored by many scholars and writers such as Professor Dulaney, and historians James Wilford Garner, Vernon Wharton, and Buford Satcher. These authors discussed data on African Americans who served in law enforcement as policemen, justices of the peace, coroners, constables, and on boards of supervisors. Like scholars listed above, Professor Dennis C. Rousey authoritatively elucidated how African Americans enjoyed the privilege of becoming lawmen in Southern States during the reconstruction period.[1] He also investigated the policing of New Orleans from 1805 to 1889.[2] Like the abovementioned authors, James Wilford Garner noted the inclusion of African Americans in law enforcement agencies in Mississippi.[3] A similar account on the employment of African Americans as lawmen was discussed by Ella Lonn in Louisiana. Lonn articulated without constraint the behavior of black police toward white people.[4] Additionally, American historians and scholars of political science have collected pertinent data on African American lawmen during the Reconstruction period.

Contrary to the work of authors listed above, this current study examines their employment in the American criminal justice system: the police, courts, and correctional institutions. Furthermore, the book discusses the elections of African Americans as mayors and their appointment as regulatory agents in local, state, and federal levels. Next, this work explores the employment of African American as lawmen under the military government enforced in the seceded states under the Congressional Act of 1867 and during their full inclusion after the ratification of the 15th Amendment of the United States Constitution. In this period, African Americans were employed in law enforcement in accordance with local, county, and state laws. Likely, as American citizens, their inclusion as lawmen followed state and national constitutional norms.

For the completion of this work, data on African American lawmen were collected from various city directories recorded on Ancestry.com. In city directories of many Southern states, the names of African American policemen and other law enforcement officers were listed. In Tennessee, I consulted the city directories of Chattanooga, Memphis, and Knoxville gathered at the State Archives. In addition to these directories, evidence indicating that African Americans served in law enforcement was documented in the Collections of the Mississippi Historical Society. Furthermore, I collected data from Reconstruction-era books written by authors such as John Rode Ficklen and Pierce Butler (1911), John Roy Lynch (1913), James Wilford Garner (1902), and William Watson Davis (1913). Moreover, the work of John Schreiner Reynolds—*Reconstruction in South Carolina, 1865–1877*—was consulted.

During the Reconstruction period, the authors examined the many titles which African Americans held as law enforcement such as sheriff, constable, magistrate, alderman, coroner, justice of the peace, county supervisor, superintendent of education, and commissioner. At the federal level, the positions held by African Americans were noted. The policy of President Grant and President Johnson regarding the appointment of African Americans in the federal law enforcement was briefly mentioned.

Notes

1. Dennis C. Rousey, *Black Policemen in New Orleans during Reconstruction*, 1987, *The Historian*, vol. 49, no. 2.

2. Dennis C. Rousey, *Policing the Southern City: New Orleans, 1805–1889*. Louisiana State University Press, Baton Rouge, 1996.

3. James W. Garner, *Reconstruction in Mississippi*. New York, London. The Macmillan Company, 1901.

4. Ella Lonn, *Reconstruction in Louisiana: After 1868*. New York, London. G.P. Putnam's Sons, 1918.

Chapter 1

Constitutional Amendments
and Inclusive Law Enforcement Policies

The inclusion of African Americans as lawmen during Reconstruction cannot be examined without tackling policies advocated by Union lawmakers, as well as President Lincoln and Andrew Johnson.[1] Also, the analysis of this topic cannot be completed without reference to the constitutional amendments advocated by radical legislators and ratified by the states of the Union and formerly rebellious states during the period under exploration. The amendments ratified during Reconstruction eliminated planned barriers for the exclusion of African descendants in American politics. With the cementing of constitutional amendments, African Americans were equal to their white counterparts to some extent. Thereafter, they became politically active in all levels of the government. Similarly, they were privileged with all the rights and responsibilities as observed in the American Constitution. Furthermore, they became active participants in American politics, as opposed to being mere spectators like they were before the Civil War and during the Civil War.

As with the three amendments to the United States Constitution, various pieces of legislation enacted by Congress had also an impact on the employment of African Americans as legislators at local and state levels. This is the case of the Reconstruction Act of 1867 elaborated by Congress for the inclusive political measures in the rebellious states. Before the enactment of the Reconstruction Act of 1867, radical congressmen passed the Civil Rights Act of 1866 for the protection of the newly freedmen. The Civil Rights Act also afforded freemen citizens of the United States with the same rights and privileges as their white counterparts.[2] Even though radical congressmen passed the Civil

Rights Act and the Thirteenth Amendment, seceded states were not restored into the Union. Therefore, a legal process was needed for the re-admission of those states into the Union. For a better understanding, it is essential to give a brief history of the policy of Reconstruction of Presidents Lincoln and Johnson.

Lincoln and Johnson's Reconstruction Policy

In 1861, when the prospect of war became imminent, Present Lincoln did not believe it was happening, as noted by George W. Julian. Likely, his cabinet members did not want to challenge the seceded states militarily. On April 10, 1861, Secretary of State William H. Seward wrote an official letter to Charles Francis Adams expressing the president's view. In the letter, Secretary of State William Seward noted that,

> the president would not be disposed to reject a cardinal dogma of this (the Secessionists), namely, that the Federal Government could not reduce the Seceding states to obedient by conquest, even though he was disposed to question that proposition. But in fact, the president willingly accepts it as true. Only an imperial and despotic Government could subjugate thoroughly disaffected and insurrectionary members of the state.... The president on the one hand, will not suffer the Federal authority to fall into abeyance, nor will he, or the other hand, aggravate existing evils by attempts at coercion, which must assure the direct form of war against any of the revolutionary states.[3]

This letter reveals the true intention of the president regarding his views on the war and rebellious states. President Lincoln preferred reconciliation or compromise rather than the use of force. Charles F. Adams was the United States minister to the United Kingdom. It is plausible to note that the letter of Secretary Seward to Minister Adams was a diplomatic way to indicate to the British government and people that the United States' actions against the seceded states were the right course of action.

Secretary of Treasury Salmon P. Chase held the same view as President Lincoln. According to Julian, Secretary Chase did not favor a policy of coercion. He believed that if rebellious states seceded peacefully, then they would return soon.[4] It is sound to note that Chase did not believe that the Southern states were serious in in their plans. Militarily, the federal government was not prepared for an armed conflict at the time.

At the legislative level, George Julian writes that the purpose of the war was to conquer or subjugate the Southern states. Likely, the war was not conducted for the overthrow of slavery. According to him, the Civil War was executed for the defense of the Constitution and the preservation of the Union.[5] The statements of both houses were also reconciliatory. These lawmakers did not want to alienate members of the Confederate government or to treat them as enemies for the sake of the Union. Regarding the overthrow of their established institution, it is clear slavery was not a subject of discussion. That means, their rights to continue the institution of slavery were undeniable. Again, members of both houses advocated a compromise rather than recourse to war.

From the beginning of the war, President Lincoln articulated honestly that Southern states should denounce the war and rejoin the Union. His policy was termed as liberal by lawmakers. As an illustration of this, Congressman James Blaine noted that "President Lincoln was anxious from the beginning of the war to re-establish civil government in any and every of the Confederate states."[6] President Lincoln was consistent regarding his liberal approach. For example, when General Fremont made his proclamation emancipating African slaves, President Lincoln did not hesitate to abolish it. There are able examples indicating the appeasement policy of President Lincoln. With respect to the integrity of the Union, President Lincoln clarified his reconciliatory spirit toward the seceded states: "if I could save the Union without freeing any slaves, I would do it; if I could save it by freeing all the slaves, I would do it; and if I could save it by freeing some and leaving others alone, I would do that."[7]

Contrary to his view, President Jefferson Davis articulated clearly that the seceded states were not part of the United States. Thus, they were not under any obligations of its Constitution. The claims of

President Davis were not taken into consideration by President Lincoln. By following his views and policy, in 1862, President Lincoln re-organized the civil government in Louisiana after the defeat of the rebel fortifications on the Lower Mississippi and Forts Jackson and Philip in Louisiana. In Louisiana, loyal inhabitants supported the causes of the Union, and they rejected secession in counties inhabited by them. In the same state, James Gillespie Blaine writes that on the third of December 1862, Benjamin F. Flanders and Michael Hahn, both natives of Louisiana were permitted to be representatives in Congress.[8] After the Thirty-Seventh Congress of February 9, 1863, Flanders and Hahn sat as members of the United States Congress.

Because of this, it is worth noting that President Lincoln advocated the admission of the former seceded states without conditions. He championed liberal and moderate policy toward former officials of the Confederate government.[9] In 1864, President Lincoln utilized the same policy for the reconstruction process in Alabama, as noted by William Archibald Dunning. Moreover, he also articulated that Lincoln's policy was observed later by President Johnson for the same purpose.[10] Like Dunning, Richard Taylor elucidated that President Johnson's aim was to restore the Union by invoking the United States Constitution. He went on to note that Johnson followed the policy envisaged by President Lincoln.[11] From the work of Charles Ernest Chadsey, data indicate that President Lincoln did not expect pre-conditions before the admission of Confederate states into the Union. In Chadsey's view, "President Lincoln at the beginning of his term in office held the then prevailing belief in the supremacy of the states in all matters not directly under the federal control, and as a matter of course [he] believed that at the cessation of hostility, each state should immediately resume its old relations to the government, [and] its local matters untouched."[12] At the end of the Civil War, President Lincoln preferred speedy restoration with minor trouble during that process. According to Thornton Kirkland Lothrop, President Lincoln wanted to restore each state into the Union separately as the conditions on the ground commanded.[13] Like Lothrop, Secretary William H. Seward noted that President Lincoln did not want to face major hardships, pains, or penalties with respect to the reunification of seceded states into the Union.[14]

The policy of Presidents Lincoln and Andrew Johnson was challenged by radical lawmakers. Even though some moderate lawmakers remained silent, vocal leaders such as Thaddeus Stevens and Charles Sumner were antagonistic to the liberal reconstruction policy advocated by President Lincoln and Andrew Johnson. After Lincoln was assassinated, Johnson applied the same policy, with the inclusion of punitive methods to selective civilians and military officers of the former Confederate government. Like President Lincoln, Johnson preferred a speedy restoration of insurrectionary states. Similarly, he was a firm believer in the preservation of the Union. He rejected the notion of secession, which his Southern brethren cherished. With such conviction, he refused the right of any state to secede from the Union.[15] It is sound to note that President Lincoln feared the disunion of the United States much more than the abolition of slavery. From its foundation, the American people described the United States as a providential land. President George Washington in his farewell advised his fellow Americans to carefully guard and preserve the Union of the whole.[16]

In addition to the conciliatory approach, President Johnson advocated a compromise design. To accomplish that plan, he campaigned for his reconstruction policy in some cities. With such an approach, his followers formed the "National Club" with an aim to disapprove the congressional reconstruction policy. According to Willison Starr Myers, on August 14, 1866, Democrats and Conservatives from various states in the nation were invited to the meeting of the National Club. Like Myers, Richard Taylor stipulates that moderates and influential Republicans were part of the convention organized by the National Club.[17] These members were from the South and the North.

According to Taylor, the object of the convention was to persuade the delegates to request the earlier restoration of the seceded states into the Union. Moreover, the president desired more support from his followers against the policy of the extremists in the Congress. Ex-members of President Lincoln's government attended the convention. During the same event, Senator James Rood Doolittle of Wisconsin was selected as permanent president. Senator Doolittle was one of the Union government officials who rejected the secession. On the right of secession during the Committee of Thirty-three, Senator Doolittle stipulated that "under this Constitution, as originally adopted, and as it now exists, no state has power to withdraw from the jurisdiction of the United States; but this Constitution, and all laws passed in pursuance of its delegated powers, are the supreme law of the land, anything contained in any Constitution, ordinance, or act of any state, to the contrary notwithstanding."[18]

Senator Doolittle was a supporter of President Lincoln during the Civil War, so he continued to embrace the same policy executed by President Johnson with regards to the restoration of Southern states into the Union. At the start of the war, he worked hard getting Republicans and Democrats to support the war effort. He continued to support the war efforts till the end of the military conflict.[19] Regarding his relationship to President Lincoln, William Frederick Doolittle, Louise S. Brown, and Malissa R. Doolittle elucidated that "he was a warm admirer and became a devoted intimate friend."[20] As a lawyer and a senator, he was well equipped with the understanding of legal implications of the reunification of seceded states into the Union. With respect to the reconstruction policy, he sympathized with Presidents Lincoln and Johnson. Accordingly, Harvey M. Harper commented that Senator Doolittle had the same political views as President Lincoln, stressing they worked together during his presidency.[21] According to many writers, Senator Doolittle was an intimate friend of President Lincoln.

After Lincoln's death, Doolittle continued to serve President Johnson. Doolittle became his close advisor during the turbulent Reconstruction period. Regarding the Southern States, he consistently voiced that they were not out of the Union, just as Senator Trumbull did.[22] Senator Doolittle served in many capacities in the federal government. He was on the Foreign Relations, Military, Commerce, and Finance committees, and served as a Chairman of the Committee on Indian Affairs. He was well instructed in constitutional law. Regarding slavery, his view was the same as lawmakers from Southern states, emphasizing that slavery was a local matter and subjected to local laws.[23] It should come as no surprise that during the administration of President Johnson, Senator Doolittle was against the reconstruction policy as advocated by members of the Congress. He was open to the speedy and peaceful restoration formulated by the executive department of the United States government. He believed in the system of qualified suffrage to all classes without regard to color instead of unlimited franchise.[24]

When members of the convention adopted resolutions that were in the interest of the early restoration, President Johnson was happy.[25] From the beginning of his presidency, Andrew Johnson sympathized with Southerners. Perhaps his connections to those states played a significant influence regarding his leniency toward them. However, President Johnson had not been a supporter of secession. He had pleaded with his fellow Southerners to reject secession. According to Frank More, Johnson even appealed to Southern senators to abide by the Constitution and remain in the Union. According to Moore, during his speech before the Senate in 1861, Johnson declared, "I feel proud. I feel that I have struct [sic] treason a blow."[26] Therefore, it is no wonder that he wanted earlier restoration of Southern states into the Union.

Another feature of Reconstruction which put President Johnson and Congress in conflict was the suffrage of newly freed African Americans. President Johnson, like his Southern brethren, did not believe in enfranchising African Americans. He also vetoed the Civil Rights Bill, which permitted the automatic naturalization of African Americans. With such a vision, radical members in Congress spoke out against the policy championed by the president. During the 39th Congress of the United States, Senator Clark lamented passionately about the policy of the president. He stated as follows:

[I]n favor of granting political rights to the negro, Mr. President, the question of the Negro has troubled the nation long. His condition as freeman troubled you. Are you sick, heart-sick of his trouble? And do you inquire when will it end? I will tell you. When you have given him equal rights, equal privileges, and equal security with other citizens; when you have opened the way for him to be a man, then will you have rendered exact justice which can alone insure stability and content. The black man has made too many sacrifices to preserve it and endangered his life too often in its defense to be excluded from it. The Common sentiment of gratitude should open its doors to him, if not political justice and equality.[27]

Like Presidents Lincoln and Johnson, Confederate officials and citizens advocated a swift restoration of the former relationship between former seceded states and the Union.

Confederate Officials and Citizens' Support of Presidential Policy

After the Civil War, Confederate officials, as well as inhabitants from the former rebellious states, requested the readmission of their states into the Union. According to Walter Lynwood Fleming, people in the South requested the repeal of the secession ordinance and the abolition of slavery so that, after convening constitutional conventions, those states would rejoin the Union.[28] Fleming believed that the perception of the inhabitants of the lower South was parallel to that of President Lincoln.

A similar view of quick restoration was championed by General Richard Taylor after his surrender at Meridian, Mississippi. Fleming stated that after he gave up fighting, he counseled the governors of Tennessee, Alabama, and Mississippi to reenter into the Union. Taylor's approach was also supported by General Canby, to whom he surrendered. Like General Canby, many generals, and other officers of the armies of the occupation also held same view.[29] During the Philadelphia Convention, the former Confederate general Richard Taylor was invited by President Lincoln. Taylor was the son of President Zachary Taylor, the 12th president of the United States.

During the Civil War, Richard Taylor had been appointed colonel of the 9th Louisiana Infantry. This regiment was stationed at a camp located on the railway a few miles north of New Orleans. He was also a brother-in-law to President Jefferson Davis. His elder sister was the first wife of the Confederate president. It is unknown whether through merit or family relations he was appointed to the rank of general in the Confederate army.[30] Taylor, in his book, mentioned worries due to his promotion to the rank of general. As he was well-connected to Confederate officials, his appointment was not contested. According to Taylor, he knew many people in both governments, Confederate and Union, due to his father's position as president of the United States. In addition to Confederate officials, some members in the United States Congress were also of the same view.

Members of Congress on Reconciliatory Policy

According to the facts collected from various documents, moderate Republicans and a majority of the Democrats championed the reconciliatory policy of President Andrew Johnson. The Philadelphia Convention is a prime example of such support. Similarly, many of them argued against the notion that seceded states were out of the Union. Based on this, it seems likely that members of Congress did not believe in using a coercive approach against rebellious states. In this case, Congressional members believed in the notion of compromise and reconciliation. In no case were they hostile to the officials of the Confederate government, and it is clear this vision was orchestrated by moderate Republicans, and Northern and Southern Democrats. Contrary to the compromise policy advocated by moderate Republicans and their Democratic allies, Radical Republicans protested such an approach. Like Democrats, General George McClellan believed in the peaceful restoration into the Union of all the seceded states. According to him, rebellious states deserved to be treated as members of the Union after the war. For him, reconciliation was a sound policy for that end. By reading his book, *McClellan's Own Story*, one will note that he sympathized with Southerners. And not only this, but during the War, he was also praised by Confederate militiamen and soldiers.[31]

Radical Republicans

To understand the views of radicals in Congress, it is pertinent to discuss their views from the beginning of the war. Historically, lawmakers identified as radicals during the Civil War and Reconstruction were devoted to the cause of the Union and African Americans before the start of armed conflict. Before the war, Northerners were against the tearing of the Union. With regards to African Americans, abolitionist lawmakers were firmly against the institution of slavery. Additionally, they believed in the protection of African Americans' human rights.

As an example of this, Congressman Thaddeus Stevens was an advocate of equal justice and defended the cause of the enslaved in court. During the Civil War, Congressman Stevens advocated the enlistment of

African Americans in the ranks of the Union to defeat the Confederate states. Similarly, Senator Charles Sumner defended many cases relating to the African race in Massachusetts. As a lawyer, he was always associated with African American civil rights defenders and antislavery agents. In addition to the lawmakers listed above, Senator Benjamin Franklyn Wade held the same views. He and others questioned the validity of the war tactics employed by General McClellan, the Commander of the Army of the Potomac at the time. After the defeat of the Union at the First Battle of Bull Run, or Battle of Manassas, McClellan was removed from the command of the Army of the Potomac by President Lincoln. The service of General McClellan was vilified by many lawmakers. They believed that he was not supportive to the cause of the Union. He was accused of having political ambitions. His war tactics were put into question. As a result, they argued for President Lincoln to remove him from being the commanding chief of the Army during the war.

At the beginning of the war, there is no data indicating that members of Congress had a planned design for the execution, management, or monitoring of the war. For the remediation of such ill-preparation, Senators Wade and Julian proposed the formation of the Joint Committee of War.

The Joint Committee of War

As in the former wars, Americans followed the military folkways of their forefathers. As an historical fact, colonists did not have a standing army or a designed plan for the execution of war. Laymen and militiamen were always called upon to defend the colonies during alarms. Similarly, during the Civil War, the Federal government did not have a standing army to repel the rebellion. Civilians were called throughout Northern states to serve as militiamen, soldiers, seamen, and spies. Confederate states did the same, even though they had many trained military men who had resigned from the United States Army. As noted already, due to the Union's defeat at the First Battle of Bull Run, lawmakers began questioning the ability of General McClellan to execute a fierce strategy against rebels. Hoping to find an answer to this question, the Joint Committee of War was formed.

The history of the Joint Committee of War has been recorded by many historians and authors, including the founder of that organization. According to Congressman George W. Julian, one of the founders and members of the committee, the Joint Select Committee on the Conduct of the War was formed on December 19, 1861. He articulated the committee was composed of three members from the Senate and four members from the House of Representatives. Among the Senators, he listed Benjamin F. Wade of Ohio, Z. Chandler of Michigan, and Andrew Jackson of Tennessee. On the other hand, the House members included John Covode of Pennsylvania, M.F. Odell of New York, D. W. Gooch of Massachusetts, and George Julian of Indiana.[32] The object of the commission was to satisfy the popular demand for a more vigorous prosecution of the war. The Committee was also empowered with instructive features. Members were entrusted with the examination of the movements of the Army and the secrets of the government's policy regarding the execution of the war.[33] This aim changed the magnitude and the approach of the war. Similarly, the status of rebellious states was put into discussion by radical members of Congress. It was also during the special meeting with President Lincoln and members of the Joint Committee of the War that Congressman Thaddeus Stevens revealed his intention on radical Reconstruction.

Congressman Stevens was not part of the founding body of the Committee of the War, but on April 13, 1862, at the meeting of the Committee, Secretary of War Edwin McMaster Stanton, Thaddeus Stevens of the House Ways and Means Committee, Mr. Fessenden of the Senate Finance Committee, and Mr. Wilson and Colonel Blair of the Senate and House Military Committees were invited. At the meeting, Congressman Stevens stated that "he was tired of hearing the Republican Cowards talk about the Constitution; that there was no Constitution any longer as the prosecution of the war was concerned; and that we should strip the rebels of all their rights, and give them a reconstruction on such terms as would end treason forever."[34] His view was applauded by Secretary Stanton. He revealed that his policy was the same as that of Congressman Stevens from the beginning of the war.[35] This was the first radical view on Reconstruction which would be carried during the Johnson administration. That means, Secretary

Stanton and Congressman Stevens had a planned approach on the reconstruction policy pertaining to Southern states even before that period was put into effect. His radicalism on the reconstruction policy can be traced from the special meeting listed above. Congressman Stevens was against the invocation of the Constitution framed by the Founding Fathers of the United States. He did not believe that instrument was fit to protect newly freed African Americans.

Another radical strategy pertaining to the restoration of seceded states into the Union was formulated by Secretary of War Chase. On December 11, 1861, during his interview with Senator Wade and Congressman Ashley, Secretary Chase lamented that any state trying to secede from the United States, or any government involved in hostility against the federal government, would fall into the status of a "Territory" and the federal government would reorganize those territories after the war.[36] He went on to stipulate that the seceded states would not be part of the Union. His policy as noted by General McClellan was applauded by politicians in the North. From the statements of Secretary Chase, it is acceptable to note that the radicals' views were the same as his.

A Constitutional Dilemma

The Civil War was a test to the American Constitution. Confederate officials argued forcefully that President Lincoln did not have a constitutional right to attack Southern states. On the other hand, members of the Union declared that no state was permitted to secede from the Union.

After the war began, the same question remained unanswered. Within Congress, some lawmakers believed that seceded states were still part of the Union. As has already been mentioned, President Lincoln was consistent in noting that the Union was unbreakable. Even though Southern states were under the flag of the Confederate States of America, there existed portions of Tennessee and Louisiana where Union support persisted. In East Tennessee and a few counties in Louisiana, loyal members were at the mercy of the de facto Confederate government. Likely, there was a special case in Tennessee where lawmakers complied with the request of the Union. Governor Andrew Johnson believed that Tennessee was still part of the Union. During his inauguration address as Vice President of the United States, he stated that the State of Tennessee had never been out of the Union. "It is the doctrine of the Federal Constitution that no State can go out of this Union, and moreover, Congress cannot eject a state from this Union. Thank God, Tennessee has never been out of the Union."[37]

It is no wonder, then, that Andrew Johnson was appointed Military Governor of Tennessee by President Lincoln. Even though he was a Southerner, he had been loyal to the Union. When Southern states seceded from the Union, he was the only lawmaker who kept his oath to the United States Constitution among the twenty Senators from the eleven Southern states.[38] According to Congressman James Blaine, Andrew Johnson was born in North Carolina and came from a poor family. He went on to note that his family was despised by the slaveholding class. Regarding his profession in North Carolina, he was a tailor by trade, and he did not learn how to read until he was fifteen.[39]

The ambiguity regarding seceded states with respect to their relationship with the Union was pronounced by Senator Jacob B. Blair on February 8, 1864. He submitted a resolution which indicated that rebellious states were still part of the Union. His resolution reads as follows: "every state which has ever been, is still a state in the Union, and when this rebellion shall have been put down, each of the so-called seceding states will have the same rights, privileges, and immunities under the Constitution as any one of the loyal states."[40] Senator Blair's vision reflects that of Presidents Lincoln and Johnson. From the beginning of the war, Lincoln always called upon his countrymen in the South to rejoin the Union and to surrender their weapons. He was a true and firm believer of the preservation of the Union.

Like President Lincoln, Senator Blair did not believe that these states formed a nation separate from the United States. His view demonstrates that he was not in favor of punitive policy toward belligerent states as radical Senators believed. Contrary to the other rebel states, in Tennessee, United States lawmakers were agreeable to its restoration to the Union. Tennessee had many loyal citizens. In East Tennessee, the secession policy adopted by state government officials was not observed. As a result, they were mistreated due to their attachments to the federal government.

Before the official end of the war, Military Governor Andrew Johnson ordered a convention on January 8, 1865, with the aim of regaining
their relationship with the Union. At the end of the convention, the
amendment of the Constitution such as the abolition of slavery was
adopted on February 22, 1865. Likely, the election of a government and
legislatures was organized on March 4, 1866. On April 3, 1865, the state
government was operational.[41] The restoration of the State of Tennessee was influenced by loyal people of that state. On August 11, 1863,
General Stephen Augustus Hurlburt communicated to President Lincoln that Tennesseans were enthusiastic about the repeal of secession
acts. Likely, they wanted to allow gradual emancipation to Africans and
join the Union. As a result, President Lincoln ordered Military Governor Johnson to organize an election for legislatures. After the election,
elected legislatures would have been empowered to call a constitutional
convention. Due to the flexibility of the citizens of Tennessee, in early
September, the federal Army vacated Chattanooga and Knoxville.[42] As
United States government officials noted above, some moderate Democrats also advocated the same reconciliatory policy.

No Constitutional Precedents

After the War, the Executive and legislative branch of the United States
faced a difficult challenge regarding the admission of former Confederate states into the Union. Authors such as William Archibald Dunning,
Congressman James Gillespie Blaine and Walter Lynwood Fleming
noted the same. Congressman Blaine articulated the obstacles of the
reconstruction process. He pointed out that "no experience of our own
had established precedents; none in other countries afforded even close
analogies."[43] He went on to stipulate that "Civil War and Rebellions
had, it is true, been frequent, but they had been chiefly among peoples
consolidated under one government, ruled in all their affairs, domestic
and external, by one central power."[45] By reading Congressmen Blaine's
statement, it seems clear that he did not support the reconstruction
policy championed by radical lawmakers.

Like other authors, Fleming notes that "there was nothing in the
Constitution to guide the president or Congress, though each sought

to base a policy on that ancient instrument."[45] His statement is logical. Contrary to Fleming, during the political maneuvering of Reconstruction, President Johnson believed that readmission of the Southern states was under the jurisdiction of the executive power which derived from the Constitution. On the other hand, Congress asserted that the United States Constitution entrusted them with the admission of any state into the Union. This conflict was difficult to remedy. As such, President Johnson and members of radical legislatures were at odds regarding the restoration of rebellious states into the Union. Lawmakers and the president could not reconcile the matter in question. Therefore, it makes sense why President Johnson and Congressman Thaddeus Stevens did not have a good rapport throughout this discussion.

The historian Walter Lynwood Fleming makes a similar claim about these challenges. In his book, titled *Civil War and Reconstruction in Alabama*, he stressed that the United States Constitution was silent in the matter of reconstructing the Union after the secession of Southern states. In his view, there was nothing in that high law of the land which could assist lawmakers in resolving this crisis. In his book, Fleming also said that

> there was nothing in the Constitution to guide the President or Congress, though each sought to base a policy on that ancient instrument. Many questions confronted them. Were the states in the Union or out? If in the Union, what rights had they? If out of the Union, were they conquered territories subject to no law but the will of the United States government, or were they United States territory with rights under the Constitution? Must they be reconstructed or restored, and who was to begin the movement—the people of the states, Congress, or the President?[46]

For him, Congress and the President could not agree in their answers to these questions.[47] The questions listed by historian Fleming are pertinent regarding Reconstruction. Since the President of the United States and Congress would not agree to the solution of the matter in question, lawmakers sought a different strategy to overcome their differences. To obtain this end, Congressman Thaddeus Stevens took the lead in constructing a very skillful approach which he and fellow radicals had to support. He understood that they did not have a majority in Congress. Therefore, a sound action was needed to get other members of the Congress onboard. For that reason, he proposed the formation of a committee for the resolution of the difficulties associated with Reconstruction. To him, members of the Joint Committee on Reconstruction were to be entrusted with full power on the administration of the process. Members of the Committee were like the administrators of Reconstruction. Therefore, the executive branch was powerless and could not enforce any policy to the contrary.

The Committee for the Reconstruction

After the passage of this act, rebel states were divided into military districts and subjected to military governors. One of the mandates of the military governors was to enforce the law in their respective states. In addition to this, the protection of all people and the maintenance of public order were also under their jurisdiction. Under these military governments, were they as their white people the conservators of peace? Were they allowed to hold law enforcement duties like their white counterparts in Southern states?

During Reconstruction, similar constitutional benefits were also given to poor whites. This group was always marginalized before the Civil War. Poor whites were considered the second class in the United States in accordance to the philosophy of the Founding Fathers. Many of them were excluded from politics throughout the United States. To illustrate this fact, poor whites were disfranchised constitutionally in many states. Contrary to the vision of the Founding Fathers, lawmakers such as Thaddeus Stevens, Henry Wilson, Charles Summers, James A. Garfield, Benjamin F. Butler, George W. Julian, Lyman Trumbull, Roscoe Conklin, Hannibal Hamlin, and Schuler Colfax did not support that policy.[48] The Founding Fathers established the country with a spirit of compromise, but these lawmakers rejected such political endeavors for the emergence of a new America. According to their views, equal justice, civil rights, and political inclusion were the ingredients of a healthy democratic government. As such, they imposed their will upon other lawmakers to design a new and free America. The enforcement of the constitutional amendments framed by the Radical Republican legislators were well-defined and executed. As Southern states were considered belligerent by Congressman Thaddeus Stevens, the enforcement of the amendments was prone to succeed. Because they seceded from the United States, Congressman Stevens believed that Southern states were subject to punishment. As conditions for their readmission to the Union, those states were forced to accept the terms and conditions set forth for their readmittance.

With respect to this policy, the executive government and the American legislative body did not reconcile. President Lincoln used a policy of appeasement toward the former Confederate states. He believed in the peaceful reunification. According to Charles Ernest Chadsey, President Lincoln supported the reestablishment of immediate relations with the seceded states after the cessation of military conflict.[49] Like President Lincoln, his successor Andrew Johnson advocated the same reconciliatory approach towards Southern states. His attachment to the policy of President Lincoln was also supported by Richard Taylor, a former Confederate senior military officer. Taylor noted the restoration of the seceded states to the Union would be accomplished through the Constitution of the United States.[50] Contrary to Taylor's views, President Johnson wanted a speedy readmission process. After the assassination of President Lincoln, he appointed provisional governors in many Southern states. He also urged his fellow Southerners to call upon state conventions for the same purpose.

In contrast to the policy of Presidents Lincoln and Johnson, Congressman Stevens fiercely rejected the restorations of seceded states under the Constitution of the United States. His opposition was recorded by Richard Taylor. In his book *Destruction and Reconstruction*, Taylor writes that Congressman Stevens said that the Constitution of the United States was worthless.[51] He went on to note that Congressman Stevens believed Southern whites would unite with their brethren Copperheads (Peace Democrats) in the North and control the entire government. Moreover, he argued that Congressman Stevens did not believe in trusting white Southerners with positions of power in the government.[52] From Taylor's account, it is plausible to stipulate that

Congressman Stevens did not have faith in the United States Constitution, which rebellious states invoked for the defense of their secession scheme. He believed in the amendment of the Constitution enacted by Republicans to incapacitate rebel states from engaging in their former traitorous behavior.

Just like Congressman Stevens, other Northern state lawmakers believed the restoration of the seceded states should be subjected to certain requirements. For example, Congressman John Bingham championed the view of Congressman Thaddeus Stevens. This lawmaker proposed a constitutional amendment for the restoration of rebel states into the Union.[53] He supported a reconstruction policy based on the observance of the United States Constitution, as well as the Law of Nations. He maintained a consistent view on his policy. He stated that seceded states had acted in a belligerent fashion, so they should be treated similarly. James Albert Woodburn notes that Congressman Stevens always considered the rebellious states as a belligerent power.[54] According to Stevens' legal theory, as rebel states disunited from the Union, they lost the privileges, immunities, and rights afforded to them by the fundamental laws of the United States. Therefore, they were belligerents and subject to the laws of war and Law of Nations.[55] In this case, he believed that the seceded states were members of a foreign nation separate from the United States. During a speech he delivered before the United States Congress on December 18, 1865, Congressman Stevens stressed the foreignness of the seceded states, continuing as a separate nation. His speech reads as follows:

> to prove that they are and for four years have been out of the Union for all legal purposes, and being now conquered, subject to the absolute disposal of Congress, I will suggest a few ideas and adduce a few authorities. If the so-called "Confederate States of America" were an independent belligerent, and were so acknowledged by the United States and by Europe, or had assumed and maintained an attitude which entitled them to be considered and treated as a belligerent, then, during such time, they were precisely in the condition of a foreign nation with whom we were at war; nor need their independence as a nation be acknowledged by us to produce that effect.[56]

His approach was approved by his Republican counterparts. On the other hand, Democrat lawmakers did not consent that the rebel states had lost their rights under the Constitution. The views of American lawmakers (both Republicans and Democrats) and President Johnson were difficult to reconcile. As a result, President Johnson lost the support of Republican lawmakers for Reconstruction. He was accused of privileging seceded officials with positions of power, so Republicans became suspicious of his intentions. They believed that the president had entrusted rebel states with local control. On the other hand, Radical Republicans advocated the occupation of the South by the Union until they had met the requirements set forth for their readmission to the Union.

Consequently, Stevens consistently argued that Southern states were conquered land and thus subject to the will of the United States Congress for reunification. Accordingly, he emphasized two articles of the United States Constitution for the admission of new states. He pointed out that "new states may be admitted by the Congress into this Union."[57] Furthermore, he argued passionately that "the United States shall guarantee to every state in this Union a republican form of government."[58] To some extent, Stevens' opinion was considered acceptable at the time. President Johnson unwillingly abided by the political thought of Congressmen Stevens regarding the reinclusion of the seceded states into the Union. Therefore, the articles of the United States advocated by Stevens for the readmission of the Confederate states into the Union were solid arguments. In the Southern states after the war, as local institutions were destroyed Union authorities had an obligation to reconstitute them. In this case, as conquerors, they employed draconian methods for the accomplishment of their designs. As a result, two years later, the Southern states were divided into military fiefs or districts.

As has already been noted, President Johnson continued the same Reconstruction policy as President Lincoln. During his administration, he appointed provisional governors for the reorganization of local institutions. After the formation of civil government in many Southern states, local lawmakers enacted legislation which infringed upon the new civil rights of African Americans. In states such as Louisiana, South Carolina, and Virginia, Black Codes were established for the oppression of African Americans.

Similarly, oppressive methods were employed by many citizens toward them, as well as white people who had remained loyal to the Union. As a result, first Carl Schurz and later Ulysses S. Grant were dispatched to the South to investigate the conditions of African Americans. Their investigations produced many pieces of evidence about the abuse of, as well as the intent to reenslave, the newly freed African Americans. Senator Schurz documented that discriminatory laws had been enacted in the Southern states against African Americans. He recorded tangible evidence that could not be refuted regarding the civil rights of African Americans.

To avoid this fate, on January 5, 1866, Senator Trumbull introduced the civil rights bill for the protection of every American citizen.[59] A week later, Trumbull's bill was taken into consideration by members of the Senate. The first Civil Rights bill introduced by Senator Trumbull read as follows:

> there should be no discrimination in Civil Rights on account of color, race, or previous condition of slavery; but the inhabitants of every race and color, should have the same right to make and enforce contracts, to sue, be parties and give evidence, to inherit, purchase, lease, sell, hold, and convey real and personal property, and to full and equal benefit of all laws and proceedings for the security of person and properties, and to none other, any law, statute, ordinance, regulation, or custom, to the contrary notwithstanding.[60]

As the first section of the Civil Rights Bill did not include African Americans, Senator Trumbull modified the language of the bill. On June 29, 1866, the senator amended the first section of the bill and declared that all people of African descent born in the United States should be citizens. But his fellow lawmakers rejected his reasoning.

For example, Senator Van Winkle of West Virginia refused to recognize African descendants in the United States as citizens. Consequently, Senator Trumbull removed the term "African descendant." After the modification of the language used in the initial bill, the first section of the bill read as follows: "all persons born in the United States, and not subject to any foreign power, are hereby declared to be citizens of the United States, without distinction of color."[61] The removal of the term "African descendant" was satisfactory to the United States lawmakers, and the bill became law. This bill was then titled, "An Act to Protect all Persons in the United States in Their Civil Rights and Furnish the Means of Their Vindication."[62]

Because the Civil Rights Act was not part of the United States Constitution, it was in danger of being repealed by another president. Therefore, Radical Republican lawmakers framed the Fourteenth Amendment to cement the language of the Civil Rights Act in the Constitution of the United States. The passage of the Fourteenth Amendment in 1868 was a success for Republicans. Accordingly, Congressman James Garfield rejoiced when the Fourteenth Amendment became a part of the law of the land. He declared, "he was glad to see that the civil rights law protected every American citizen." He went on to note that:

> the Civil Rights Bill is now a part of the law of the land. But every gentleman knows it will cease to be a part of the law of the land whenever the sad moment arrives when that gentleman's party [Democrats] comes into power. It is precisely for that reason that we propose to lift that great and good law above the reach of political strife, beyond the reach of the plots and machinations of any party, and fix it in the severe sky, in the eternal firmament of the Constitution, where no storm of passion can shake it, and no cloud can obscure it.[63]

The prophetic language of Congressman Garfield is unquestionable. Constitutionally, the Fourteenth Amendment became and has remained one of the pillars of the American legal system. After the ratification of the Fourteenth Amendment, lawmakers reached a consensus and framed the 15th Amendment, which enfranchised African Americans. After the ratification of the 15th Amendment in 1870, African Americans became full citizens of the United States.

During the Civil War, members of the United States Congress voted for an act that would allow the enlistment of Africans (both free and enslaved) in the United States Army. Like the members of the United

States Congress, in 1863 President Lincoln ordered a proclamation with the object of enlisting African Americans in the ranks of Union soldiers. Even though the proclamation's aim was to include African slaves in the army, the strategy which was utilized to satisfy that design was different. To explain, the president used punitive measures against slave owners by liberating their bondsmen. As such, they were declared to be freedmen. The president did not have any constitutional power to end slavery in the United States. For that reason, his proclamation was directed to the states which had seceded from the United States. On the other hand, in the states where the proclamation was not enforced, slavery was not abolished.[64]

In the states subjected to President Lincoln's proclamation, free African Americans and slaves were denied the rights granted to whites. James Ford Rhodes, in *History of the United States*, also noted that freed bondsmen were subjected to severe penalty and denial of certain rights by Southern legislatures.[65] Similar discriminatory methods were also enforced in Texas. Charles William Ramsdell writes, "there was a disposition in some of the remote districts to keep the Negroes in bondage and to treat with cruelty those who endeavored to exercise their freedom."[66] The accounts of these writers reveal the reasons why the Civil Rights Bill of 1866 was enacted.

As noted above, President Lincoln was not constitutionally permitted to free the enslaved. His order was not enforced in the states under the Union flag. In a like manner, African Americans in the South held the same status as they had before the war and the Emancipation Proclamation. In 1865, members of the United States Congress amended the Constitution to abolish the institution of slavery. From then on, slavery became illegal in the United States. The Thirteenth Amendment of the United States declares: "Neither slavery nor voluntary servitude, except as punishment for crime whereof the party shall have been duly convicted, shall exist within the United States, or any place subject to their jurisdiction."[67]

After 1865, African slaves were free by law, but this liberation did not give them the same privileges and immunities as European Americans. In the South after the Civil War, Union supporters such as African freedmen and poor whites were mistreated and discriminated against.

As a result, the Civil Rights Act of 1866 was enacted for the protections of the American people, especially freedmen. In addition to the protection clause, free bondsmen were declared citizens of the United States.

The employment of African Americans as lawmen in the United States during the Reconstruction was a constitutional process. First, they were freed from slavery. Thereafter, they were given protection. Following their protection, they were made citizens of the United States. Finally, they were enfranchised. After the completion of this process, they were finally included as lawmen at the local, state, and federal levels. Prior to their inclusion in American politics, military governors, with the powers vested to them by Congress, allowed the appointment of African Americans as lawmen in jurisdictions subjected to the reconstruction policy.

Notes

1. President Andrew Johnson advocated the same policy as President Lincoln for the restoration of rebel states into the Union. These two Presidents invoked the Constitution of the United States for the reunification of the South with the North. See Richard Taylor, *Destruction and Reconstruction. Personal Experience of the Late War in the United States.* William Blackwood and Sons. Edinburgh and London, 1879, p. 339.

2. William Archibald Dunning, *Reconstruction, Political and Economic, 1865–1877, vol. 2,* Harper & Brother, 1877, 61. Professor Dunning notes that "the Civil Rights bill was designed to secure to the freedmen through the normal action of the courts the same protection against discriminating state legislation that was secured in the early bill by military power. It declared the freemen to be citizens of the United States, and as such to have the same civil rights and to be subject to the same criminal penalties as white persons."

3. George W. Julian, *Political Recollections.* Chicago: Jansen, McClurg & Company, 1884, p. 189.

4. Ibid., p. 190.

5. Ibid., p. 197.

6. James G. Blaine, *Twenty Years of Congress from Lincoln to Garfield, with a review of the events which led to the political revolution of 1860.* Library of Alexandria, 1844, p. 35.

7. Julian, 1884, p. 223.

8. Ibid.

9. Ibid., p. 8.

10. Dunning, 1877, p. 61.

11. Richard Taylor, *Destruction and Reconstruction: Personal Experience of the Late War*. New York: D. Appleton and Company, 1879, p. 251.

12. Charles Ernest Chadsey, *The Struggle Between President Johnson and Congress over Reconstruction, Issue 19*. Columbia University, 1896, p. 14.

13. Thornton Kirkland Lothrop, *William Henry Seward*. Houghton, Mifflin, 1899, p. 366.

14. William H. Seward, *William H. Seward, 1861–1872*. Derby and Miller, 1891, p. 283.

15. See Andrew Johnson and Frank Moore, *Speeches of Andrew Johnson, Presidents of the United States*. Little, Brown, 1865, p. xviii.

16. George Washington, *Washington's Farewell Address to the people of the United States*, 1796. Houghton, Mifflin, 1913, p. 11.

17. Wilson Starr Myers, *The Self-reconstruction of Maryland, 1864–1867*. Johns Hopkins Press, 1909, p. 81., The same information was recorded by the contributors of the book titled *Two Americans: Their Complete History, from the Earliest Discoveries to the present Day*. J. Andrews, Decker & Company, 1881, p. 601.

18. Edward McPherson, *The Political History of the United States of America*. Solomons & Chapman, 1876, 63.

19. See William Frederick Doolittle, Louise S. Brown and Malissa R. Doolittle, *The Doolittle Family in America, Issue 4–7*. Press of National Printing, 1904, p. 670.

20. Ibid., p. 666.

21. Ibid., p. 668. See the quote of Harvey Harper.

22. Ibid., pp. 668–670, 672–674,678.

23. Ibid., p. 663.

24. Ibid., p. 672. As his views were the same as President Andrew Johnson's with respect to the reconstruction policy, he became his close friend and advisor during his antagonistic period with radical United States lawmakers.

25. Taylor, 1879, p. 253.

26. Johnson and Moore, 1865, p. xviii.

27. Quote from Senator Clark. See William Horatio Barnes, *History of the Thirty-ninth Congress of the United States*. Harper & Brother, 1868, p. 390.

28. Walter Lynwood Fleming, *Civil War and Reconstruction in Alabama*. Columbia University Press, 1905, p. 262.

29. Ibid.

30. Taylor, 1879, pp. 16, 23.

31. George B. McClellan, *McClellan's Own Story. The War for the Union, the Soldiers who fought It, the Civilian who Directed it and His Relation to it and to Them*. New York: Charles L. Webster & Company, 1887, p. 35.

32. Julian, 1884, p. 201.

33. Ibid.

34. Ibid., p. 213.

35. Ibid.

36. McClellan, 1887, p. 7.

37. Blaine, 1884, 52.

38. Ibid., p. 7.

39. Ibid., p. 3.

40. Charles E. Chadsey, *The Struggle Between President Johnson and Congress over Reconstruction*, Issue 19–22. Columbia University, 1896. p. 12

41. See Report of the Joint Committee on Reconstruction, at the First Session, Thirty-ninth Congress. U.S. Government Printing Office, 1866, p. 1.

42. James Walter Fertig, *The Secession and Reconstruction of Tennessee*. University of Chicago Press, 1898, pp. 44–45.

43. Blaine, 1884, p. 2.

44. Ibid.

45. Fleming, 1905, p. 333.

46. Ibid.

47. Ibid.

48. The Honorable Stevens called the Constitution a worthless bit of old parchment. It appears that the Constitution was not inclusive and subjected to discriminative clauses. For these reasons, Stevens firmly rejected the reentry of rebel states into the Union under the Constitution. See Chadsey, 1896, p. 328.

49. Chadsey, 1896, p. 14.

50. Richard Taylor, *Destruction and Reconstruction: Personal Experiences of the Late War*. D. Appleton, 1879, p. 339.

51. Ibid., p. 328.

52. Ibid.

53. William H. Barnes, *History of the Thirty-Ninth Congress of the United States*. NY, Harper & Brothers, Publishers, 1868, p. 517.

54. James Albert Woodburn, *The Life of Thaddeus Stevens: A Study in American Political History, Especially in the period of the Civil War and Reconstruction*. Bobbs Merrill Company, 1913, p. 212.

55. Ibid., p. 219.

56. See the speech of the Honorable Stevens, *Reconstruction: Speech of Hon. Thaddeus Stevens, of Pennsylvania, Delivered in the House of Representatives of the United States, December 18, 1865*. H. Polkinhorn & Son, Printers, 1865, pp. 1–2.

57. Ibid.

58. Ibid.

59. Henry Wilson, *History of the Reconstruction Measures of the Thirty-ninth and Fortieth Congress, 1865–68*. Hartford: Published by Subscription Only, By

The Hartford Publishing Company, 1868, p. 117. Senator Wilson notes that the bill introduced by Senator Trumbull had as its goal "to protect all persons in their civil rights, and to furnish the means for their vindication referred in the committee in the judiciary."

60. Ibid., p. 119.

61. Ibid., p. 121.

62. Ibid., p. 147.

63. Barnes, 1868, p. 438.

64. See "Message of the President of the United States Communicating in Compliance with a resolution of the Senate." Government Printing Office, 1865, p. 38. President Andrew Johnson declared that "slavery was impracticable, at least where the military arm of the government has enforced emancipation. Others are still trying to go on in the old way, and that old way is in fact the only one they understand, and in which they have any confidence. Only a minority is trying to adopt the new order of things."

65. James Ford Rhodes, *History of the United States from the Compromise of 1850; 1864–1866*. Macmillan, 1904, p. 580.

66. Charles William Ramsdell, *Reconstruction in Texas, issues 95*. Columbia University, 1910, p. 62.

67. The Charters of Freedom "A New World is At Hand" Constitution of the United States. Amendments 11–27.

Chapter 2

Constitutional Amendments at the State Level

Founding Fathers of the United States set forth that the country was a federation of many states in the Union. As such, the states were empowered with self-governing features. Each state has its own Constitution and laws. A dual judicial system was observed in much of the country. In accordance with the United States Constitution, the federal government was restricted from interfering in the domestic affairs of a state in the Union. But contrary to the Constitution, after the Civil War the law of the land was no longer enforceable in the seceded states. As a result, the rebel states were sometimes called "states out of Union" or "dead states." Because of this status, the states out of Union had to undergo legal process before their readmittance into the Union.

As there was no precedent in the United States Constitution regarding the readmission of seceded states into the Union, United States lawmakers were obligated to formulate a viable mechanism for that end. As a result, the seceded states were at the mercy of the United States Congress. Clearly, both Presidents Abraham Lincoln and Andrew Johnson did not have a planning strategy for the readmission of the seceded states. Historian Benjamin B. Kendrick argued that "President Lincoln refused to commit himself to any general plan of reconstruction, but thought it best to act separately on each state according to the conditions existing in it."[1] President Johnson advocated the same approach as his predecessor. Historically, during the war, Union officials did not enact laws for the reinclusion of seceded states into the Union. After the death of Lincoln, President Johnson continued the same procedures as Lincoln.[2] Contrary to President Lincoln and Johnson, Congressman Thaddeus Stevens was antagonistic to the unconditional readmission of seceded states into the

Union. Like him, other radical congressmen also objected. As a result, Congressman Stevens intelligently orchestrated a conditional plan for the reinclusion of rebel states into the Union. The opposition against President Johnson's policy on Reconstruction was also shown during the 39th Congress. According to Kendrick, in December of 1865, a large number of this body negatively viewed the unconditional re-admission of seceded states into the Union set forth by the executive department.[3] To meet this end, Congressman Stevens proposed the formation of a Joint Committee of fifteen members for the manage-ment of Reconstruction affairs.

The Joint Committee of Fifteen on Reconstruction

To remedy their plight, Southern states were forced to amend their Constitutions by adding the Fourteenth Amendment. In a similar man-ner, after convening a constitutional convention, each state framed a new Constitution that included both races. In these new constitutions, African Americans were recognized as citizens of their respective states.

On April 30, 1868, Congressman Thaddeus Stevens presented to the Committee of Fifteen a joint resolution for the protections of citizens at the state level. The language utilized for the protections of the Citizens as noted by the United States Constitution after its amendment reads as follows:

> Sec.1. No state shall make or enforce any laws which shall abridge the privileges or immunities of citizens of the United States; nor shall any state deprive any person of life, liberty, or property without due process of law; nor deny to any person within its jurisdiction the equal protection of the laws.[4]

This amendment was critical after the Civil War because the newly emancipated Africans and Northern men were ill-treated in the former Confederate states. Therefore, such a measure was imperative for the standardization of the American judiciary at each level of the govern-ment. After this, previously enacted Black Codes were repealed, and

African Americans enjoyed to some extent the same justice as their white counterparts in Southern states.

Before the Fourteenth Amendment, African Americans did not benefit from the protection of the local and state laws. Legal cases regarding African descendants were adjudicated before the slave court. Just like people of the African race, poor whites were also denied due process. This was visible during the 1850s in the Northern states. As in the North, in the South, poor whites were also subjected to the same conditions. Oligarchs enjoyed the full privilege of the law in contrast to poor citizens.

As the protection advocated by Congressman Stevens, when each former seceded state framed its constitution, due process rights were incorporated into that law. Trial by jury, right of the people to secure their persons, houses, and papers against unreasonable search were inviolable for both races. Moreover, self-incrimination and double jeopardy were also prohibited. Furthermore, excessive bail, fines, and cruel or unusual punishment were rendered illegal.[5] Finally, African Americans were recognized as citizens of the states where they were born or in their adopted state.

In the states under Reconstruction, slavery was also prohibited for the first time in accordance with the newly framed Constitution of 1868. Each state constitution declared that "neither slavery nor involuntary servitude, except as a punishment for crime, whereof the party shall have been duly convicted, shall exist."[6] Furthermore, each state set forth the declaration of rights for the protection of all Americans. The declaration of rights of each state reads as follows:

All men are born free and equal – endowed by their creator with certain inalienable rights, among which are the rights of enjoying and defending their lives and liberties, of acquiring, possessing and protecting property, and of seeking and obtaining their safety and happiness.[7]

Even though there were few differences in the language of this article among the states under Reconstruction, the aim of this article was the same. Georgia's Constitution explicitly noted that every United States citizen born in that state was her citizen, stating,

> all persons resident in the state, born in the United States or naturalized, or who shall have legally declared their intention to become citizens of the United States, are hereby declared citizens of the state of Georgia, possessing equal, civil, and political rights and public privileges.[8]

From the language of Georgia's constitution, African Americans would have been allowed to be part of the body politic of that state and able to hold political offices like their white brethren. A large number African Americans were excluded from state politics during the Reconstruction era.

The constitution of each state framed in 1868 enfranchised people of African descent. To illustrate, in South Carolina, the constitution noted that "all elections shall be free and open, and every inhabitant of this commonwealth possessing the qualifications provided for in this constitution shall have an equal right to elect officers and be elected to fill public office."[9] During the same period, African Americans had the same election privileges in the states under Reconstruction. As members of the American body politic, African descendants were able to elect local officials from among themselves. Contrary to the Southern states, in the North African Americans were enfranchised after the ratification of the Fifteenth Amendment in the Constitution of the United States in 1870.

With regards to the judicial system, with the implementation of the due process law at the state level, the components of the state criminal justice system were shaped. Procedural and substantive laws of the state took on a different connotation. To explain, trial by jury was applied in cases pertaining to whites and blacks. Moreover, African Americans were permitted to sue and to be sued just like their white counterparts. Furthermore, they were permitted to serve as witnesses in civil and criminal cases.

In addition to those judicial privileges, African Americans served as lawmen at the state or local level. As the state constitution recognized them as citizens, their inclusion in law enforcement was not a matter of discussion in many regions under reconstruction enforcement. On the contrary, it appears that African Americans were only employed as lawmen in the states of the Union. Accordingly, they were employed in that capacity in Illinois, Indiana, Tennessee, and the District of Columbia. The employment of African Americans in Northern states was materialized after the ratification of the Fifteenth Amendment of the United States Constitution. They were not employed as such in Southern states or states under Reconstruction until 1868, when each former Confederate state framed its constitution. In 1867, African descendants were employed as lawmen under the military governors under the jurisdiction of the United States. In this period, the constitution of each state was abolished, and former confederate states were considered dead states.

Unlike other Southern states, Reconstruction policy was not enforced in Tennessee. Its state legislature voluntarily ratified the Thirteenth Amendment. In a similar manner, the Fourteenth Amendment was also adopted. According to data, on February 22, 1865, the 13th Amendment to the Tennessee Constitution was adopted, abolishing slavery.[10] This was the first time that slavery was legally abolished in the South. After the Fourteenth Amendment was ratified in 1866, African American men were allowed into the American body politic. With the ratification of the Fourteenth Amendment to the United States Constitution, the state of Tennessee was restored into the Union. On July 24, 1866, during the first session of the 39th Congress, lawmakers approved the restoration of Tennessee into the Union.[11] At the state level, on February 25, 1867, African Americans were enfranchised in Tennessee.[12] As in Tennessee, on June 8, 1867, in the District of Columbia, Congress passed a bill which enfranchised African Americans.[13]

Reconstruction amendments also had effect on the state level. In the newly framed constitutions, slavery was abolished, and African Americans were recognized as citizens of the states where they resided. Likewise, they enjoyed the same judicial privileges as their white counterparts. Furthermore, the newly framed constitution of 1868 enfranchised every citizen of the United States without regard to color or previous conditions. It was also in 1868 that the Fourteenth Amendment of the United States constitution was ratified at the state level.

Notes

1. Benjamin B. Kendrick, *The Journal of the Joint Committee of Fifteen on Reconstruction: 39th Congress, 1865–1867*. Columbia University, 1914, p. 133.

2. Ibid., p. 134.

3. Ibid., pp. 17–18.

4. William H. Barnes, *History of the Thirty-ninth Congress of the United States*. Harper & Brothers, 1868, pp. 435–436.

5. See *Florida Constitutional Convention, Journal of the Proceedings of the Constitutional Convention of the State of Florida; Begun and Held at the Capital at Tallahassee, on Monday, January 20th, 1868*. E.M. Cheney, Printer, 1868, p. 72.

6. Charles W. Ramsdell, *Reconstruction in Texas, Issue 95*. Columbia University, 1910, p. 3.

7. See *The Constitution of South Carolina, Adopted April 16, 1868: And the Acts and Joint Resolution of the General Assembly Passed at the Special Session of 1868, Together with the Military Orders Therein Re-enacted*. John W. Denny, 1868, p. 3.

8. "Journal of the Proceedings of the Constitutional Convention of the people of Georgia." E.H. Pughe Book and Job printer, 1868, p. 158.

9. *The Constitution of South Carolina*, 1868, p. 3.

10. See *Joint Select Committee on the Affairs in the Late Insurrectionary states in the House Documents, vol. 1–2; vol. 267*. USA House of Representatives. US Government Printing Office, 1872, p. 461.

11. John T. Moore and Austin P. Foster, *Tennessee: The Volunteer State, 1769–1923*, vol. 1, S.J. Clarke Publishing Company, 1923, p. 530.

12. Ibid., p. 533.

13. See *Negro Year-Book: An Annual Encyclopedia of the Negro*. Negro Year-Book Publishing Company, 1914, p. 144.

Chapter 3

African Americans as Law Enforcement Agents during Reconstruction

The maintenance of law and order by African Americans in the states subjected to the Reconstruction policy has not been fully discussed by historians as well as law enforcement professionals. Historians have, from time to time, recorded the employment of African Americans in law enforcement during the Reconstruction, but there is not a concentrated work on the subject in question. Professor Marvin Dulaney, Bobby L. Lovett, Eric Foner, Canter Brown, and Frank Lincoln Mather have recorded law enforcement duties performed by African Americans, but they did not fully discuss their inclusion in the components of the criminal justice. Similarly, the impact of politics in the enforcement of law in the South during the same period has not been deeply explored. For the reasons noted above, students in law enforcement as well as those majoring in criminal justice, including history and political science have been deprived of salient information on the subject in question. Therefore, it is essential to explore the enforcement of law and order maintained by African American law enforcement officers during the Reconstruction period. The examination of the employment of African Americans in Southern states during Reconstruction reveals vivid information about the approach political parties used for their inclusion.

In 1865, at the end of the war of secession, the political culture and folkways of Southern states were redefined. Northern states through the auspices of the Radical Republicans imposed a new political discipline in the occupied states. First, slavery, which was a sizeable segment of the Southern economy, was abolished by law, in addition to the proclamation signed by President Lincoln. The Thirteenth Amendment was a blow to the Southern societies. Culturally, in the South, African slaves were the property of men. But after the ratification of the Thirteenth Amendment of the Constitution of the United States, by law, Africans in the Confederate states to some extent were no longer considered as such. They were free from bondage. In addition to the Thirteenth Amendment, the Civil Rights Act was enacted in 1866, aiming for the protection of the newly freed Africans as well as white people. Although the Thirteenth Amendment and the Civil Rights Act of 1866 were in force, an enforcement mechanism was needed for their validation. As a result, the Fourteenth Amendment to the Constitution of the United States was ratified by the United States lawmakers. Contrary to the United States government, in the former Confederate states, strenuous political gymnastics were needed before the ratification of the Fourteenth Amendment. In the Confederate states, African Americans endured oppression and terrorism post Reconstruction.

Therefore, the Fourteenth Amendment guaranteed their citizenship, as well as protecting their due process rights. Even though African Americans became citizens of the United States, they were still not enfranchised. As result, in 1870, the 15th Amendment was ratified to the Constitution of the United States. With the ratification of the 15th Amendment, African Americans were fully accepted in the political body of the United States and in the states where they lived.

The history of the involvement of African Americans in law enforcement during Reconstruction began with the enforcement of the Military Reconstruction Act passed by the United States Congress on March 2, 1867.[1] In each district of Alabama, two whites and one black were appointed as registrars in accordance with the act, which ordered the election for the selection of members of the Constitutional Convention. As a result, Royal, Finley, William, Alston, Turner, Kapler, and King, or Godwin were among African Americans appointed members of the board of registrars.[2] Fleming notes that African American members of the board of registrars were of better quality than their white counterparts.[3] As in Alabama, in other states there were African Americans appointed as election registrars. Eric Foner notes that in 1869, in Wilmington, North Carolina, Miles Armstrong was registrar and election judge.[4] In Mississippi, Garner tells us that many registrars were freedmen, military officers, and ex-Union soldiers who had resided in the state before the war.[5] Before this date, African Americans were excluded from any civilian law enforcement duties by the provisional governors of Confederate states. Similarly, they were not allowed to have any political responsibilities. They were not allowed to vote or conduct political meetings. The political attitude of local Southern government officials was a generalized suspicion of both people from the North and members of the United States lawmakers.

Therefore, fearing their reenslavement in the South, radical legislators in the U.S. House and the Senate passed the Reconstruction Acts of 1867. According to the *Congressional Serial Set*, on March 2, 1867, "no legal governments existed in states subjected to the Reconstruction enforcement."[6] Therefore, military commanders were obligated to appoint local law enforcement officers of their choices. To illustrate this, in Mississippi, a military governor named Adelbert Ames had the appointive power of civil officers in the state.[7] Similarly, in North Carolina, Governor Holden had the power to appoint civil officers. During his administration, many African Americans were appointed as justices of the peace.[8] As a reminder, many Union generals were against the status quo, advocating for the citizenship of African Americans, as well as for their right to vote. For example, Maj. Gen. Q. A. Gilmore, commanding the Department of the South headquartered at Hilton Head, declared that "the people of the black race are free citizens of the United States, whose rights must be respected accordingly."[9] With respect to the generals charged with the Congressional Reconstruction, Generals Sickles, Canby, Griffin, Sheridan, and Swayne were associated with the blacks during the execution of the Civil War. General Swayne was the head of the Freedmen's Bureau. As head of the Freedmen's Bureau, he was familiar with blacks, and appointing them to minor positions in the local law enforcement was not a problem. Possibly, General Swayne was also an advocate of the political rights of African Americans. On the other hand, General Sheridan was a loyal Union advocate who detested the policy of President Johnson, which rejected any attempt to franchise African Americans. He was also a close ally of General Grant. These generals were familiar with the sacrifices made by African Americans during the war. Therefore, they had no objections in appointing them to minor law enforcement duties at the local level. When many former Confederates who had been local law enforcement officers were removed from offices, African Americans were among those who were appointed law enforcement officers to replace them. In some cases, when the Confederate sympathizers rejected the offer from the generals asking them to serve in law enforcement, African Americans were also appointed instead. Much of the appointment of African Americans by the commanding generals charged with the administration of Congressional Reconstruction will be discussed in the following paragraphs.

At the end of Congressional Reconstruction, African Americans were finally fully included in the American body politic with the ratification of the 15th Amendment of the United States Constitution in 1870. The 15th Amendment guaranteed the right to vote to every American without regard to color, race, and previous conditions. This was the year when African Americans were given the same full rights as their white brethren. Even though the law secured the right to vote for every American, there were always obstacles from those who denied African Americans such rights. From 1870 to the end of Reconstruction in 1877, African Americans faced many challenges with respect to their voting rights. Political parties affiliated with them made various efforts in protecting their voting rights, but the resistance of the opponents of the enfranchisement of African Americans was strong. Many conditions were created to render such enfranchisement difficult. White Southerners formed organizations such as the Ku Klux Klan, the Night Riders, and White Camelia. These groups not only threatened African Americans to keep from the polls and from political action, but they also terrorized them for any perceived "transgress" against white supremacy. Similarly, white supporters of the Republican Party were also sometimes abused by the same domestic terrorist organizations. Even though African Americans faced strong challenges from whites in their respective states, they did not give up their voting rights. They always participated in the American political life and elected people of their choice in local law enforcement agencies. Similarly, they elected white Republican candidates of their choice till the era when they were legally disfranchised. For a better understanding how African Americans were included in law enforcement during both periods—which were the Military Reconstruction, and the full rights after the ratification of the 15th Amendment to the Constitution—it is better to examine each period separately. During the full rights, African Americans were also employed by many law enforcement agencies in the loyal states.

The Appointment of African Americans by Military Commanders

In the previous sections we discussed law enforcement duties performed by African Americans before and during the Civil War under the rules of military generals. Similarly, the maintenance of law and order by black soldiers during the occupations of the Confederate states were related. But after the war, the conquered territories became part of the Union. Therefore, the preservation of the Union was to be put into action through legal means. The loyalty to the federal government and the observation of the citizenship of freed slaves were taken seriously by Union supporters before the readmission of the seceded states to the Union. On the contrary, these states excluded African Americans from the local and state body politics before the Congressional Acts. Black Codes were also enforced for control of the behaviors and movements of the newly freed blacks. The institutionalization of the Black Codes was viewed in the North as the plan to restore the enslavement of the blacks.[10] The view of Professor William Archibald Dunning was that "the Black Codes seemed to be the expression of a deliberate purpose by the southerners to nullify the result of the war and the re-establishment of slavery."[11] The perception of Professor Dunning and Savage was also signaled by William Watson Davis, who stipulated that the enforcement of the black codes in Florida "was deliberate and diabolical attempts" to return the blacks to slavery "by means of legal subterfuge, in defiance of the results of the war."[12] Due to the Black Codes and the concept of the nullification of the result of the war, radical lawmakers feared the return of the status quo in the South. As a political strategy, they challenged the appeasement of Reconstruction theory advocated by President Johnson and enforced a more radical and inclusive reconstruction policy for the welfare of the Union. Clearly, the plans of President Johnson and that of the radical Republicans were at odds. Johnson advocated the reconstruction plan of President Lincoln, and the radical lawmakers believed in a plan for the destruction of the status quo to prevent the reemergence of the former Confederate officials to power, fearing the continuation of war. With this philosophy, the radicals invoked draconian methods for better results of the Reconstruction process, which were the franchise of every American citizens, and the full inclusion of every male of the American society into the body politic of the conquered states. In the South, before the Civil War, poor whites were always excluded from the political fabrics of the states. Therefore, Reconstruction was also an avenue for their involvement in the American body politic. Similarly, the observance of constitutional rights, as well as the civil rights of every American citizen, was to be taken into account in the conquered states.

The philosophy of the Reconstruction of President Lincoln was the readmission of the Confederate officials through a loyalty approach. Those who freely rejected the policy of the Confederate government and supported the reunification of the United States were free to join the Union after taking an oath of loyalty. In addition, desertion from the Confederate Army was also a possible venue for a toleration of the misdeeds they committed during the Civil War. Unlike President Lincoln, President Andrew Johnson, his successor, believed in supporting Southerners who were loyal to the Union. His Reconstruction design was to appoint loyal provisional governors in the Confederate states who would reorganize civil institutions. To accomplish his architecture, he proclaimed an amnesty and appointed provisional governors. According to John Savage, President Johnson appointed William M. Sharkey as the provisional Governor of Mississippi. The Hon. James Johnston was appointed provisional Governor of Georgia. In Texas, the Hon. Andrew Hamilton was appointed provisional governor. In Alabama, the Hon. Lewis E. Parsons was appointed provisional governor. On July 1, 1865, Benjamin F. Perry was appointed provisional Governor of South Carolina.[13] In North Carolina, Professor William Archibald Dunning notes that W.W. Holden was appointed provisional governor. Like Savage, Professor Dunning notes that on May 9, 1865, Francis H. Peirpoint was recognized as Governor of Virginia by President Johnson. In Arkansas, Isaac Murphy remained governor, and James Madison Wells became Governor of Louisiana.[14] Among the newly appointed governors, there were those who supported the de facto government of the Confederacy.

To explain, Benjamin F. Perry of South Carolina was the district judge in the Confederate de facto government a few weeks before its fall. The governors appointed by President Johnson did not have support from the radical lawmakers in Washington, D.C., because of their sympathies for the Confederacy.

The reappearance of former high-ranking Confederate officers in Southern politics was unwelcomed by the Northerners.[15] They believed that Confederate governors would reinforce the status quo as well as the reemergence of slavery. Possibly, people in Northern states feared the reinstitution of the Confederate government. Therefore, many radical members of the House and Senate were troubled by President Johnson's policies. He was suspected of supporting the causes of his Southern brethren. While in the North, there were lamentations on the political behavior of President Johnson, in the South, government officials and the people were pleased by his policy for the readmission of former Confederate states into the Union. But the conditions of the newly freed slaves and loyal whites in the South revealed that the policy of President Johnson was not healthy for the nation. It was very divisive and prone to return the country to the same conditions that had prevailed before the Civil War. He did not believe that African Americans were fit for political offices or being part of an electorate body in the nation.

Similarly, Northern people who resided in the South were sometimes subjected to mistreatment. These revelations deepened the mistrust the radicals had about the reconstruction policy of President Johnson. Like Southerners, President Johnson rejected any notions of enfranchising African Americans. President Johnson did not believe in political equality between the whites and black people.

From 1865 to 1866, with the mustering out of many Union soldiers from Southern towns, many cities descended into lawlessness. Therefore, there was no feasible mechanism for the protection of properties and people. Due to the lack of security, in 1866 many African Americans who resided in cities in former Confederate states were abused or mistreated. Militia forces formed in these states abused freedmen consistently. Similarly, loyal members of the Union were ill-treated. In cities such as Memphis, New Orleans, and Richmond, there were riots against people of color.[16] During these riots, many African Americans were killed. After these riots, an investigation was conducted by members of the United States House of Representatives.[17] Similarly, in other cities in the same regions, African Americans were sometimes reenslaved with the support of the local officials in the former Confederate states. Hoping to verify the conditions of the South, in 1865 and later that year President Johnson dispatched Carl Schurz and Ulysses S. Grant to investigate the conditions of the South. The investigation of Schurz revealed troubling realities with respect to the free blacks and whites who had been loyal to the Union. The co-habitation of the blacks and their former masters was antagonistic. The newly freed African Americans were always denied access to the economic privileges, as well as access to basic needs. The movements of African Americans were also limited due to the attacks against them. Like the blacks, Northern whites were also abused or mistreated in the conquered states.

According to the Schurz report, African Americans endured prejudice from Southern people. Additionally, physical mistreatments were common for the blacks who refused to work. Pertaining to slavery, Carl Schurz notes that the attempt to preserve slavery in its original form as much as possible was present among Southerners. He went on to stipulate that people believed in the preservation of slavery, or in the introduction a new form of slavery.[18] Possibly due to these abuses and the attempt to reintroduce slavery, radical members of the House of Representatives took a different stance to force the South to comply with the Emancipation Proclamation, the Thirteenth Amendment, the Civil Rights Act of 1866, and the ratification of the Fourteenth Amendment to the United States Constitution. Tennessee, which ratified the Fourteenth Amendment in 1867, was not subjected to the same Congressional enforcement as other Confederate states. Similarly, Kentucky was not punished with the Reconstruction enforcement imposed upon the Rebel states.

The abuse of African Americans and loyal Union subjects was taken very seriously by radical lawmakers in both houses. Congressman Thaddeus Stevens and Senators Henry Wilson and Charles Sumner were furious at the treatment to which African Americans and Union loyalists were subjected. In addition, the establishment of the Black Codes in the South was considered the return of slavery. Hoping to change the course of the Reconstruction policy, radical law makers requested the involvement of lawmakers in the administration of Southern political affairs. As many members of the House and the Senate were legally literate, it was easy for them to challenge the policy of President Johnson. As law and order was somewhat nonexistent and African Americans were not enfranchised, the radical lawmakers passed a Military Reconstruction Act on March 2, 1867, for the management of the Reconstruction. With this act, Congress became directly involved in that process.

The Military Reconstruction Act of March 2, 1867

This act ordered the United States Congress to oversee the process of the Reconstruction, as well as the appointments of military generals as governors of the states which had rejected the ratification of the Fourteenth Amendment to the Constitution, and the inclusion of African Americans into the United States government. Dunning credited Governor William Brownlow for the ratification of the Fourteenth Amendment in Tennessee. According to him, "Parson Brownlow, the governor who controlled the legislature, facilitated the ratification of the Amendment to the Constitution."[19] The Fourteenth Amendment was ratified July 19, 1866, and a bill for the restoration of Tennessee to the Union became law on July 24, 1866.[20] With the ratification of the Fourteenth Amendment, Tennessee was readmitted to the Union. Even though the Fourteenth Amendment was ratified, African Americans were not enfranchised. A similar process of disenfranchising former Confederate officials and sympathizers was enforced in the ten states subjected to the Congressional Reconstruction policy.

In 1867, African Americans were enfranchised and small numbers of them were elected to minor position of power. In Tennessee, when Davidson County was governed by three commissioners, an African American named Randal Brown was one of them. According to J.C. Napier, Brown had much experience and common sense, but he had a limited education. In addition, he had much influence among other African Americans. This led to him being highly respected by people of both races.[21]

For refusing to ratify the Fourteenth Amendment, Virginia, South and North Carolina, Georgia, Alabama, Florida, Mississippi, Arkansas,

Louisiana, and Texas were divided into five military districts under the command of military officers. The first district was formed from Virginia. South Carolina and North Carolina were in the second district. The third district was formed out of the state of Georgia, Alabama, and Florida. The fourth district was composed of Mississippi and Arkansas. The fifth district was made of Louisiana and Texas.[22] Military officers were empowered with the administration of civil and criminal cases. Similarly, the administration of political and economic affairs of the rebellious states was under the administration of the military governors. In addition to that, they organized elections for the selections of participants for the constitutional conventions. According to the act, African Americans were to be included among those who would have framed the new constitutions of these states. Furthermore, the act ordered that the sympathizers of the Confederate to be disenfranchised.

The Appointment of African Americans in Local Governments during 1867

The enforcement of the Reconstruction process was difficult due to the conflict which resurrected between President Johnson and radical United States lawmakers in both houses. The president was not in favor of including freedmen in the American political process as noted earlier. Furthermore, he did not believe that African Americans were ready to be electors like their white brethren. On the other hand, radical United States members of the House and the Senate advocated full inclusion of African Americans in the American body politic. Like President Johnson, the political and military leaders in the South opposed the enfranchisement of African Americans. They were against any process leading to the equality between them and their former slaves. As result, radical Senators and Congressmen such as Charles Sumner and Stevens, among others, enforced the Reconstruction Acts of 1867 as legal means for the enfranchisement of African Americans. The Act of March 2, 1867, entrusted the generals with the registration of electors and the organization of elections for the selection of members of the convention without regard to race or previous status. They were instructed to register only legal voters, because members of the Confederate government were restricted from participating in the framing process of the constitutions of the states under Reconstruction. In addition to this, elected officials were empowered with the framing of state constitutions.[23] The Act of March 2, 1867, is considered one of the most important acts established after the Civil War. This act has historical merit in the United States, since it is the first of this sort that eliminated old political folkways in Southern states.

As for the Civil War generals, those appointed for the enforcement of the Reconstruction acts had different views and approaches as to the involvement of African Americans in law enforcement. Generals who believed in the Reconstruction design of members of the United States Congress appointed African Americans in law enforcement. On the other hand, supporters of President Johnson were less likely to involve African Americans in the political process. To illustrate, General Hancock (who succeeded General Sheridan in Louisiana) was a supporter of the reconstruction policy of President Johnson, advocating against the elevation of African Americans to positions of power. During his administration, when the city council provided seven blacks and two whites for the election to the office of recorders, General Hancock removed the names of the seven African Americans and substituted white candidates. Due to his opposition to blacks, General Grant requested an explanation for their removal and ordered their reinstatement. General Hancock found himself to be uncomfortable, so he resigned as military governor of Louisiana.[24] Generals such as Sheridan, Ord, Canby, Pope, Griffin, Ames, and Sickles were supporters of Reconstruction. In fact, President Johnson disliked General Sheridan because of the latter's determination to enforce congressional policies. Ultimately, he was removed from his post because of his opposition to the president's Reconstruction policy. General Grant was also one of the generals who had much impact on the success of the Reconstruction Act of 1867. He worked diplomatically against President Johnson's goal of disenfranchising African Americans. He was sympathetic to the Secretary of War, General Rufus Saxton, who was a fierce supporter of the enfranchisement of African Americans. General Saxton had the same views as radical lawmakers regarding the implication of African Americans in the American political landscape.

In 1867, with the enforcement of the Military reconstruction, African Americans were again under the protections of military officers as they were during the Civil War. They became political partners of those who believed in the restoration of the Union. As a result, they were entrusted with minor law enforcement duties in their respective districts or towns. From Reconstruction authors such as Walter Lynwood Fleming, John Schreiner Reynolds, Charles William Ramsdell, James Wilford Garner, John Rose Ficklen, and Pierce Butler, this author discovered that military commanders in the newly established districts in the South appointed African Americans as police officers, aldermen, justices of the peace, election board members, sheriffs, and in one case, a mayor. African Americans were also appointed as regulators in many cities.

In Mississippi, when General Edward Otho Cresap Ord was appointed commander of the military district, he appointed Benjamin T. Montgomery as justice of the peace.[25] Buford Satcher recounts how the appointment of Montgomery was opposed by a white subject in Davis Bend, but his son Isaiah T. Montgomery assured them that his father would not adjudicate cases pertaining to white people.[26] Davis Bend was a small village near Vicksburg, and it was the former plantation of Joseph Emory Davis and his brother Jefferson Davis. Montgomery, the father of Isaiah Montgomery, was a reputed African American planter in Mississippi. He was also a plantation manager at Davis Bend when the plantation belonged to Joseph and Jefferson Davis.[27] While Satcher and William Harris note that Military Governor General Ord appointed Benjamin T. Montgomery justice of the peace, James Wilford Garner recorded that he appointed Isaiah T. Montgomery as justice of the peace. Possibly, this confusion was due to the recording process of the time. From historical records, data indicate that Benjamin Montgomery was appointed justice of the peace, but his son Isaiah Montgomery was not.

As to the appointment of African Americans in law enforcement, in the history of Mississippi, Benjamin T. Montgomery was the first African American to hold the position of justice of the peace. It is important to note that at Davis Bend, many inhabitants were people of his race. Therefore, Montgomery adjudicated minor cases involving them. In addition to the appointment of Montgomery, Harris tells us that "later General Ord decreed that blacks could serve as clerk and judges of election."[28] Similarly, Thornton William Montgomery, the son of Benjamin T. Montgomery, was appointed constable at Davis Bend by General E.O.C. Ord.[29] In addition to the titles listed above, blacks were also appointed as election registrars. The appointment of African Americans as registrars was done in accordance with the act of March 1867 which ordered an inclusive and republican form of government.

Just like General Ord, in Alabama, General Pope shaped the organization of the local provisionary government. He disbanded the militia of the state and appointed new officers loyal to the Union. When General Pope ordered General Swayne to appoint new officers at the local level, he included black officers. General Swayne first attempted to appoint the most respected and influential blacks as police officers, but they [blacks] rejected the offer, suggesting to the general that white officers were fit for the positions. Fleming notes that black police officers were appointed by General Swayne in Mobile and Selma.[30] In these two towns, possibly there were many African Americans. Like General Swayne, General Canby authorized the formation of the police force in North Carolina composed of loyal whites and blacks according to the ratio of registration.[31] In North Carolina, Hamilton did not indicate in which town black police officers were appointed. We can stipulate that in the towns where African Americans were the majority, more than likely they were included in the police force. During the administration of Governor William W. Holden, African Americans were also appointed as law enforcement agents to minor positions. The presence of African Americans was always detested by their white brethren. It is important to note that they were appointed in towns such as Wilmington and others, where African Americans were the majorities. African Americans were also empowered with prison services. In South Carolina, data showed that black troops were employed as prison guards in Charleston, working under the administration of Major General Daniel E. Sickles. According to Reynolds, after the killing of a Union trooper in Edgefield, "several citizens of Edgefield, including Gen. M. W. Crary, were arrested on the charge of complicity in the killing of the trooper, huddled into an ambulance, taken to Columbia in the nighttime, and there incarcerated." The arrestees were thereafter released without charges."[32] In Florida, whites who committed any infractions against

Union officers were also guarded by black soldiers after their arrests.[33] Following the war, Union soldiers, specifically black soldiers, were always attacked by the enemies. The presence of black soldiers in South Carolina and other Confederate states as agents of law enforcement was humiliating to whites. In Wilmington, North Carolina, African American soldiers entrusted with law enforcement were at odds with the population, often being accused of arresting white subjects without cause.[34]

When General Canby was appointed commander of the Second Military District, he followed the same philosophy as his counterparts in other military districts. He removed former local law enforcement officers and appointed new ones. In 1867, among the aldermen appointed by him, half were African Americans. In addition, in Columbia, he appointed W. Beverly Nash as justice of the peace. Nash succeeded magistrate J. T. Zeaby. As the plan of the election was underway, General Canby ordered the registration of election board members from both races.[35] Election board members were given the power to supervise the elections, including registering voters and informing voters of their election rights. During Reconstruction, African Americans were also authorized to act as election inspectors by the order of the generals. In North Carolina, data showed that General Nelson A. Miles, who commanded the post at Raleigh, issued a circular ordering the selection of African Americans as election inspectors.[36]

The appointment of black law enforcement officers in 1867 by the military commander also happened in Louisiana. In this state, after the removal of Governor Wells, General Sheridan, the commander of the Fifth Military District, discharged the board of aldermen from their duties. Among the newly appointed aldermen were African Americans. During their term, these councilmen appointed three black and one white assistant recorders. They also appointed two black physicians. General Sheridan was dissatisfied with the work of the local officials in New Orleans. According to him, "they impeded the execution of the reconstruction acts and had brought the credit of the city into a disorganized condition."[37] It appears that local officials did not comply with the enforcement of the Reconstruction laws. When General Sheridan allowed the appointment of African Americans to minor governmental positions, black constituents were delighted. It appears that Sheridan broke the custom of the past, which denied African Americans any access to positions of power after the War. Possibly due to his opposition to President Johnson's policy, General Sheridan was removed from his governorship in his district. Even though he was disliked by the president, Sheridan was a favorite general of General Grant, who admired him.[38] General Sheridan was always faithful to General Grant.

In 1867, data revealed that Pinckney Benton Stewart Pinchback, an African American, was appointed inspector of customs in New Orleans. Pinchback was a son of a white man and had some education. He had been educated in Cincinnati with his brother Napoleon by the request of their father. He had been born in Macon, Georgia, in 1837. He was a businessman, as well as an influential person of African descent. He fought during the Civil War for the defense of liberty and freedom. Pinchback was the son of Major William Pinchback, who lived in Holmes County, Mississippi. According to Booker T. Washington, his mother Eliza Stewart claimed to have mixed blood of black and Indian.[39] During the Reconstruction period, he was deeply involved in politics, getting elected to the Senate of Louisiana and being appointed Lieutenant Governor of the same state after the death of Lieutenant Governor Dunn, who was also a person of color.

African Americans as Elected and Appointed Local Officials in 1868

In 1868, African Americans were enfranchised in accordance with the Military Reconstruction Act of March 2, 1867. In the newly divided military districts, African American men were permitted to register and vote for a candidate of their choice. Before the election, military commanders assured their physical as well as ballot protections. The agents of the Freedmen's Bureau were also the architects who educated blacks on their voting rights. In the states such as Mississippi and Alabama where the election for the convention failed, military governors still appointed African Americans to the local level. But in 1868, during the administration of General Alvan Cullem Gillem, who was both a resident of Tennessee and a friend of President Johnson, African

Americans were not appointed to the local government. There is no obvious data indicating the names of African Americans appointed by Governor Gillem. In 1869, under Military Governor Adelbert Ames, who was from Maine, supporting data indicate that African Americans enjoyed the same privilege as their white counterparts in the local level. They were appointed as local law enforcement officers. According to James Wilford Garner, because there were not enough qualified white people to fill the ranks of local officers, Governor Ames was obligated to appoint freedmen and white strangers. Among the 25 appointees of Governor Ames, eight were African Americans.[40]

In the states where the Reconstruction constitutions were framed in 1868, African Americans were elected or appointed to the state and local levels. In Florida, Louisiana, South Carolina, and North Carolina, African Americans held positions of power. Governors Reed in Florida, Scott in South Carolina, and Warmoth in Louisiana included African Americans in their governments. For example, in Louisiana, Dunn was appointed Lieutenant Governor in 1868, and he served as commissioner of the police. In Florida, Governor Reed appointed Jonathan Clarkson Gibbs Secretary of State. These are a few examples of African Americans who were elected or appointed in 1868. At the local level, African Americans were also appointed as constables, justices of the peace, clerks and chancery of the court. Similarly, others were appointed as police officers.

In 1870, African Americans were also fully involved in the local political process. In the former Confederate states in counties and towns where the African Americans were the majority, they managed to elect some local law enforcement officers. On the other hand, in the counties where they were minorities, it was difficult for them to elect an officer of the law. Meanwhile, in diverse counties and towns, African Americans were more likely to elect law enforcement officers. In Mississippi, where many counties were majority-black, the elections of officers of their own race were not a matter of question. In counties such as Washington, Yazoo, Bolivar, Madison, Hinds, and Wilkinson, there were African Americans elected as law enforcement officers. Garner, who examined the elections of African Americans to the local level in Mississippi, agrees that "where the colored voters were in the majority in a county, the office was often held by a black [man], though more generally by a northern white."[41] Garner's account indicates that African Americans were not the dominant political force in counties where they were in the majority. They shared law enforcement offices with their Northern white counterparts. In Mississippi, there were 33 counties where African Americans were in the majority. Out of the 61 total counties, whites held the majority in 28 of them.[42] John Roy Lynch, an African American, who served as justice of the peace in Mississippi, stipulates that "in no county or municipality African Americans [controlled the] government, but on the 72 counties, in the state at the time, blacks elected an average of 28 officers to a county."[43] The statement from Lynch disputes the accounts of many authors who recorded that the South was Africanized during Reconstruction. Regarding the numbers of Mississippi's counties, data from Garner and Lynch do not match up.

Similarly, in Beaufort, South Carolina, where African Americans were the majority, they elected many local officers. From the account of Sir George Campbell, a British traveler, data indicate that Beaufort was a majority black county while under the reign of the Republican Party, with African Americans sharing elective offices at the local government with their white counterparts.[44] In Virginia, in towns where African Americans had a large population, it was not a major hurdle to elect one or more people of their race. With respect to process, candidates were sometimes selected based on color-line [divide between races] in the former Confederate states. As in other states, in North Carolina and Arkansas, African Americans during the Republican reign had the privileges to elect some of them to law enforcement positions.

In addition to the geographical aspects, the political ideology and philosophy of the party's platform had an impact on the elections of African Americans to minor law enforcement positions at the local level. To illustrate, African Americans supported by the Republican Party were more often elected as justices of the peace or any other law enforcement positions. As for the governors, those who received political support from the black electorate were more than likely to support their candidacy for local law enforcement positions. In Mississippi, for example, during the administration of Governor Ames, there were many African Americans elected at the local level. Similarly, in Arkansas during the rule of Governor Garland, African Americans were privileged to serve as law enforcement agents at the local level. Like the governors listed above, in South Carolina, Governor Scott owed his election to the African Americans who supported the candidacy of African Americans in some positions in the government. In Louisiana, Governor Warmoth and Kellogg appointed many African Americans to the police force. Elisha Benjamin Andrews tells us that "Kellogg had a body of Metropolitan police, mostly colored, paid by the city of New Orleans, but under his personal command, which formed a part of his militia."[45] Similarly, Governor Davis of Texas appointed many blacks in the Texas State Guard formed under his regime. Governor Reed of Florida also followed the same policy of appointing African Americans to minor law enforcement positions. Many of the elections and appointment of African Americans in Mississippi, Arkansas, Louisiana, South Carolina, Florida, Alabama, North Carolina, Virginia, and Texas will be discussed as we explore each law enforcement title held by them during the administrations of the governors named above. Contrary to the Republicans, Democrats were less likely to appoint or support the candidacy of African Americans to law enforcement positions. In some instances, a few African Americans were elected or appointed under the government held by Democrats. But, as a general rule, Democrats enforced the policy of reducing the number of African Americans in law enforcement.

During the period of full rights, African Americans were elected lieutenant governors, senators, and congressmen. They were appointed as Secretaries of State, Secretaries of Treasury, Superintendents of Education, Adjutant-Generals, Commissioners of Immigration, county magistrates, and associate justices. To illustrate, Oscar Dunn, Pinchback, and Mitchell were lieutenant governors in Louisiana. Davis and Rapier were lieutenant governors in Alabama. In South Carolina, Richard H. Gleaves was lieutenant governor from 1872 to 1876. Lieutenant Gleaves was from Pennsylvania. As for the Secretary of Treasury, an African American held that position in Louisiana and South Carolina. Likewise, Francis L. Cardozo was appointed Superintendent of Education in South Carolina. In 1874, Cardozo was listed as treasurer in the Charleston city directory.

At the local level, there were African Americans elected as board of supervisors, sheriff, constables, justices of the peace, and coroners. Others were appointed by governors in the positions such as commissioners of land, police officers, court clerks and chancery. As during the Military Reconstruction, governors of states such as Louisiana, South Carolina, North Carolina, Arkansas, Texas, Florida, Virginia, and Alabama appointed many black police officers for the protection of their localities. In Georgia, however, it appears that African Americans were excluded from performing police work. Similarly, it appears that few African Americans held minor offices in Georgia during the Reconstruction period. African Americans were also appointed as regulators at the state and federal levels. The appointments and elections of black regulators will be discussed later in this text.

Through historical documents, data indicate that African Americans were employed as local law enforcement in Southern states during the military government of 1867. Before this date, they were included in this capacity only under the Civil War and during the occupation period. In Southern states, it was against the culture (folkways) of the time to employ an African American as lawman. This culture was temporarily suppressed with the execution of the Civil War and the conquering of the rebellious states. As already noted in chapter one, legal procedures were enforced before their entrance in the American body politic. The inclusion of African Americans in the larger political landscape was imposed upon Southerners by threat, not undertaken voluntarily.

Notes

1. See Walter Lynwood Fleming, *Documentary History of Reconstruction, Political, Military, Social, Religious, Educational, Industrial, 1865 to the present.* A. H. Clark Company, 1906, p. 174. This act granted the political right to everyone in the former confederate states. With the division of the states into military districts, African Americans were appointed registrars of the elections.

2. Walter Lynwood Fleming, *Civil War and Reconstruction in Alabama*, p. 488.

3. Ibid., p. 488.

4. Eric Foner, *Freedom's Lawmakers: A Directory of Black Officeholders during Reconstruction.* Oxford University Press, N.Y., 1993, p. 9.

5. James Wilfort Garner, *Reconstruction in Mississippi.* Macmillan, 1902, p. 172.

6. See *Congressional Serial Set.* Act of March 2, 1867, U.S. Government Printing Office, 1922, p. 90.

7. John Roy Lynch, *The Facts of Reconstruction.* Neale Publishing Company, 1913, p. 261.

8. For the justices of the peace appointed by Governor Holden of North Carolina, see Eric Foner, *Freeedom's Lawmakers*, Oxford University Press, N.Y., 1993.

9. John Schreiner Reynolds, *Reconstruction in South Carolina, 1865–1877*. State Company, 1905, p. 4.

10. William Watson Davis, *The Civil War and Reconstruction in Florida*, *vol.53*. Columbia University, 1913, p. 424.

11. See William Archibald Dunning, *Reconstruction, Political and Economic, 1865–1877, vol. 22*. Harper & Brother, 1877, p. 57.

12. Davis, 1913, p. 424.

13. John Savage, *The Life and Public Services of Andrew Johnson: including His State Papers, Speeches and Addresses*. Durby & Miller, 1866, pp. 370–388.

14. Dunning, 1877, p. 36.

15. Ibid., p. 45.

16. Ibid., p. 79.

17. See the Memphis Riots, 1866 House Documents, volume 223–224, 166, pp. 6–23.

18. See Report of General Carl Schurz. The Condition of the South: Extracts from the Report of Major-General Carl Schurz, on the states of South Carolina, Georgia, Alabama, Mississippi, and Louisiana: Addressed to the President, 1866.

19. Dunning, 1877, p. 69.

20. Ibid., pp. 69–70.

21. J.C. Napier, "Some Negro Members of the Tennessee Legislature during Reconstruction Period and After," *The Journal of Negro History*, 1920, p. 115.

22. Dunning, 1877, pp. 95–96. The ten states were divided into five military districts; Virginia constituted the first district.

23. See *Congressional Serial Set of the United States*, March 2, 1867 Act. United States Government Printing, 1922, p. 90.

24. John Rose Ficklen and Pierce Butler, *History of Reconstruction in Louisiana*. Johns Hopkins Press, 1911, p. 200.

25. William C. Harris, *The Day of the Carpetbagger: Republican Reconstruction in Mississippi*. Louisiana State University Press, 1979, p. 7.

26. Buford Satcher, *Blacks in Mississippi Politics, 1865–1900*. University Press of America, 1978, p. 74.

27. Harris, 1979, p. 7.

28. Ibid.

29. Foner, 1993, p. 152.

30. Fleming, 1905, pp. 482–483.

31. Joseph Gregoire de Roulhac Hamilton, *Reconstruction in North Carolina*. Presses of Edwards & Broughton, 1906, p. 217.

32. Reynolds, 1905, p. 42.

33. John Wallace, *Carpetbag Rule in Florida*. Da Costa Printing and Publishing House, 1888, p. 19.

34. Ibid., p. 145.

35. Reynolds, 1905, p. 71.

36. Hamilton, 1906, p. 204.

37. Ficklen and Butler, 1911, p. 190.

38. Ibid., p. 191.

39. Booker T. Washington, *The Story of the Negro*. Doubleday, Page & Company, 1909, p. 22.

40. Garner, 1902, p. 232. General Adelbert Ames was a Brevet Major. During the Civil War, he was Lieutenant Colonel of the 24th Infantry. He was friendly to the freedmen and protected their voting rights as well as civil rights.

41. Ibid., p. 305.

42. Ibid., p. 175.

43. Lynch, 1913, p. 93.

44. See Sir George Campbell, *White and Black*. Applewood Books, Jan 1, 2007, p. 330. First published in 1889 by Worthington Campny

45. See Elisha Benjamin Andrews, *The History of the Last Quarter-Century in the United States, 1870–1895*. C. Scribner's, 1896, p. 155.

Chapter 4

Black Police in the States under Reconstruction Enforcement

Police officers are the guardians of peace who are empowered with the maintenance of law and order. More specifically, they enforce local ordinances, make arrests, conduct investigations, and perform many emergencies services such as guiding tourists, searching for missing people, and protecting civilians during major events. Controlling crime, as well as deterring criminals from committing crimes in the first place, is also part of the mandates of police officers. In some countries, as well as in the United States, police officers escort high-ranking government officials during political and national events. To illustrate, when the president visits any state, the local and state police are among the security agents entrusted with the security of the president in addition to the United States Secret Service. In some developing countries, police officers are under the command of the president or the governor of the state. In addition to controlling crime, they protect the regime that is in power and its associates. In this type of political environment, police officers always overlook the abuses committed by government officials and their political supporters. On the contrary, in a democratic nation, police officers do not protect the regime in power, but the people and their property.

As it often happens in developing countries, during the American Reconstruction, police officers were under the jurisdiction of governors who were commanders-in-chief. From various documents examined, records indicate that in Texas, South Carolina, Arkansas, North Carolina, Florida, Alabama, and Louisiana the police forces were under the control of the governors. The constitutions of these states empowered governors with unlimited power regarding the administration of the components of criminal justice. Similarly, legislatures of each state listed above consented to the power entrusted to the governor regarding the appointment of law enforcement agents. Regarding the police force, governors such as Edmund J. Davis in Texas, Henry Clay Warmoth of Louisiana, and Davis Scott of South Carolina were the architects of the emergence of the state police in their respective states. The governors listed above had total control of the police force. The appointment of the police, promotions, and purchase of police equipment were by their orders. As these governors received political support from African Americans, they were challenged politically by their opponents on the inclusion of African Americans in their states' political bodies. Therefore, for the protection of the political system enforced at that time, a loyal police force was needed to keep the opponents of Reconstruction governors under control. In South Carolina, Louisiana, and Texas, loyal whites and African Americans were appointed to the police force to meet that purpose. In Georgia, the appointment of black policemen was refused by legislatures. According to historian Howard N. Rabinowitz, Georgian legislatures rejected the inclusion of African Americans in the police force.[1] As a result, during the Reconstruction period, African Americans were politically paralyzed. They did not have any influence on the appointment of people of their color to minor functions in law enforcement. For better understanding on the employment of African Americans in the police during the period under examination, it is essential to discuss each state separately.

Louisiana

In 1868, the police system of this state was transformed into a political tool by the governor and legislature. To accomplish this mandate, the legislature enacted laws which empowered the governor with full control over the police force. Likewise, the governor was given the power to appoint police board members. As a result, Governor Warmoth appointed five police commissioners for the city of New Orleans, Jefferson, and St. Bernard Parish, three of whom were African Americans.[2] From the account of Henry Mills Alden, we discovered that when the police force of Louisiana was taken from the control of the mayor, the force was placed under authority of the board of six commissioners, three of whom were white and three were black.[3] Alden also writes that the board appointed a total of 373 police officers. Of this number, there were 243 black and 130 white officers.[4] As with the Louisiana police commissioners, they were entrusted with much power, which included the appointment and revocation of members of the police force. In addition to this, they were authorized to assess various corporations for the sums necessary to carry out the law. Similarly, they had the power to lease and purchase property for the purposes of the bill, and to pass enactments pertaining to its function.[5]

The mission of the board was also noted in the *Official Journal of the Proceedings of the House of Representative of the State of Louisiana.* According to the journal, "each member of the board had the power to supervise a police district under his jurisdiction." Moreover, a board member had the legal power to fill the vacancies in the police force.[6] The power entrusted to the board for the administration of the police was opposed by the council, which termed the bill as illegal. For that reason, the council formed a police force according to the old law. The formation of the police by the council was rejected by General Steedman, the superintendent of the police, who argued that the power of the commissioners would be superseded by the council. At the time when General Steedman was superintendent of the police, Louisiana was under the military power of General L. H. Rousseau. With the support of General Rousseau, the police organized by General Steedman was legitimized after the refusal of the state militia by Members of the United States Congress.[7] Refusal of the establishment of state militia was critical to avoid violence between the two races. It appears that whites in Louisiana feared the arming of African Americans. A similar fate was also reserved to former Confederate soldiers. Reconstruction officials in Louisiana opposed the enlistment of Confederate soldiers in the militia which could be disastrous to the state.

In Louisiana, under the law of 1869, the lieutenant governor was ex-officio president of the police board.[8] Oscar J. Dunn, an African American, was the lieutenant governor of the state. Therefore, he was the president of the board of the police as well as the head of the police force. He was also the president of the senate. Dunn was an educated African

American who devoted time and energy fighting for the rights of people of his race. He was also among the black elites in Louisiana. Historically, Lieutenant Dunn was born a slave in Louisiana in 1826. His father was also in bondage and was emancipated in 1819. With respect to his government positions, he served as an investigating agent of the Freedmen Bureau. One of his duties in this position was to protect the rights of free people of his race. Politically, in 1867, he was appointed as member of the board of aldermen in the city of New Orleans. During the Civil War, he was enlisted in the Louisiana Native Guard as a private. While fighting for the Union, he was promoted to the rank of captain.

In addition to Lieutenant Governor Dunn, Octave Rey, an African American, was a member of the Board.[9] Dusseau Picot and Emile Farrar were members of the Board, also.[10] A similar black commissioner of the New Orleans police was James Lewis. This African American was also nominated for Congress at Large. According to John Wymard, Lewis was respected in Louisiana. He was appointed to the office of Commissioner of the Police and Commissioner of Improvement in the Council of New Orleans. Mr. Lewis was also a Jury Commissioner on the Metropolitan Police Board, which members of the Louisiana legislature believed was in direct violation of the law. The appointment of Mr. Lewis was made by Governor Kellogg with full knowledge of the violation of the law.[11] The new police board enacted the Metropolitan Police Bill. In Ascension Parish, Pierre "Caliste" Landry was president of the police jury.[12]

The entrance of African Americans in the police force after many years of exclusion happened in 1867. During the administration of Mayor Heath in 1867, African Americans were privileged with inclusion in the police force of the city of New Orleans. According to Professor Dennis Charles Rousey, on May 30, 1867, Rousseau Picou and Emile Farrot were employed as policemen in the Second District by Mayor Heath. They are believed to be the first African Americans to serve in the police in New Orleans. Rousey also noted that after a week, more than a dozen African Americans were appointed as policemen in New Orleans by the same mayor.

In 1869, in the city directory of New Orleans, nine African Americans were listed as policemen. Additionally, many of them were identified as city policemen. It seems that Mayor J.R. Conway observed an inclusive policy in the police force. Due to his policy, African Americans were able to serve as policemen in New Orleans. In this year, Paul Blouson was identified as policeman in the city directory of New Orleans. Similarly, Mideron Bowles also served as police. Like Bowles, William Bradford was listed in the city directory of the same city as policeman. While the African Americans listed above were recorded as patrolmen in the city directory, H. Baptiste, D. Butler, A. Daniel, F. Dede, and L. Dumarquies were listed in the city directory as city police. In addition to the city police, African Americans also held the position of corporal. Information on African American police corporals is discussed in Chapter 7, which discusses promotions of black police during Reconstruction. According to the data from the city directory, in 1869, it appears that many African Americans served at the Tremé Station. Even though many African Americans served in the suburb of Tremé, few others were recorded in the city directory as policemen in St. Philip and St. Ann. It is reasonable that many African Americans were appointed policemen in Tremé because this suburb was inhabited by many of African descent.

In 1870, in the city of New Orleans, numerous African Americans served in the police. In the city directory, 40 people of that group were identified as policemen. Moreover, eight were listed as special patrol officers; 37 African Americans were listed as patrolmen. These African American policemen worked at the police station and one of them was at the police court. In this year, African American policemen and patrolmen served in various precincts. Data from the New Orleans city directory of 1870 reveal that many African American patrolmen, special police, and policemen served at the 4th station. In the same city, 13 African American officers served at the 6th precinct. In the same city directory, one African American police officer was listed as working at the 11th precinct, and two were stationed at the 3rd precinct. Possibly, the 4th and 6th precincts were in the areas where African Americans were the majority. Among African American policemen listed in the city directory in 1870 were: Gustave Bang, Allen Bibb, Mathias Bias, Charles Chevalier, Paul Blunson, and William Bradford. Charles Bergeron was identified as special patrolman. Another African American who served as special patrolman was William B.

Barrett. Like Barrett, W.J. Harrison was a special patrolman. With respect to patrolman, William Hawkins, P. Isabelle, and Joseph Tholmer served in that capacity. Tholmer served the New Orleans police for many years. He was retained even during the administration of the Democrat governor. After the Reconstruction period, he performed police work in New Orleans.

It appears that in Louisiana, from 1868 to the end of Governor Warmoth's term in 1872, many black men were appointed to the Louisiana police force. Under the administration of Governor Pinchback, African Americans were still employed in the police force. He was acting governor when Governor Warmoth was impeached. The appointment of African Americans to the police board was noted in *The Official Journal of the Proceedings*: "a good many of the colored men were put on who could neither read nor write. Most of them were appointed through political influence."[13] During the governorship of William Pitt Kellogg, African Americans continued to serve in the police force. In 1875, Edward King, during his travel to Louisiana, recorded that black police stood armed with clubs and revolvers at the doors of the Mechanical Institute, the seat of Governor Kellogg and the legislature during the session.[14] Like previous governors, S.B. Packard employed the service of African American policemen when he was in political disputes with the Democrat Governor Francis T. Nichols. At this time, two men claimed to be the duly elected governor until Packard was removed from office. His lieutenant governor was C.C. Antoine, a black man, and the appointment of African American policemen was not a matter of question. According to *The Official Journal of the Proceedings of Louisiana*, Lieutenant Governor C.C. Antoine employed a special detective to watch over the efficiency of the force, and the said detective reported directly to him alone.[15] It is unknown whether or not African Americans were appointed in the special force. During this period, politics had a serious impact in the employment of police officers; more than likely Lieutenant Governor Antoine elected people of his color for political gains. Similarly, black police were appointed during the interim administration of Governor Pinchback. From the *Congressional Serial Set* published in 1922, we discovered that "Pinchback's police were composed almost wholly of colored men, and were ordered to disarm whites who were under General Campbell, the commander of the state militia."[16] Possibly, Governor Pinchback ordered the African American police to disarm the whites fearing attack from them. Lieutenant Governor Pinchback was acting governor pending the inauguration of Kellogg. He became lieutenant governor when Oscar Dunn, an African American who held that position, died in November 1871. After his death, Pinchback was chosen president of the senate and ex-officio lieutenant governor.[17] Under the rule of Pinchback as acting governor, the metropolitan police brigade was at the absolute disposal of the governor in any part of the state as noted by Fortier.[18]

The African Americans listed above were empowered by law to be the president of the board, as well as the head of the police. Therefore, appointing members of their own race was a political asset for them. In this era, police officers were the arm of the government employed to intimidate those who were against the agenda and political strategy of the party in power. During the elections, police officers were always dispatched in the areas where the governor and his party believed that their associates and supporters were subject to intimidation, brutality, and abuse at the polling stations. Governor Henry Clay Warmoth was politically supported by the blacks for his election to the office.[19] Therefore, it was his duty to protect black constituents against his opponents who always attempted to incapacitate them from voting for the Republican Party.

The employment of black police officers in Louisiana has been noted by many authors such as Professor Dulaney, Fortier, Ficklen, and Professor Arnold "Slick" Moore. Professor Marvin Dulaney notes that in 1868, Octave Rey was promoted to the position of police captain by Mayor Heath. This African American was more than likely among the first appointed black police in the police force in the Reconstruction era. As a respectable man, it was easy for the mayor to promote him to that position. The enforcement of law during the regime of Governor Kellogg was noted by Fortier. According to him, there was an incident which happened in September in which three black policemen on horseback arrested an old gentleman during the administration of Governor Kellogg.[20] In Monroe, Louisiana, blacks were employed in the police force from 1871 to 1874, as noted by Arnold "Slick" Moore, a retired major. According to him, when G.W. Hamlet was appointed Mayor of that city, the town had one white officer and four black officers. The names listed by Major Moore were: Frank Terrell, G.B. Hamlet, Vic Valley Moore, and Ben James. On the other hand, the white police officer was called Dr. J.E. Newman. During this era, police officers were armed with an army pistol and a nickel star badge.[21]

From 1874 to 1877, African Americans were still serving as policemen in New Orleans in a small number. In the city directory of that year, few African Americans were listed as patrolmen or policemen. As listed in the city directory, they were not identified by color; the names of African Americans listed in the city directory as "colored" in 1870 were matched to the names recorded in the city directory of 1874, as well as during the years preceding the end of the reconstruction. As a result, data showed that Charles Bergeron, an African American, was serving as police corporal in New Orleans in 1874. Charles Butler was listed as police patrolman. Similarly, Joseph Craig was recorded in the city directory as policeman.[22] Bergeron, Butler, and Craig were listed as "colored" policemen in the city directory of New Orleans in 1870.[23] In 1876, Bergeron was also listed as police sergeant in 3rd Precinct in New Orleans. In this year, his address was listed as 219 N. Claiborne. Charles David was another African American who served in the New Orleans police department. He was recorded in the city directory of 1876 as policeman in 4th Precinct. In addition to David, Charles Elgard, an African American, served as policeman in 4th Precinct in New Orleans. Moreover, Tolbert Ewell was recorded in the city directory as policeman.[24]

South Carolina

In South Carolina, where African Americans were numerous, especially in the city of Charleston, they were frequently appointed to the police force. During the administration of Governor Davis K. Scott, Professor Reynolds recorded that African Americans were included in the constabulary force.[25] In 1869, General Hendricks, the chief of police of Charleston, accompanied almost 25 African American policemen patrolling on Tradd Street where people were gathered. African

American policemen desired to know the reason why people were congregating on the street.[26] Likewise, during the administration of Mayor Pillsbury, African Americans were appointed to the Charleston police force. This mayor was not new to African Americans. He was a freedmen agent in Hilton Head, South Carolina.[27] His brother Parker Pillsbury was an ardent abolitionist and was close to Lloyd Garrison. With respect to the appointment of African Americans to the police force, Professor Reynolds writes that the state constabulary under Governor Scott was formed of many blacks. From 1868 to 1872, black police were appointed in cities such as Charleston, Columbia, and Beaufort. To illustrate, the Charleston guard house was protected by white and black police as noted by Edward King. Police officers of both races worked on term of amity.[28]

Contrary to the record of the Carolina Rifle Club of 1904, data from 1869 city directory of Charleston indicated that five African Americans were listed as policemen during the tenure of Mayor Gilbert Pillsbury, the first Charleston mayor during Reconstruction. The number of black policemen recorded in the city directory is not a conclusive number. Perhaps, some African American policemen worked in the Charleston police force but resided in the suburbs of the town. In addition to police officers, B.E. Holloway served as a detective. The names of African Americans listed in the Charleston city directory of 1869 were Julius Bing, J. Desverney, William Fox, Wm Simpson, and W. M. Viney.[29] Holloway was a descendant of free African Americans in South Carolina. He was born free and possibly had access to education. The account on the appointment of African American policemen during the administration of Mayor Pillsbury was also recorded in the *Charleston Year-Book of 1909*. According to the *Yearbook*, when Mayor Pillsbury organized a day police with 25 men, African Americans were also included.[30] In the *Yearbook*, data on African American or white policemen were not recorded. Consequently, it is difficult to ascertain how many African American policemen were among the 25 appointed police officers.

In 1871, a political deal was convened between the conservatives and African Americans, which led to the election of Mayor John A. Wagner to the mayoral office in Charleston.[31] In this election, African Americans made a visible impact. They voted for the conservative. In the *Yearbook*, data indicated also the conservative African Americans helped with the election of the Hon. John A. Wagner to the executive office of the city of Charleston.[32] As reward, many African Americans were appointed as law enforcement officers. In 1872, in the city directory of Charleston, 20 African Americans were identified as policemen. On the other hand, more than 50 white men were listed as policemen in the same city. In addition to the policemen, B.E. Holloway was a detective in 1872 in Charleston as recorded in the city directory of that year. Like African Americans, their white counterparts had police detectives in Charleston.[33] Mayor Wagner was born in Germany, and he came to Charleston, South Carolina before the Civil War. He was recorded as being part of the men enlisted in the German Artillery battalion in Charleston. In addition to the position of mayor, he was Commissioner of Immigration in Charleston, South Carolina, on July 17, 1867.[34] Regarding Mayor Wagner, the *Charleston Year-Book* notes that he reorganized the police force. The day force was assisted by many night police officers fashioned as the old city guard. During his term, the salary of night police force was collected from half of the fines collected from the arrests they made. During daytime, members of the night force had different occupations than the police work. The *Yearbook* also indicated that officers of the night force made arbitrary arrests to increase their salaries.[35]

In 1873, when the Hon. George L. Cunningham was elected mayor of Charleston, the police force was reorganized once again. The city was patrolled by a day and night police force. These forces were combined as one unit.[36] In 1874, a portion of African Americans were still serving in the Charleston police force. In the city directory, about 35 African Americans were identified as policemen. In addition to the number of African American policemen listed above, there were also high-ranking officers such as lieutenants and sergeants. The accounts of African American high-ranking officers will be discussed in the chapter covering their promotions. In addition to the policemen, two African Americans served as detectives. William Hord and George Shrewsbury were African American detectives listed in city directory. With respect to policemen, William Simpson, James A. Williams, James Wright, and Francis Weston were among the 35 African American policemen listed in the city directory of 1874.[37]

In 1875, still during the administration of Mayor Cunningham, the number of African Americans in the Charleston police force increased. In the city directory of that year, about 50 African Americans were listed as policemen in a force of 135 men.[38] The yearly salary of a private was $720, and the patrolman was paid $720 yearly. The sergeant of police was paid $750 yearly. On the other hand, the first lieutenant received $1,200 yearly.[39] The second lieutenant was paid $1,000 a year. In addition to the policemen, others were identified as detectives. The records in the city directory indicate six African Americans performed the duties of a police detective in Charleston. In the directory, one of them held the rank of chief detective. George Shrewsbury was an African American chief detective as noted in the Charleston city directory in 1875. It appears that he had been promoted in the same year because, in 1874, he was listed in the city directory as detective. The promotion of Shrewsbury was due to the increase in the number of African American detectives. According to the Charleston city directory of 1875, a chief detective had six detectives under him. In this year, Robert Fields, Augustus Green, Primus Green, John H. Hardy, and William E. Elliot were African American police detectives in Charleston. It is reasonable to note that Chief Detective Shrewsbury supervised the work of his fellow African American detectives. Possibly, he was experienced and talented among those who served in the department, and he was probably literate. Among the policemen, Francis Bunno, William H. Bennett, Henry Baker, and Tobias Dawson were African Americans listed in the city directory of 1875.[40]

In 1876, Mayor W.A. Sales was elected to office. Under his administration, African Americans continued to serve in the police force. As the information regarding the police force during this period was not well documented, data regarding African American policemen were collected from the city directory as in previous years. In the city directory of 1876, more than 50 African Americans were listed as policemen. In the same year, a few African Americans at the police department of Charleston held the positions of drayman, hostler, and sentinel. The city directory indicates that Henry Carroll held the position of drayman at the police department. In the same city directory, James Stoker was identified as an African American hostler at the police department, and John Legare was a sentinel at Upper Police Station. In this year, some African Americans were also police detectives. In the city directory, records indicate seven African Americans served in the police department in addition to the chief detective. It appears that the number of police detectives increased. In 1876, John C. Clausen was the chief detective over the African American detectives. According to the city directory, William Doyle, William E. Elliott, Primus Green, John J. Hardy, and William A. Hord were African American police detectives in Charleston. William Fields was listed as special detective in the same city. Among the police officers, African Americans had high-ranking police officers as in 1875. In 1876, the names of Richard Foreman, H. Fludd, Francis Gadsden, William Gadsden, and Furman appear in the city directory as African American policemen, among the others. James Mason was listed in the city directory as an African American special policeman.[41]

In 1877, the last year of Reconstruction, African Americans maintained their presence in the police force. In the city directory, many names of African Americans were identified as policemen, detectives, and draymen at the police department. Moreover, some African Americans held the position of sentinel at the police departments. According to the data collected from the city directory, more than 50 African Americans were identified as policemen. Among them were: Moses Brown, Benjamin Crawford, Edwin G. Crocker, George Cuthbert, and Tobias Dawson. Additionally, six of them were mentioned as being detectives. In 1877, John C. Claussen was noted as being the chief detective. William Elliott and William Doyle were also listed as detective in the city directory.[42] African Americans who held the position of detective in 1876 continued to perform the same duties. As in the previous years, high-ranking African American policemen were also listed in the city directory. It appears that in 1877, many African Americans performed police duties in Charleston. It is difficult to conclude whether or not some African American policemen resided in the suburbs of Charleston. If they did, the number of African Americans identified in the city directories can be considered as exact.

In Beaufort, where the population of blacks was high, the appointment of black police officers was not questioned. As the police was employed for the protection of election's stations, Northern officers more than likely appointed many black police in this town to serve that purpose. In Columbia, the capital of the state and the place of residence of the governor, black police were suited to protect the institutions of the government. Edward King, who traveled to Southern states in 1875, agrees that there were black policemen in Hilton Head. At the time of his visit, there were almost 3,000 blacks and possibly 100 whites in Hilton Head. On St. Helena's Island, there were 6,000 blacks and about 70 whites. On the other hand, 3,000 blacks and 200 whites resided on the island of Yemassee. In Edisto Island, 3,000 blacks occupied that island.[43] It appears that there were no white people residing there. From this data, we can stipulate that numerous police officers in these places were black.

Texas

In 1870, when Governor Edmund J. Davis was elected in Texas, the state was in turmoil. Lawlessness was rampant. Criminals committed crimes without fear of the law. According to Edward King, from 1865 to 1868, there were 900 reported homicides in the state.[44] For the sake of law and order, Governor Davis, with the assistance of his Republican legislature, established a state police force. In the newly formed state police, African Americans enjoyed the privilege of being appointed. According to various data, African Americans were appointed as policeman in the city of San Antonio, Dallas, Austin, Galveston, Houston, and Fort Worth during the period under examination. Likely, in counties inhabited by many African Americans, Republican officials appointed qualified men among them as county constables or marshals. On April 5, 1870, Dave Pettis, an African American, was elected to the Board of Police Commissioners.[45] In the same year, T. Madden, an African American, was appointed policeman in the city of Houston, as was recorded in the city directory. His address in the city directory was listed as 107 Main.[46] The accounts on the appointment of blacks in the Texas State Police have been recorded by authors such as James B. Gillett, Charles William Ramsdell, Thomas S. Thrall, and William J. Hughes, among others. These writers agree that the Texas state police under the administration of Governor Davis were composed of many African Americans. From his entrance to the office of governor in 1870 until 1873 when he left office, African Americans, with their white counterparts, maintained law and order in many cities in Texas. In the city directories, the names of African American policemen were also listed.

In 1870, in the city of Galveston, P. Burns, an African American, was identified as policeman in the city directory. He was employed during the administration of Mayor Joseph A. Mckee. He worked at the City Hall, which was located over the 2nd Ward Market.[47] It seems that Burns was the only African American appointed to the Galveston police force in this year. In 1872, the number of African American policemen in the Galveston police force increased. In the city directory, five African Americans were listed as policemen. G. Allen, Edward Brown, and William H. Butler were among the African American policemen recorded in the city directory. A. Chandler and James Wallace were also African Americans who held the position of policeman in Galveston in 1872.[48] In 1873, the previously appointed African American policemen were not listed in the city directory; it seems that they were replaced by new recruits. Anderson Chandler, Andrew Hightower, Charles Johnson, and Steve Paschall were African American policemen in Galveston as listed in the city directory.[49] In Austin, during 1872 and 1873, Christian Fisher and G.G. Fleming were both African Americans who served as policemen.

In 1875, Anderson Chandler continued to serve as policeman in the city of Galveston. Like Chandler, Andrew Hightower was also an African American policeman in Galveston in 1875, as recorded in the city directory. In the same year, Charles Johnson was another African American policeman listed in the city directory. Like Chandler, Paschall was still in the police force in Galveston in 1875. In the following year, African Americans were also listed in the city directory as policemen. Chas Johnson was recorded as a policeman in the city directory of 1876. His address was listed as SS Av. L, bet 26 and 27th. In the same city directory, another African American by the name of Chas S. Johnson was recorded as detective. He lived on Av. L, bet 19th and 20th. It is unknown whether Chas S. Jonson and Chas Johnson were related.[50] In 1877, in Houston, African Americans also served in the police force. In the city directory, David William and Nathan Thompson were listed as African American policemen. In 1877, David resided on SS Carolina bet Polk and Dallas. On the other hand, Thompson lived on "S Robin W of Saulnier."[51] In Fort Worth, Hagar Tucker, an African American, was recorded as the first special police ever appointed among people of African descent in that city. In 1877, in the city directory of San Antonio, Anderson Harris was listed as policeman.

The Texas State Police was formed by the 12th Legislature in 1870 for the apprehension of criminals and the control of violence.[52] In 1867, crime was prevalent in Texas, and violence against blacks was a daily occurrence. According to Ramsdell, the irritation against black people developed rapidly. Sometimes, they were attacked or killed due to their relation to the Loyal League.[53] Possibly, due to the violence against the blacks, Governor Davis was obligated to include them in the police both for their own protection, and that of the government which they supported. When the police force was formed in each county in the state, the state police and the militia were under the control of the Governor. The state police force was composed of some two hundred and fifteen men under the jurisdiction of a chief of police.[54] In this force, the number of African American police officers was higher than that of their white brethren. Gillett tells us that "in Texas the state police force formed by Governor Davis was unpopular because many of the body were African Americans."[55] Gillett's account was supported by Hubert Howe Bancroft's. According to Gillett the large portion of the police force during the administration of Governor Davis was African American.[56] Similarly, Ramsdell notes that in the police force of Texas under the administration of Governor Davis, there were many black police officers.[57] Governor Davis was supported by the blacks for his election. As the blacks were disliked in Texas, the appointment of black officers to the police force was humiliating to the whites. Blacks were servants to the whites before the Civil War; as they became equal, or sometimes had more power than the whites at that period, conflicts were unavoidable.

As to the function of the Texas State Police force, crime data from the work of Barr showed that they made over 7,000 arrests and recovered $200,000 of property in four years.[58] The outcome of the duties performed by the Texas police was satisfactory. Edward King notes that the corps of state police formed in Texas maintained order throughout the state and combated crime against outlaws and murderers.[59] In addition to crime prevention and other police duties, officers of the Texas police were entrusted with the security of the voting stations. The account recording the protections of the polling booths was noted by Ramsdell. According to him, many black police officers and militiamen surrendered the polling booths during election time.[60] This is true because the police enforced the voting rights of people of their color who would be denied access by the registrars who were against Governor Davis. The election of Governor Davis depended on the black population who supported him. The Loyal League worked hard for his election. Although Governor Davis was vilified for appointing black police in the Texas State Police, Edward King credited him for doing phenomenal work in restoring order and maintaining peace in the state during his four years of service.[61] Like Governor Davis, state police officers deserve credit for reducing the level of crime in Texas during Reconstruction. It seems that they acted professionally to satisfy the mandates expected from them. Charles William Ramsdell also notes that police in Texas under the Davis administration assisted with combating crime against the desperados. According to Ramsdell, police made 978 arrests within a period of six months. Despite these arrests, Ramsdell writes that Texas policemen were tarnished by a group of desperados who joined the police force. According to him, such policemen were engaged in robberies and, sometimes, murders. They also made illegal arrests and committed outrages. After the complaints, the worst classes of the policemen were removed from service by the governor and the adjutant general. In addition to the misbehavior of the police, the inclusion of African Americans in the police force was irritating to the whites.[62] As former slaves, entrusting them with the arrests of white lawbreakers was provocative. With such perceptions, white people did not believe African Americans could fulfill the duties of law enforcement.

Mississippi

As in Texas, African Americans in Mississippi were also entrusted with police duties. In this state, African Americans were appointed as members of the police board in counties such as Lafayette, Carroll,

Bolivar, and Yazoo. In 1870, Henry Money, an African American affiliated with the Democratic political platform, was appointed to the
board of police in beat No.1. Money was an educated African American, and he was an editor of a newspaper in Winona, the site of the
county government.[63] In 1869, in Lafayette County, an African American named Jerry Fox was appointed to the board of police. In 1870
and 1871, he was a member of the board of supervisors. He continued
in the same position in 1872 as a member of the board of supervisors.[64]
In addition to counties, in 1873, in the town of Columbus, Mississippi,
Mitchell Simon and Johnson Wiley were listed as members of the police board.[65] It is unknown whether or not members of this race were
appointed as police officers. In the city directory of this year, none of
them was recorded as police officer.

During the administration of Governor J.L. Alcon, Rev. G.W.
Gayles, an African American, was appointed to the board of police for
district No. 3, of Bolivar County. Rev. Gayle was also appointed as supervisor for district No. 5 on September 17, 1869. He was a native of Mississippi, born in Wilkinson County on June 29, 1844.[66] Buford Satcher
writes that Rev. Gayle was educated in New York under the care of
Elizabeth Powell. After finishing his instruction, he became a Baptist
minister in 1867. He is also credited with organizing the Altar Church in
Bolivar County between September 1869 and November 1870.[67] In addition to police services, he was appointed the justice of the peace of Bolivar County for a short period of time. Satcher noted that he was justice
of the peace for only a month. It appears that when he was no longer a
justice of the peace, he was appointed to the board of supervisors.[68]

Charles Caldwell, an African American who was a former slave
and a blacksmith, also served as a member of the police board in Hinds
County.[69] According to Satcher, Caldwell was a brave African American among the leaders of his race. This native of Hinds County resided
in Clinton, as noted by Satcher. It appears that he was a self-educated
person, as there are no records showing that he attended a formal school.
Even though he lacked a formal education, he was entrusted with as-
sessing taxes, including police duties. According to Satcher, his duties
as police board member ended in 1870. Even though Satcher noted the

end of Caldwell's police work, he failed to reveal when he was appointed to the police board.[70]

Regarding policemen, Satcher recorded that African Americans were appointed as policemen in some counties.[71] He did not list any counties where African Americans served as policemen. From the records, data showed that in Marshall County, where the population of blacks was almost more than 50 percent, African Americans were privileged to have three people in the board of police in 1874. According to Ruth Watkins, who investigated the appointment of blacks in the county during Reconstruction, the three blacks who served on the board were from different political platforms. One was a radical, and the second believed in social equality and was consistent to his belief, while the third was a black police board member who was a conservative. Watkins also noted that they served on the board until the election of 1875, when the Democrats overthrew the radical rule.[72] In Aberdeen, Mississippi, Ed William, a black man, was appointed to the police force during Reconstruction. In Yalobusha County, Mississippi, African Americans were also elected to the board of police. In 1872, Henry Vann, a former slave of John O. Vann, was a member of the board of the police for one year. In 1874, two African Americans were elected to the board of the police. Samuel Carr and Randolph Eggleston were elected to serve on the board.[73] In the same state, in the city of Columbus, Simon Mitchell and Wiley Johnson were members of the police board.

In 1876, Eggleston was elected again to the board. His reelection was more than likely successful because of his good moral character and good work.[74] In Yazoo County, Robert Bowman recorded that there were many African Americans on the board of police, but they did not enlist any. In Aberdeen, Ed William, an African American, was a police officer.[75] Satcher notes also that there were some counties in Mississippi where black policemen were appointed. He also notes that one in Jefferson, the chief of police, was an African American.[76] He did not specify the name of the black chief of police in Jefferson or the year in which he served. Countelow Bowles, an African American, was elected president of the board of police in Bolivar County.[77] Like other African Americans listed above, W.H. Foote was also a member of the police board in Yazoo County. Robert Bowman recorded that he was an uneducated mulatto.[78]

Alabama

Fleming writes that "there were African American police officers in the larger towns such as Selma, Montgomery, and Mobile."[79] While Fleming does not list the names of black police who served in one of the towns cited above, the city directory of Mobile recorded African American policemen. In 1870, about 29 African Americans served as policemen in the city of Mobile. According to the city directory, James Allen, Lewis Brazley, Henry Chapman, and Hugh Chavanaugh were among the 30 African American policemen recorded.[80] In 1872 and 1873, African Americans were not listed in the city directories as policemen. It seems that they did not hold that position during both years. In 1874, under the administration of Mayor John J. Reid, ten African Americans were recorded in the city directory as policemen. The number of African Americans was tremendously reduced when compared to 1870. The following are a few names among African American policemen in Mobile, Alabama, in 1874: James Blue, Abram Brown, Adam Burke, Samuel Diggs, and Robert J. Europe were listed in the city directory as policemen among the others.[81] In 1875, George Holly was the only African American policeman listed in the city directory.[82] It is unknown if there were other African American policemen in the city who were not listed in that year's city directory. It is possible that those policemen resided in the suburbs of Mobile. In 1877, no single African American was listed as policeman in the city of directory of Mobile. Related to police behavior, Fleming writes that whites were irritated when they were arrested by a black police officer.[83]

Florida

In Florida, African Americans were not excluded from performing police work during Reconstruction. From the work of Professor Canter Brown, JR, data shows that African Americans also served as city and county constables and marshals. In the city directory of Jacksonville,

African Americans were listed as policeman. Similar records were also mentioned by Patricia Kenney. In 1990, Kenney listed names of African Americans who served as marshals in LaVilla. Governor Reed also appointed African American policemen. Data indicated that in 1871 Alexander Lee served as city police in Jacksonville. In the 1876 and 1877 Jacksonville city directory, African Americans were identified as African. Due to this identification, it was easy to determine those who served as policemen in Jacksonville. In the city directory of Jacksonville of 1876, five African Americans were identified as policemen: John Belote, Robert Hearn, Frank Bendy, Harrison Morris, and Fortune Simmons were listed as policemen in the city directory of 1876.[84] In the city directory, they were listed as Africans. The same African Americans continued to serve as policemen in the following year at the end of the Reconstruction process. The city directories from 1872 to 1875 were not accessible at the time of this investigation. It is possible that during those years African Americans served as policemen in Jacksonville. Additionally, in counties where African Americans were in the majority, they were possibly appointed to the police force. In localities such as Gainesville, Lavilla, and Pensacola, where African Americans were elected mayors, it is possible that African Americans were appointed to the police force.

Arkansas

The population of African Americans in Arkansas was not large as in South Carolina and Louisiana. Similarly, the population of this group of people was less in Arkansas in comparison with Alabama. With respect to the African American policemen, in 1871 during the administration of Mayor J.G. Botsford, Cyrus Hill held the position of policeman in Little Rock, Arkansas, as noted in the city directory of that town.[85] It seems that Hill was the only African American policeman listed in the city directory. In 1872, the number of African American policemen was increased. In the city directory of that year, about six African Americans were identified as "colored" policemen. Geo Champ, A.J. Handy, Henry Pryor, and Lacey Woods were among African American policemen recorded in the city directory. Cyrus Hill was also retained in 1872. His name was also listed in the city directory. His retention in 1872 may be correlated to police work he performed in previous year. In 1872, George Champ, an African American, was recorded in the city directory as a "colored" policeman. He resided on Corner Center and Fourth. Like Champ, Henry Pryor, also an African American, served as policeman in Little Rock, Arkansas. Furthermore, in the 1872 city directory, Isaiah Sinclair and Lacey Woods, both African Americans, were listed in the city directory as policemen.[86] If there were African Americans who resided in the suburbs of Little Rock, the names of such persons were not listed in the city directory.

In 1875, when Charles Nordhoff visited Little Rock, he witnessed that African Americans and their white counterparts maintained law and order in the city. In the city directory of 1876, two African Americans were listed. Perhaps, African Americans lived around Little Rock. In 1876, Alexander Benson and Robert F. Parish, both African Americans, were identified in the city directory as policemen.[87]

Virginia

In 1994, Howard N. Rabinowitz discovered that in Petersburg, Virginia, black police were enrolled from 1872 to 1874.[88] The account of Rabinowitz was also noted by Professor Luther Porter Jackson. According to Jackson, all the cities in Virginia during Reconstruction had black police officers. But the city of Petersburg had a great number of them in 1872.[89] Because African Americans were slightly in the majority in Petersburg, it is understandable that there were many black police officers employed in the force. Possibly, the police patrolled the black beats. Professor Jackson listed a few names of those who served in the Virginian police force such as Harris Artis, Joseph Colman, and Thomas Jackson.[90] In the city directory of Petersburg of 1872–1873, two African Americans were listed as policemen. Aaron Dodson and William R. Penn were African Americans recorded in the city directory as policemen.[91]

In Virginia, African Americans were politically inactive; it appears they did not have any political impact. From the city directories of towns such as Richmond, Lynchburg, and Norfolk, data indicated that African Americans did not hold law enforcement titles such as sheriff, constable, policeman, city marshal, or coroner. Additionally, they were not appointed as city regulators, with an exception in Norfolk. In 1872, in the town of Norfolk, P.G. Morgan was listed in the city directory as assistant assessor at large. At this time, he was residing in Petersburg.[92] In Lynchburg, in 1875, no single African American was listed in the city directory as a law enforcement officer or city official. It seems that in Virginia, pre-Civil War folkways were maintained, and African Americans were not fully integrated in the body politic of the state. As there is no data on African American policemen in the suburbs of Virginia, it is difficult to ascertain whether African Americans were included in the police. In addition, at the time of the investigation of this topic, no facts were found elucidating the appointment of African American policemen at the county level in Virginia.

North Carolina

Blacks were also included in the police force of many North Carolina cities, such as Raleigh and Tarboro. In 1872, William Battle, an African, was a police officer in Tarboro. Frank Redmond served as policeman in Tarboro for two or three years, as noted by Joseph Kelly Turner and John Luther Bridges. Redmond was credited as a good policeman in the city. He maintained good relationships with his clients. The chief of police was pleased with his style of working. He said that Redmond was better than any other police officers in solving problems. In addition, he worked for two or three years in the Tarboro police.[93] The comment of the chief of police shows that Redmond was more likely praised by whites and blacks, whom he encountered. In Tarboro, the blacks had a majority of the population during Reconstruction.[94] Furthermore, the comments of the Tarboro chief of police indicate that there were black officers who enforced the law and maintained order without taking race or other external or internal influences into account. Joseph Gregoire de Roulhac recorded, "General Canby authorized the formation of a police force composed of loyal whites and blacks in the ration of registration in North Carolina."[95]

In Wilmington, North Carolina, African Americans were also included in the city police force. There, the population of African Americans was large. Historians have supported this account regarding the majority of African Americans in the county. In 1869, Governor W.W. Holden appointed J.H. Neff as mayor of Wilmington. He was assisted by the board of commissioners, which included William Kellogg and G.W. Price, both African Americans. The newly formed board of commissioners, when they established a police force, appointed many African Americans to the force. The Trinity Historical Society and Duke University note that white policemen were removed from the force and African Americans were instead employed.[96] It is certain that African Americans continued to serve as policemen in the city of Wilmington because they were in the majority. In 1875 and 1876, under the administration of Mayor W.P. Canady, ten African Americans were active policemen in the city. In addition to the policemen, Richard Sherwood was a police detective. In the city directory, Lewis Bryant was listed as policeman. Joseph J. Cutlar was another African American recorded in the city directory of 1875–76. John Curtis also held the position of policeman in Wilmington. Another African American who served in the Wilmington police was Daniel Haynes. Similarly, Walter Henderson was recorded in the city directory as African American policeman. Like the African Americans listed above, Abraham McKenzie served in the city of Wilmington as a policeman. Edgar Miller was also an African American listed as a policeman in Wilmington. Moreover, Simon Richardson and Jeffrey Wise were African American policemen in Wilmington in 1875 and 1876.[97] The existence of African American policemen in Wilmington was also recorded by Duke University and Trinity College Historical Society.

In 1875, in Raleigh, North Carolina, several African Americans held the position of policeman. In the city directory, ten African Americans were identified as "colored" policemen. These African Americans also served in 1876, as noted in the city directory. To illustrate, Sampson Anderson, Jefferson Butler, Henry Biggs, and William Durham were among the African Americans who served in Raleigh in the capacity of policemen. Additionally, Hinton H. Lane, Alexander Mitchell, and James Shepard were African American policemen in Raleigh, North Carolina, in 1875 and 1876. Moreover, Edward Semmes was also another African American policeman in the same city during the same period. Similarly, Edward Syme and Oscar Winters were policemen in Raleigh.[98]

During the period under examination, African Americans were appointed as policemen in many cities throughout Southern states. The percentage of black policemen swayed local politics. In localities or states under the control of Republicans, African Americans were privileged to serve as policemen. To some extent, Democrats also appointed African Americans in the same capacity in exchange for votes. Even though Democrats allowed the appointment of African Americans as policemen, it was during the reign of Republicans that African Americans served in large numbers in various police departments. Furthermore, at local levels where African Americans were in the majority, from time to time, they served as policemen under Republican or Democrat administrations. However, with the hostilities from the opponents of Reconstruction, the numbers of African American policemen were reduced progressively from the police force in many towns. In some cities, they were excluded from police functions before the end of Reconstruction. This was the case in many localities in Mississippi, Louisiana, Virginia, and South Carolina. In addition to the position of policemen, African Americans were also appointed or elected as constables and city marshals.

Notes

1. Howard N. Rabinowitz, *Race, Ethnicity, and Urbanization*. University of Missouri Press, 1994, p. 169

2. Ficklen and Butler, *History of Reconstruction in Louisiana (Through 1868)*. John Hopkins Press, 1911, p. 208.

3. Henry Mills Alden, *Harper's New Monthly Magazine*, vol.28, vol.38, 1869, p. 278. See "The Police in Louisiana."

4. Ibid.

5. Ficklen and Butler, 1911, p. 209.

6. See *Official Journal of the Proceedings of the House of Representatives of the State of Louisiana*, Legislative, House of Representatives State of Louisiana, 1876, pp. 189, 194 See the Commissioner of Police.

7. Ficklen and Butler, 1911, p. 209.

8. See the *Official Journal of the Proceedings of the House of Representatives of the State of Louisiana*, 1876, p. 194

9. Dulaney, *Black Police in America*. Indiana University Press, 1996, p. 11.

10. Ibid.

11. See *Official Journal of the Proceedings of the House of Representatives of the State of Louisiana*, 1876, p. 195.

12. Glenn R. Conrad, *A Dictionary of Louisiana Biography*, vol.1, Published by The Louisiana Historical Association in cooperation with the Center for Louisiana Studies of the University of Southwestern Louisiana.

13. See *Official Journal of the Proceedings of the House of the Representatives of the State of Louisiana*, 1876, p. 195.

14. Edward King, *The Great South*. American Publishing Company, 1875, p. 97.

15. *Official Journal of the Proceedings of the House of the Representatives of the State of Louisiana*, 1872, p. 195.

16. See *Congressional Serial Set*, 1922, pp. 125-126, P.B.S. Pinchback, a colored man of some ability and lieutenant governor of the state.

17. See House Document "Condition of Affairs in Louisiana." U.S. Government Printing Office, 1873, p. 83.

18. See Alcee Fortier, *A History of Louisiana, vol.4*. Gougil & Company of Paris, 1904, p. 134.

19. King, 1875, p. 92.

20. Ibid., p. 138.

21. See Arnold "Slick" Moore, *The History of the Monroe Louisiana Police Department*. Negro Carpet Bagger, 1993, p. 4. These black police were appointed when G.W. Hamlet was appointed mayor of the city. At his time, Monroe had one white officer and four black officers. Arnold Moore was a retired major.

22. See *New Orleans, Louisiana, City Directory*, 1874, pp. 143, 191, and 237.

23. See *New Orleans, Louisiana, City Directory*, 1870, pp. 71, 111, and 152.

24. See *New Orleans, Louisiana, City Directory*, 1876, pp. 134, 226, 264, and 270. Also see *New Orleans City Directory*, 1870, pp. 71, 163, 201, and 207.

25. John Schreiner Reynolds, *Reconstruction in South Carolina, 1865–1877*. State Company, 1905, p. 114.

26. Corenelius Irvine Walker, Carolina Rifle Club, Charleston, S.C., July 39th, 1869. The Club, 1904, p. 72.

27. E.S. Stearns, *Genealogical and Family History of the State of New Hampshire*. Punon Knaccuk, 1908, p. 556.

28. King, 1875, p. 446.

29. See *The Charleston City Directory*, 1869, pp. 90, 115, 126, 140, 203, 213.

30. See *Charleston, S.C. Year-Book*, 1909, p. 14.

31. Edward King, *The Great South*. American Publishing Company, 1875, p. 447.

32. See *Charleston, S.C. Year-Book*, 1909, p. 14.

33. See *Charleston City Directory*, 1872, pp. 18, 28, 36, 55, 59, 63, 70, 72, 81, 88, 92, 93, 96, 98, 99, 113, 116, 128, 202, and 216.

34. See James Dunwoody Brow De Bow, John A. Wagner, *De Bow's Review, Industrial Resources, Statistics, Etc...* Vol. 4 J.O.B De Bow, 1867, p. 218. In the Southern Historical Society papers. R. A. Broock, 1897, p. 233. It was mentioned that Colonel John A. Wagner was in the German Artillery battalion in Charleston. William L. King, *The Newspaper Press of Charleston, S.C.: A Chronological and Biographical History, Embracing a period of one Hundred and Forty Years.* Lucas & Richardson, 1882, p. 137. In this book, the author notes that John A. Wagner was the founder of the newspaper named the Teutone in Charleston, South Carolina.

35. *Charleston, S.C. Year-Book*, 1909, p. 14.

36. Ibid.

37. See *Charleston, South Carolina City Directory*, 1874, pp. 48, 53, 63, 75, 76, 91, 96, 97, 99, 101, 104, 129, 141, 155, 163, 165, 178, 180, 182, 185, 205, 208, 218, 232, 236, 246, 249, 272, 277, 278, 281, and 286.

38. *Charleston, South Carolina City Directory of 1875.*

39. *Charleston, South Carolina City Directory of 1876*, p. 39.

40. *Charleston, South Carolina City Directory of 1875*, pp. 48, 52, 55, 60, 64, 67, 71, 92, 97, 99, 100, 102, 103, 104, 105, 114, 119, 124, 126, 127, 132, 136, 137, 140, 142, 146, 161, 162, 163, 175, 179, 181, 183, 185, 186, 210, 212, 214, 228, 246, 250, 262, 270, 273, 274, 289, and 297.

41. *Charleston, South Carolina City Directory of 1876*, pp. 113, 158, 183, 193, 194, 196, 200, 202, 204, 209, 218, 223, 224, 227, 229, 230, 232, 234, 235, 242, 248, 249, 253, 257, 261, 266, 272, 273, 282, 285, 286, 305, 306, 308, 310, 311, 326, 329, 330, 343, 346, 351, 366, 371, 373, 390, 394, 398, 401, 410, 415, 420, 421, 424, 425, 429, 437, 449, and 475.

42. *Charleston, South Carolina City Directory*, 1877, pp. 127, 133, 158, 175, 183, 193, 194, 196, 200, 202, 204, 209, 218, 224, 224, 227, 229, 230, 232, 234, 235, 242, 248, 249, 253, 254, 261, 266, 272, 273, 282, 285, 286, 305, 308, 310, 311, 326, 329, 330, 346, 351, 366, 371, 373, 390, 394, 396, 398, 420, 421, 424, 425, 437, 449, 455, 457, 459.

43. King, *The Southern States of North America*, Blackle & Son, 1875, p. 427.

44. Ibid., p. 130.

45. See *Jacksonville Sheriff's Office*, 1822–2001, Turner Publishing Company, Paducah Kentucky, 2002, p. 42.

46. *Houston, Texas, City Directory, 1870–71*, p. 44.

47. *Galveston, Texas, City Directory, 1870*, p. 30.

48. *Galveston, Texas, City Directory, 1872*, pp. 26, 38, 40, 43, and 133.

49. *Austin City Directory, Texas, 1872–1873.*

50. *Galveston, Texas, City Directory, 1876*, p. 82.

51. *Money and Morrison's Directory of the City of Houston*, 1877–78, pp. 86, and 193.

52. Alwyn Barr, *Black Texans: A History of African Americans in Texas, 1528–1995.* University of Oklahoma Press, 1973, p. 48.

53. Charles William Ramsdell, *Reconstruction in Texas*. Columbia University, 1910, p. 227.

54. Homer S. Thrall, *A Pictorial History of Texas*. N.D. Thompson & Company, 1883, p. 430. See also Ramsdell, *Reconstruction in Texas*,1910, p. 205.

55. James B. Gillett, *Six Years with the Texas Rangers, 1875 to 1881*. Van Boeckmann – James Co., 1921, p. 108.

56. Hubert Howe Bancroft, *The Works of Hubert Howe Bancroft: The Native Races 1882*. A. L. Bancroft & Company, History Co, 1889, p. 507.

57. Ramsdell, 1910, p. 310.

58. Barr, 1973, p. 43.

59. King, 1875, p. 130.

60. Ramsdell, 1910, p. 310.

61. King, 1875, p. 130.

62. Ramsdell, 1910, pp. 302, 307.

63. See Free M. Witty, "Reconstruction in Carroll and Montgomery Counties" Publications of the Mississippi Historical Society, 1909, pp. 119, and 126.

64. Julia Kendall, "Reconstruction in Lafayette County" Publications of the Mississippi Historical Society, 1913, p. 265.

65. See *Columbus, Mississippi, City Directory*, 1873.

66. A. W. Pegues, *Our Baptist Ministers and Schools*. Willey & Company, 1892, p. 214.

67. Buford Satcher, *Blacks in Mississippi Politics 1865–1900*. University Press of America, 1978, p. 77.

68. Ibid., pp. 76–77.

69. Ibid., p. 72.

70. Ibid.

71. Ibid., p. 38.

72. Ruth Watlkins, "Reconstruction in Marshall County" Publication of the Mississippi Historical Society, Mississippi Historical Society, 1912, p. 182.

73. Frank Smith "Reconstruction in Yalobusha County" Publications of the Mississippi Historical Society, vol.12. Mississippi Historical Society, 1912, p. 244.

74. Ibid., p. 245

75. See Publications of the Mississippi Historical Society, vol.9. Mississippi Historical Society, 1906, p. 62.

76. Satcher, 1978, p. 38.

77. Foner, 1993, p. 22.

78. Robert Bowman, "Reconstruction in Yazoo County" Publication of the Mississippi Historical Society, 1903, p. 121.

79. Walter Lynnwood Fleming, *Civil War and Reconstruction in Alabama*. Columbia University Press, 1905, p. 765.

80. *Mobile, Alabama City Directory*, 1870, pp. 3, 17, 30–31, 33, 40, 45–46, 49, 55, 60, 72, 75, 77, 82, 86,-87, 100, 124, 128, 138, 154, 156–57, 164, 169, 171–72, 177–79, 186, and 199.

81. *Mobile, Alabama City Directory, 1874,* pp. 15, 20, 24, 49, 134, 140, 165, 179, and 197.

82. *Mobile, Alabama City Directory, 1875*, p. 90.

83. Fleming, 1905, p. 765.

84. *Webb's Jacksonville, FL, City Directory, 1876–77.*

85. *Little Rock, Arkansas, City Directory, 1871*, p. 75.

86. *Little Rock, Arkansas, City Directory, 1872, pp. 57, 90, 120, 127, and 143.*

87. *Little Rock, Arkansas City Directory, 1876*, pp. 56, and 126.

88. Howard N. Robinowitz, *Race, Ethnicity, and Urbanization: Selected Essays.* University of Missouri Press, 1994, p. 169.

89. Luther Porter, *Negro Office Holders in Virginia, 1865 – 1895.* Guide Quality Press, Norfolk, Virginia, 1945, p.ix.

90. Ibid., p. 86.

91. See *Petersburg, Virginia, City Directory*, 1872–73, pp. 52, 109.

92. See *Norfolk, Virginia, City Directory*, 1872, p. 124.

93. See Joseph Kelly and John Luther Bridgers, *History of Edgecombe County, North Carolina.* Edwards & Broughton Company, 1920, p. 276. William Battle and Frank Redmond are noted as police officers in the city of Tarboro, North Carolina.

94. Ibid., p. 253.

95. Joseph Gregoire de Roulhac Hamilton, *Reconstruction in North Carolina.* Columbia University, 1914, p. 239.

96. Duke University and Trinity Historical Society, Historical Papers, Trinity College Historical Society, 1915, pp. 99–100.

97. *Sheriff and Co's Wilmington, NC Directory and General Advertiser*, 1875–76, pp. 40, 50, 74, 75, 86, 98, 104, 122, 129, and 152.

98. *Chatainge's Raleigh City Directory*, 1875–1876, pp. 43, 50, 55, 85, 93, 109, 115, and 127.

Chapter 5

Community Views on African American Policemen

Historically, the relationship between policemen and the community is critical for the maintenance of law as well as combating and controlling crimes. Without the assistance of community members, policemen are hampered in their police duties. They cannot fully investigate crimes and make arrests in many cases. Like the police, prosecutors are also paralyzed and cannot bring charges against the accused person without the assistance of witnesses. Consequently, community leaders play a vital role in terms of community policing and problem solving within their respective communities. In cities where law enforcement officers and community members are prone to unhealthy relationships, a volatile attitude is always present between lawmen and community members. In this case, law enforcement officers establish a subculture for their own protection. As police officers observe such patterns of behavior, the entire process of criminal justice is viewed as being flawed. For the reasons mentioned above, the views of community members on the work, culture, and performance of police officers are important to bridge a better line of communication between them. In the precincts where lawmen and community members communicate effectively, many crimes are solved in a timely manner.

Contrary to law enforcement norms on community relations, during Reconstruction, police officers were viewed as insolent and brutal. They were labeled as unprofessional and prone to malfeasance. They were disliked because some of them were African Americans. To illustrate, in states such as Texas, Louisiana, and South Carolina black police were perceived negatively. Many white inhabitants were offended to be under the police jurisdiction of blacks who were once their servants.

As black police represented power of the regimes, in states and cities where they were appointed white citizens felt humiliated. Therefore, resistance methods were sometimes employed to challenge their police power. One occasion in South Carolina, the appointment of African Americans to the police force was observed with anxiety, fear, and suspicion.[1] It seems that white inhabitants of Charleston feared vengeance from their former bondsmen. This view was noted by Lieutenant P. Cantwell in his *History of the Charleston Police Force*. In the compilation of that history, Lieutenant Cantwell writes, "the apprehension of the negro policemen was verified in the exciting times of 1876, when our citizens were clubbed on the streets and shot to death from the windows of the main Guard House Corner Broad and Meeting Street."[2] The account of Lieutenant Cantwell indicates that the Charleston police force used excessive deadly force to quell the riot of 1876. As African Americans were members of the police force, they were subjected to the same blame. Concerning the guards, it is unknown whether the police at the guard house were a mixed force between whites and African Americans. Furthermore, the lieutenant did not mention whether African Americans or white policemen defended themselves against armed militiamen.

Contrary to the police brutality which he noted above, Lieutenant Cantwell did justice to African American policemen. He believed in their police performance. In his book, he notes that

> I am far from condemning all the Negro policemen, as I know from experience that there were many at the time who used their best endeavors to preserve the peace and protect the people in this trying time, many of them were retained on the force after the overthrow of the radicals in 1877, when the Hon. W.W. Sale was elected mayor. While reorganizing the force, he dropped about sixty members and the newly elected mayor replaced the missing members by men who passed through the trying times of the Reconstruction and riots, and also the men who had gone through all the changes of the police force from the City Guard up to that time.[3]

The testimony of Lieutenant Cantwell is a tangible account indicating police professionalism of African Americans. As in Charleston, African American policemen performed their police work the same.

In Alabama, Fleming tells us that black police were disliked because they employed discriminatory methods while enforcing laws. They favored people of their own color in many cases. Fleming notes that black police in towns such as Selma, Montgomery, and Mobile irritated the whites by their methods of arrests.[4] They arrested more whites than blacks. It is possible that if black police employed those methods, conflicts between white citizens and black police were prevalent. Perhaps, resistance against black police was common in Selma, Mobile, and Montgomery, Alabama. As police represent the power of the local government, white inhabitants in Alabama were likely against the inclusion of African Americans in law enforcement.

In Texas, black police were disliked because they represented the power of Governor Davis. Francis Richard Lubbock noted that during the administration of Governor Davis, people were harassed by African American policemen. He also noted that due to police brutality and misconduct, the notion of freedom did not exist.[5] In the same state, Charles B. Pearre documented that Lieutenant W. T. Prichett, along with three white and four African American policemen, searched the house of James J. Gathings without warrant. During the search, family members of Gathings were alarmed and terrified.[6] Like the other authors listed above, Hilary Abner Herbert writes that in Texas, "the state police was a terror to every community, and in the name and by the authority of the state, they perpetrated crimes of every description. They searched any place, or seized any person or thing, and without probable cause supported by oath or affirmation. The governor held that uniform which was worn by the state Guard and state police, together with their silver badge of office, supplied the place of affidavits and warrants, and authorized persons wearing the same to search any place, or to seize any person or thing"[7]

Similarly, in South Carolina where Governor Scott employed many black police officers, the relationship between police officers and the whites was not friendly. In Louisiana, black police were treated as they were in other states, and the tension between them and the white inhabitants was also high. Louisiana historians have recorded numerous complaints against African American policemen during Reconstruction. Ella Lonn, author of *Reconstruction in Louisiana after 1868*, characterized black policemen as being insolent and as behaving in oppressive and threatening ways. According to her, prominent citizens were always arrested by black police without probable cause, without court-issued warrants, and ordinary people were arrested for trivial matters.[8]

Even though whites felt humiliated by the presence of black police in Southern cities, in small towns where racial conflicts were minimized, the relationship between black police and whites was sometimes cordial. A good example is in Tarboro in North Carolina where Frank Redmond was identified as a good police officer who performed his police duties professionally. Joseph Kelly Turner and John Luther Bridgers write that "he [Redmond] stood well with the people."[9] It seems that he was liked by white inhabitants. In reference to the behavior of black police officers toward the whites, it is difficult to determine whether they were impartial in their crime control strategies. With no accounts from black subjects with respect to the performance of African American policemen, their attitudes and professionalism can't be measured with certainty. Similarly, due to the racial tensions of the time, it is difficult to label the behavior of black policemen as brutal or insolent. Perhaps, some white subjects had a misconception toward the performance of black policemen.

The employment of African Americans as policemen was not welcomed by white constituents in Southern states. These officers were detested and challenged on many occasions. They were sometimes prohibited from patrolling in the white areas. Historian Howard N. Rabinowitz recorded that African American lawmakers were against black policemen patrolling white areas.[10] It is certain that black lawmakers feared the increase of tensions between black police and white citizens. Contrary to the white inhabitants, African American policemen collaborated well with people of their own race in general. At the time of this writing, no evidence showed that blacks in Southern states were antagonistic to African American policemen. As literature on this subject is limited, it is arguable for researchers to explore whether African Americans were pleased with the work of lawmen of their own color during the period under investigation.

However, it is clear from the period under study that communication between African American policemen and white constituents was always antagonistic. It appears that their work performance was always underestimated wherever they were appointed in that capacity. Likely, they were denied the opportunity to conduct police work in white neighborhoods with few exceptions. Moreover, their power to arrest white people was also limited. Mayors and chiefs of police did not approve the arrest of white suspects by black policemen because they feared violent encounters.

Notes

1. *Charleston (S. C.) Year-Book*, 1909, p. 14.

2. Ibid.

3. Ibid.

4. Walter Lynwood Fleming, *Civil War and Reconstruction in Alabama*. Columbia University Press, 1905, p. 765.

5. Francis Richard Lubbock, *Six Decades in Texas: Or, Memoirs of Francis Richard Lubbock, Governor of Texas in War Time, 1861–63. A Personal Experience in Business, War, and Politics*. A.C. Jones & Company, Printers, 1900, p. 605.

6. Chas B. Pearre, *Twelfth Legislature*. J.D. Lipscomb & CO., Printers, 1872, p. 87.

7. Hilary Abner Herbert, *Why the Solid South? Or, Reconstruction and Its Results*. R.H. Woodward, 1890, p. 374.

8. Ella Lonn, *Reconstruction in Louisiana after 1868*. G.P. Putnam's Sons, 1918, p. 254.

9. Joseph Kelly Turner and John Luther Bridgers, *History of Edgecombe County, North Carolina*. Edwards & Broghton Printing Company, 1920, p. 276.

10. Howard N. Rabinowitz, *Race, Ethnicity, and Urbanization: Selected Essays*. University of Missouri Press, 1994, p. 172.

Chapter 6

African American Policemen
in Other States of the Union

The impact of the Civil War was not witnessed in Southern states only. In Northern states, after the ratification of the Civil Rights Act of 1866, and the Thirteenth and Fourteenth Amendments, African Americans were included in the political body. After the ratification of the Fifteenth Amendment of the United States Constitution, they were also fully included as law enforcement officers in a few states. With respect to the entrance of African Americans to the police force, authoritative data reveal in Washington, D.C., that they were employed as police officers by the mayor in almost the same period as in the states subjected to the Reconstruction policy. As in Washington, D.C., in Chattanooga and Memphis, Tennessee, African Americans were also entrusted with the maintenance of law and order for the first time in 1867. Furthermore, in Indianapolis, Indiana, African Americans were also privileged to serve as police officers. Finally, in Chicago, a Republican mayor also appointed an African American to the police force. At the time of the writing of this chapter, data do not indicate that in other states, African Americans were included in the police force from 1867 to 1877 at the end of Reconstruction.

Policemen in Washington, D.C.

Data on African American policemen during the Reconstruction period have been recorded by many writers. Sandra K. Schmidt conducted outstanding research on the inclusion of African Americans in Washington, D.C. Her work remains prominent in regard to the African Americans' police work in the District of Columbia. In addition to the work of

Schmidt, in Washington, D.C.'s city directory, African Americans were also listed as policemen. To illustrate this, in the 1870 Washington, District of Columbia, city directory, African Americans were identified as "colored" policemen. On the other hand, in 1871, the asterisk symbol (*) was used for the identification of African Americans. With the use of this symbol, African American policemen were identifiable.

In 1870, nine African Americans were listed in the Washington, D.C., city directory as "colored policemen." According to the city directory, Calvin Caruthers, Walter A.P. Cooper, Abraham Dyson, Robert Fleet, Francis Jenifer, George L. Mabson, William Simpson, James H. Smith, and Charles Tilman were African Americans who served as policemen. In the city directory of this year, Tillman was listed as police detective. On the other hand, Charles H. Butler was a fireman at the Washington, D.C. police headquarters.[1] While the listed African Americans were policemen, Perry Carson worked as a watchman at the City Hall.[2] The account on African American policemen noted in the city directory of 1870 was not similar to that of 1869. In the later directory African Americans were not mentioned as colored or by a symbol such as an asterisk.

In 2011, Schmidt wrote an article, "On Being Black in an Overwhelming White Police Department." In this work, the names of African American policemen who served in that city from 1869 to the end of the Reconstruction period and thereafter were recorded.[3] While previously African Americans were identified in the city directory by the term "colored" or an asterisk, those two terms were omitted after 1871. Therefore, the names of African American policemen found in the city directory of 1870 and 1871 were used to see whether some of them continued to perform police duties in the following years. Evidence showed that some African American policemen performed police work for many years after their initial employment date. It is difficult to accurately ascertain if other African Americans were appointed to the police, due to the omission of the term "colored." In addition to the documents listed above, Mayor Richard Sylvester and superintendent of the D.C. police recorded authoritative data on African American policemen who served under him.

In the District of Columbia, the national capital with a large African American population, the mayor of that town included some members of that race on the police force. There is no doubt that African American policemen were primarily employed for maintaining law and order in their own communities. Before the Civil War, no evidence indicates that they were employed in the police force in Washington, D.C. It was in 1869 that the first African Americans were employed as policemen in the D.C. police force. Schmidt writes that three African Americans were appointed to the police force in that year. In 1869, Sayles J. Bowen was elected mayor of the District of Columbia. In that capacity, he was a member of the Board of the Police as ex-officio. According to Schmidt, African American policemen were appointed by Mayor Bowen in 1869. As free men, it is plausible to note that people of the African race supported the mayor for his election. As a Republican candidate, Mayor Bowen received unconditional support from African Americans.

The account of Schmidt on the employment of African Americans in 1869 is ascertainable because in the 1870 Washington, D.C. city directory, few African Americans were recorded as "colored policemen." As noted at the beginning of this chapter, nine African Americans were appointed as policemen. For a better understanding, it reveals pertinent data of each African American policeman in the District of Columbia. In 1870, Calvin C. Carruthers was an African American police officer in D.C. This name was mentioned twice in the city directory. On a different page, the name was spelled as Calvin Carothers. He resided on 1401 7th NW.[4] On a different page, his name was spelled correctly.[5] It is unknown whether the name represented one person. Carruthers was born in Tennessee around 1839. He was 31 years old in 1870 when he was working as a policeman, as noted in the U.S. census of 1870. The same information was also noted by Schmidt. He was married to Mary J. Carruthers.[6] It seems Carruthers was a good police officer. His name appears for many years in the city directories as policeman, except in 1877. In the following year, his name reappeared in the city directory with the same position. Even though Carruthers served for many years in the District of Columbia police department, he was not promoted. It seems that the promotion of African American to high police rank was not permissible, or the department policy was not in favor of such action. Little is known regarding his employment before the Civil War. On the contrary, during the Civil War, he served in the colored infantry in the Union. There is no doubt that he was an experienced policeman. During the Civil War, many African American soldiers were entrusted with military police duties.

Another African American who served as a policeman in D.C. was Walter Cooper. In 1870, he 30 years old; he was born in D.C. around 1840. In the United States Census, he was listed as residing in Washington Ward 5, Washington, D.C., and he was married to Eliza Cooper.[7] Similarly, Abraham Dyson was a policeman in Washington, D.C. He was 29 years old in 1870, as noted that year in the United States Census. He resided in Ward 2 in the District of Columbia.[8] In the city directory of 1870, he was listed as residing on 1422 12th nw.[9] Robert Fleet served in Washington, D.C., in the same capacity in 1870. It appears that he worked at building 1101 on 21st NW as recorded in the city directory.[10] He was possibly born in 1842 and was 28 years old in 1870. He resided in the Ward 1 in D.C. As in the city directory, in the United States census, his occupation was listed as police officer.[11] In 1873, Fleet was recorded as a policeman in the D.C. city directory. During the same year, he lived on 2126 K NW.[12] Fleet was a biracial person born from a union of an African American and a white person.

Francis Jenifer (or Janifer), also an African American, was a police officer in Washington, D.C., in 1870.[13] His name was also recorded in the city directory of 1873 as a policeman. In 1873, he lived on 127 L NW.[14] Furthermore, George L. Mabson was recorded in the city directory of 1870 as an African American policeman. Similarly, William Simpson, another African American, served as a policeman in Washington, D.C., in 1870. In addition to policemen, Charles Tillman was a detective in D.C. in 1870. He resided on 1007 16th NW.[15] In the city directory, he was the only African American listed as detective. Due to his police occupation, it appears that Tillman had some education. He was a literate African American. Without having some education, police officials would not appoint him as police detective. Charles H. Butler, an African American, was fireman at the police headquarters in Washington, D.C. Possibly, the fire department during this time was under the jurisdiction of the police department.[16] In 1870, George L. Mabson was recorded as capital policeman.[17] It seems that Mabson was the first African American listed as capital police in the national capital. There is no indication that before his assignment to the position another African American was appointed as such. As capital police, it is sound to note that Mabson worked with his white counterparts. In the same year, James H. Smith was also an African American who served as policeman in the city of Washington, D.C. He resided at 1701 L NW Cor.[18]

In 1870, Charles Tillman, an African American was mentioned in the city directory of Washington, D.C., as police detective. He was the only African detective in that town in that year. In 1871, his name appears in the city directory in the same capacity. Schmidt noted that he died in 1871 due to heavy drinking. After his death, African Americans did not hold the title of detectives. African American policemen recorded in the city directory of 1870 were educated as mentioned by Schmidt. Their level of education was not noted by any writers, and it is difficult to accurately determine if they were college graduates or had some education from formal training. As a fact, they were able to write and read.

In 1871, according to the District of Columbia directory, John F. Brown, an African American, was a policeman in Washington, D.C. Just like Brown, Joseph Cuney, another African American, held the position of policeman in the District of Columbia. Likely, Abraham Dyson was also an African American policeman in D.C. in 1871. His address in the city directory was mentioned as 1422 12th NW. Moreover, Robert Fleet was also a similar African American who held the position of policeman in the District of Columbia as noted in the city directory. In 1871, Eugene Johnson, an African American, was recorded in the city directory as intelligence officer at 1706 12th NW. His home address was listed as 2141 F NW. His duties as intelligence officer were noted in the city directory.[19]

William Jackson was recorded in the city directory as an African American policeman in 1871. Charles Proctor was also an African American employed as policeman in the District of Columbia. As the other African American policeman noted above, John A. Seaton was a policeman in the same city in 1871 as recorded in the city directory. It appears that he was the first person of that race to hold such position. From the records of the District of Columbia, data indicated that African

American policemen were also retained to the police force for more than one year. During the period under investigation, African Americans were still employed in the police force. With respect to the data of the African American policemen in 1872, data collected in 1871 and 1872 was cross-checked in the following years. In 1871 and 1872, African Americans were identified as "colored." On the contrary, in 1873 as well as the following years, the epithet identifying African Americans was omitted. Therefore, the names listed by other researchers, as well as the previous city directory, served as a catalyst for further research in the city directories of the District of Columbia.

In 1872, John W. Bailey and David E. Chase were added to the D.C. police force. In the city directory of 1871, these two African Americans were not listed as policemen. In 1873, the name of Robert Fleet appeared in the city directory as an African American police-man. In 1877, Thomas J. Clark, an African American, was a D.C. po-liceman. In 1873, African Americans were also appointed as policemen in Washington, D.C., as noted by Schmidt. In the same period, Philip Thompson was also appointed as a policeman. This African Amer-ican served also under Mayor Richard Sylvester. In 1870, in the city directory of Washington, D.C., he was listed as coachman. On the other hand, in the 1880 United States census he was mentioned as a policeman. In this year, he was 55 years old and he was a native of the District of Columbia. With respect to his police work, Major Syl-vester noted that he lost his eyesight when a sailor kicked him in his eye. Due to that incident, he was discharged from the police force.[20] Through the account of Mayor Richard Sylvester, it is notable that African Americans in D.C. continued to serve on the police force even after Reconstruction. In her research, Schmidt listed the names of African Americans who served as policemen in the District of Co-lumbia close to the end of Reconstruction.

While several African Americans were listed as policemen in Washington, D.C., Eugene Johnson was mentioned in the city direc-tory of 1871 as an intelligence officer. In this capacity, it is unknown if he served as a detective. In the United States census of 1870, Johnson was identified as a mulatto born in the District of Columbia. In 1870, he was 22 years old, and held the position of laborer.[21] In addition to the black policemen in the District of Columbia listed above, William H. West was noted for his work performance.

William H. West

William West, an African American policeman, is one of the officers who deserve credit in the District of Columbia Police Department. Before his appointment as policeman, Officer West served as messenger at the Treasury Department. According to the 1870 United States census, he was married to Catherine West. In the same census he was identified as a 26-year-old black male, and his personal assets were valued at $100. During his service as a policemen, he was credited for arresting President Grant for traffic violations. His was speeding while riding his horse on a public road. According to *The Sunday Star* of September 27, 1908, Policeman West arrested President Ulysses S. Grant and took him to the police station. This incident happened in Washington, D.C., in 1872. Even though Grant was the president of the United States, Policeman West executed his duties according to the city ordinances. After his arrest, President Grant commended Policeman West for his attention to his duty. For that reason, he was free from any repercussions for his actions. *The Sunday Star* noted also that President Grant had warm regard toward Policeman West even after his arrest.[22]

Regarding his years of police service, Policeman West served for many years in the city of Washington. In the District of Columbia city directories, his name appears for a long period as policeman. In 1872, he was listed in the city directory as policeman and resided on 1025 3rd NW in Washington, D.C. He resided in the same address for many years. In 1876, he was listed as policeman and resided in the same address as in 1872. In the same year, he was in a picture with police members of the Third Precinct. Contrary to *The Sunday Star*, in the Washington, D.C., Metropolitan Police site from 1866 to 1899, his name appeared as "Simon West, the colored officer, who arrest President U.S. Grant for riding a horse too fast down Pennsylvania Avenue." Data from the site stipulate that President Grant paid a fine for his violation. After Reconstruction, Policeman West continued to serve as a policeman in the same city. In 1900, he was still listed in the city directory as policeman and resided at the same address as in the previous years of his police work.

Police officer West was born in Maryland. At 26 years, he resided in D.C.'s Ward 4. If his age listed in the 1870 United States census is correct, it is sound to note that he was born in 1844 in Maryland. In the Company Descriptive Book recorded by Union officials, William West was listed as a member of the 7th Regiment of United States Colored Infantry. He joined this regiment at 22 years old, before which he was a farmer. In the same document, his place of birth was mentioned as Accomac, Virginia. In 1863, he enlisted for three years in the service of the United States at Camp Staunton. In the Company Muster Roll of July 1864, he was identified as a free man. According to the muster roll, he was emancipated on or before April 19, 1861. During the Civil War, he served his term honorably and was mustered out in Indianola, Texas, on October 13, 1866. He also received his last salary of $17.68 on June 30, 1866. His Civil War services were also noted by Michael S. Rosenwald on December 16, 2018, in an article discussing the arrest of President Grant by a police officer.[23]

Policemen in Tennessee

While the State of Tennessee seceded from the Union like other states under discussion in this investigation, its legislature ratified the Fourteenth Amendment early than any other Confederate states. Upon that ratification, Tennessee was readmitted to the Union. As a result, the inhabitants of Tennessee did not witness the radical enforcement policy of Reconstruction to which South Carolina, Georgia, Louisiana, North Carolina, Arkansas, Mississippi, Alabama, Virginia, Texas, and Florida were subjected. Even though Tennessee was not placed under the Reconstruction policy, the platform of the Republican Party emerged as it did in the states listed above. Republicans in Tennessee also valued the input of African electorates.

In 1866, the Metropolitan Police Act was enacted in Tennessee. With the establishment of the act, modern police structures and features were also introduced in the force. When the police act was materialized, African Americans were not entrusted with the maintenance of law and order as civilian police officers. From the documents consulted during the investigation of African American policemen in Memphis, records showed that it was in 1870 that an African American was appointed to the police. On the contrary, in Chattanooga, in 1867, five African Americans were empowered with the enforcement of law and order, having the same duties as their white counterparts. In Chattanooga, five white policemen were also appointed in the same year as those African Americans. In addition to the policemen, in 1869, Albert Butcher served as night clerk police at the 2nd district in Memphis. In 1870, V.H.R. Decker, an African American, was listed in the city directory as policeman.[24] It seems that he was the first African American policeman employed in Memphis. In 1873, when the Chattanooga police force was organized, among the six appointed policemen, three were African Americans.[25] In addition to Tennessee and the District of Columbia, African Americans were appointed as policemen in Indiana and Illinois.

Policemen in Indiana and Illinois

In Indiana as well as in Illinois, during slavery Africans slaves were permitted to establish settlements. In Illinois, African Americans were economically self-sufficient to some extent. In this state, they established the town of Brooklyn. Perhaps due to their political contributions to the local government, they were entrusted with police work. In the Union, African Americans were denied access to police work, even though the advocacy of the liberation of slaves was strong in Northern states. Conversely, in the South people were antagonistic to the inclusion of African Americans in politics. In many cities, people of that race held the position of policeman during Reconstruction. In the North, only the states listed above allowed the employment of African Americans as police officers.

In Indianapolis, African Americans were employed as policemen during the period under examination. According to the *Indianapolis Daily News* of May 15, 1876, "white policemen had difficulties in serving the arrest warrants for the arrest of colored men."[26] The journals also noted that numerous warrants were stalled in the criminal and city courts because white officers were incapable of identifying African American criminals.[27] It appears that due to this lack of trust, the Indianapolis mayor was obligated to employ African American policemen.

From authoritative documents, data showed that African Americans were first appointed to the Indianapolis police department in 1873 and were entrusted with jail duty.[28] The account of the African American jailor in Indianapolis will be discussed in the chapter covering African American correctional officers. In the same state—on May 13, 1876—six African Americans were appointed to the police force. According to Patrick R. Pearsey, the first African American policemen to be appointed in 1876 were Benjamin Thornton, John Minor, William Whittaker, Carter Temple, Jr., Philip Franklin, and Thomas Hart.[29] In the *Indianapolis Daily News* of May 15, 1876, data showed that the first appointed African American policemen were assigned to ward's division.

On this date, the newspaper writes that Thornton Hart, Carter Temple, Jr., and William Whittaker reported to duty on Saturday. They were empowered with patrolling Bucktownites and going after criminals such as Blood Lums, Cloud, Goode, and Smith. The journal feared that Goode and Cloud gang members would look after them. While the three African Americans reported to work, Benjamin Young was absent on that day.[30] The reason of his absence was not recorded in the journal. In the city directory, African Americans were not recorded as "colored" or any other racial identification. In 1876, Carter Temple, Jr., was identified as a policemen. As in 1876, in the city directory of Indianapolis, Carter Temple, Jr., and Thomas Hart, both African Americans, were listed as policemen. Temple, Jr., resided at 182 Minerva and Hart lived at 74 Margaret.[31] These two African Americans were policemen in Indianapolis in 1878, as recorded in the city directory.[32]

Before 1876, African Americans were not designated by race in the city directory. In 1877, after the name of each African American, the term "colored" was added. Therefore, it was possible to determine that both policemen were African Americans. In Chicago, in 1872, Mayor Joseph Medill, a Republican, appointed an African American to the police force as officer.

Reconstruction policies and amendments to the United States Constitution revolutionized the political landscape both in the former Confederate states and in those which had remained loyal to the Union. In the case of the former, African Americans were also included in Tennessee's police force, even though this state was not subjected to the same punishments as other rebellious states after the Civil War. As for the latter, in Illinois, Indiana, and the District of Columbia, African Americans were also authorized to serve as policemen. Beyond the states listed above, data do not reveal that African Americans served as policemen in Northern states before 1878.

Notes

1. *Washington, District of Columbia, City Directory*, 1870, pp. 58, 62, 66, 87, 118, 133, 202, 254, 349, 354, and 378.

2. Ibid., p. 65.

3. Sandra K. Schmidt, "On Being Black in an Overwhelmingly White Police Department." 38th Annual Conference on D.C. Historical Studies, November 5, 2011.

4. *Washington, District of Columbia, City Directory*, 1870, p. 62.

5. Ibid., p. 66.

6. *United States Census*, 1870 for Calvin Caruthers.

7. See *United States Census*, 1870 for Walter Cooper.

8. See *United States Census*, 1870 for Dyson C Abraham.

9. See *Washington, District of Columbia, City Directory*, 1870, p. 118.

10. Ibid., 1833.

11. *United States Census*, 1870 for Robert Fleet.

12. See *Washington, District of Columbia, City Directory*, 1873, p. 189.

13. See *Washington, District of Columbia, City Directory*, 1870, p. 202.

14. Ibid., p. 262.

15. Ibid., pp. 254 and 354.

16. *Washington, District of Columbia, City Directory*, 1870, pp. 62, 66, 87, 118, 133, 202, 254, 349, 354, and 378.

17. See *Washington, District of Columbia, City Directory*, 1870, p. 254.

18. Ibid., p. 354.

19. *Washington, District of Columbia, City Directory*, 1871, p. 176.

20. See Richard Sylvester, District of Columbia Police. *A Retrospective of the police Organizations of the City*, 1894, p. 222.

21. See *Washington, District of Columbia, City Directory*, 1871, p. 187. *United States Census of* 1870 on Eugene Johnson.

22. See *The Sunday Star*, Washington, D.C., September 27, 1908-Part 4.

23. Michael S. Rosenwald, "The Police Officer who arrested a President," *The Washington Post*, December 16, 2018.

24. *Memphis, Tennessee, City Directory*, 1870, p. 94.

25. Alrutheus Ambush Taylor, *The Negro in Tennessee*, Associated Publishers, Incorporated, 1941, p. 248.

26. Ibid.

27. Ibid.

28. Patrick R. Pearsey, *Guardians of the Avenue 2: Biographies of African American Legends of the Indianapolis Police Department*, vol. 2, 2017, p. 11. Conrad Burley, an African American, was jailor at the Indianapolis Police Department.

29. Ibid., pp. 11–32.

30. See *The Indianapolis Daily News*: Monday Evening, May 15, 1876. Account on African American policemen, Hart, Young, Temple, and Whittaker, p. 3.

31. *S.E. Tilford and CO's Indianapolis, City Directory*, 1877, pp. 184 and 406.

32. *Polk's Indianapolis (Marion County, Ind.) City Directory*, 1878, pp. 266 and 502.

Chapter 7

The Selection, Recruitment, and Promotion
of African American Police Officers

The account regarding the selection and recruitment of African Americans in law enforcement has been related by many Reconstruction historians. Additionally, local historians have recorded the names of African Americans promoted to higher ranks in law enforcement. From various historical collections, the selection and recruitment methods employed by Republicans and Democrats for the inclusion of African Americans in law enforcement were noted. To illustrate, in the document from the Mississippi Historical Society, data shows that Republicans appointed illiterate African Americans to the positions of sheriffs and justices of the peace. In a like manner, Walter Lynwood Garner, the Alabama historian, recorded that African Americans recruited for law enforcement were ignorant. Even though these authors related the qualifications of African Americans employed in law enforcement, they failed to fairly explore the subject in question.

Historically, law enforcement institutions in Southern states were not strongly affected by the political era before the Civil War. Political philosophies and policies observed in the South were not the same as in the North. When local politicians in the North observed the patronage system in the South, the aristocratic design was in force. As such, democratic norms were not fully implemented. On the contrary, the open system was observed throughout many cities in the North. As a result of that system, local institutions were used as an arm of the government to generate money for political bosses. Like other institutions, police departments were also employed for the protection of the political machine's interests. With respect to the selection and recruitment of African Americans in law enforcement in the South, it is pertinent to

stress the concepts of the political era. In the South, the behavior, strategies, and the culture observed during the political era in the states such
as New York and Illinois were also imported during Reconstruction.

Political Era Concepts in Northern and Southern States

From the 1840s, ethnic conflicts were prevalent in New York City, Chicago, and Philadelphia. Political upheaval was the norm. Disorders
were also observed during elections. Data indicate that law enforcement officials protected the interests of political bosses and those who
had ties to the elites. The municipal government was under the auspices
of state legislatures. To illustrate, in 1857, in New York, the police force
fell under the control of the state by the order of the legislature. With
the transfer of the city police to the state, political influence was accen-
tuated, and political corruption became legitimized. The police force
was employed for political design.[1] As in the North, during Reconstruction, the same political strategies were observed in the South. This
political culture was imported from the North, with the police forces
being placed under the control of state governors. In Texas, Louisiana,
and South Carolina, the New York approach was institutionalized in
law enforcement. With the implementation of these political strategies, corruption became part of the political system. The appointment
of law enforcement officers was politically oriented. Candidates affiliated with political bosses obtained law enforcement positions with or
without merit. This was observable throughout the states subjected to
Reconstruction policy. The system was new but spread rapidly in many
Southern cities where African Americans and white inhabitants were
evenly represented. On the contrary, in cities where white Democrats
were in the majority, politics did not play a major role in the selection
of local officials as well as policemen. In counties where African Americans were in the majority, local officials competed for the votes. For
that reason, the patronage system and clientelism were also observed
during the selection of law enforcement officers. Candidates and appli-
cants affiliated with the political bosses were often rewarded for their
contributions to the election of their bosses to political positions.

In New York with the Act of legislatures of 1857, the police force was under the control of five appointed commissioners. The same procedure was also put into force in Louisiana. The Constitution of 1868 empowered the police board of five commissioners with the management of the police force. The commissioners were appointed by the governor. In both cities, the police force was no longer under the jurisdiction of the municipal government. In New York City and New Orleans, the mayors likely refused to obey the orders of the newly appointed police commissioners.[2] In general, the police force in both cities was politicized. As in those cities, in Philadelphia, before the administration of Mayor King, the police force was politicized. During his administration, he enforced methods aiming to take the police force out of politics.[3] The illustration noted above indicates that the police was an instrument of the political machines.

Reconstruction historians have recorded many cases where political elites abused their power in municipal and state governments, but they failed to mention that political corruption in the South was a national problem. Instead, they blamed it on African Americans and the Northern political elites appointed in the states under Reconstruction. Contrary to many historians, Professor William Archibald Dunning established a parallel regarding the corruption under the leadership of the Tweed Ring and that of Reconstruction governors such as Franklin Israel Moses Jr., Henry Clay Warmoth, and R.K. Davis of South Carolina.[4] In his opinion the methods utilized by the Reconstruction governors in generating financial gains through corrupt methods were universal in any other democratic governments. In New York as well as in the states under Reconstruction, vouchers and bonds were utilized as a method for embezzling state money. In the South, the use of railroad bonds for personal gains was common. In Mississippi, Walter Lynwood Fleming recorded the statement of H.R. Revels, an African American and former United States senator, also supporting the claim that corruption, theft, and embezzlement were prevalent among office holders in his era.[5] Northern men introduced corrupt political methods in law enforcement in the South, where the autocracy had prevailed for many years. But when Southerners internalized those practices, corruption in local institutions became rampant during the period under investigation.

The methods of selecting law enforcement as well as municipal officials employed in New York, for example, were also enforced in the South. A popular candidate received much support even though he did not have a decent education. George Walling, a New York police captain, notes that during the 1850s, police justices were illiterates both in terms of basic reading skills and legal analyses.[6] The account of Walling reveals that in the United States, literacy was not a requirement of gaining a law enforcement position. Instead, selection, recruitment, and promotion were based on the individual's attachment to a political party. Police officers who served the interest of the political machines were frequently appointed to high rank.

In the South, violence was always employed by political parties for political gains. Sometimes, parties associated with the main political platforms (Republican and Democrat) were eager to utilize violent methods to affect the elections. To illustrate, in Mississippi, in many counties Democrats and Republicans used violence in the hopes of intimidating their opponents' supporters. In Oktibbeha County, Democrats armed their supporters and positioned them at the station polls, where they intimidated African Americans. With violence, other strategies were also observed, such as stuffing ballot boxes.[7] Attacking voters was another means employed to stop their political rivals from voting. The same procedures were utilized in New York as early as 1837. According to John Isaacs Davenport, fraud and violence were prevalent in New York during the election. He notes that in 1857, during the election of Mayor Daniel F. Tiemann and Fernando Wood, violence was utilized. In 1866, the Tweed Ring used all kinds of fraud and violence during the election.[8] While in New York violence was orchestrated in large cities only, in the South, political violence was prevalent in counties and small towns.

In 1857, in New York City, the municipal government was controlled by political machines. In this year, the legislature established the board of supervisors as an elective body. This body was empowered with the levy of taxes and the management of building. When the board was established, William Magear Tweed, a Tammany Society partisan, was

elected president of the board. Thereafter, Tweed controlled the appointment of all city government officers. During his years in the common
council, employment was obtained through patronage. Walling writes
that William M. Tweed, Peter B Sweeney, and Richard B. Connolly,
and all members of the Tammany "Ring," were robbers and masters of
corruption.[9] They controlled the Board of Audit and plundered mil-
lions of dollars. Through fraudulent vouchers, they made a lot of money
for personal gain. Tweed and his associates were in the same political
party as mayor Abraham A. Oakey Hall of New York. Connolly was the
comptroller of the city of New York and Sweeney was the president of
the Department of Public Parks in 1861. In the same year, Tweed was
Commissioner of Public Works.[10] These practices were also prevalent
during Reconstruction in the South.

In 1868, the board of supervisors was also introduced in Southern
states with the same power as those of New York. In the South, the
board of supervisors was termed differently. Sometimes this board was
called board of commissioners. With the power entrusted to them, corrupt methods were common. Relating to the appointment of law enforcement officers, members of the board were eager to select members
of their own party or people who were loyal to them. Education and
moral character were not always taken into consideration. Additionally,
members of the board of commissioners overlooked violations of the
duties entrusted to their partisans.

In South Carolina, Governor Moses was named the "Robber
Governor." He utilized the same methods as the Tammany officials in
generating money for personal interests. In Mississippi, the case of mismanagement and corruption was recorded by Robert Bowman, the author of *Reconstruction in Yazoo County*. Bowman detailed the explicitly
political behavior of Lt. Gustavus Cheyney Doane in Yazoo County, an
Ohio carpetbagger and mayor. After being appointed to the local government, he amassed a large amount of money through corruption and
spoliation. He robbed African Americans and whites. He enforced law
arbitrarily by illegally fining anyone who held a gun. According to Bowman, he collected $2.00 from each African American who owned a gun
and a pistol. Bowman also pointed out that he confiscated the weapons from African Americans who did not pay the $2.00 as required.

To reach his goal, he employed his own bailiffs, who enforced the gun law he had enacted. He was a native of Ohio and was appointed to that position by Governor Ames.

The Color Line or Division between Races

In 1867, when African Americans were enfranchised by military governors, they made an important impact in shaping the political landscape in many Southern states. In Louisiana, South Carolina, Mississippi, Arkansas, Florida, and Alabama, which had large populations of African Americans, leaders of political parties vigorously sought their political supports. Candidates for governor and mayor were always after the African American votes. Republicans and Democrats used the same strategy. Even though Democrats courted African Americans' political support, their efforts failed to some extent. African Americans tended to vote for Republican candidates. To reward them, they were offered minor positions in the local government. In city governments, the elected mayors sometimes appointed law enforcement officers by following the color line approach. This was true in South Carolina during the administrations of Mayors Wagner and Cunningham. In Mississippi, historian James Wilford Garner recorded that African Americans, due to their failure to secure enough state officers in 1870, established the color line approach in the following years. In Mississippi, African Americans sometimes divided city and county offices with their white Republican counterparts. To illustrate this, in 1873 African Americans and their white Republican brethren had nine members in the Mississippi Senate each. In the House, African Americans elected 55, while their Republican white counterparts had 60 members. In counties where African Americans were in the majority, they always tended to vote for another African American. This was the case of Issaquena County in Mississippi. In 1875, the entire county board was formed of African American officers. Likewise, the sheriff, clerks, and justices of the peace were African Americans. The color line was observed in counties where both races had numerous electors. Sometimes, African Americans supported white Republicans even in the localities where they were in the majority. Walter Lynwood Garner notes that in a county where African

Americans were in the majority, the office was often held by a black person, though in general by a Northern white. Garner's account indicates the trust African Americans invested in their white counterparts. In many cases, when the Republicans abused that trust, African Americans were prone to seek a fusion ticket with another party which they believed would satisfy their political concerns. There were also instances where African Americans were not rewarded after rendering political support to a white political boss.

Loyalty to the Party and Patronage

Party loyalty was an important political ingredient for African Americans who had political ambitions. The support which African Americans provided to political parties was always appreciated by the elected officials of both parties, Republicans and Democrats. Political rewards depended on the elected officials' political and social beliefs. For example, in South Carolina, Governor Daniel H. Chamberlain—a Republican and an abolitionist from Massachusetts—did not object to the election of an African American to the Supreme Court in 1874. He believed in social equality. In Louisiana, Governor Henry C. Warmoth, Governor William P. Kellogg, and Governor Stephen B. Packard were elected on the same ticket with African Americans. During the administration of Governor Warmoth, an African American named Oscar James Dunn was his lieutenant governor. On the same ticket, other African Americans were also elected to high positions. Similarly, under the administration of Governor Kellogg, there was an African American lieutenant governor named Caesar Carpenter Antoine. In Mississippi, African Americans enjoyed the same privilege in the beginning of Reconstruction until 1874, when Democrats removed Republicans from political supremacy through violence and fraud. At the federal level, patronage was observed. Possibly, many African Americans and white Republicans obtained their federal positions through the patronage approach. In North Carolina, Joseph Gregoire de Rhoulac Hamilton writes that Governor Holden, while filling minor offices in North Carolina, always ensured that African Americans were appointed because he valued their political contributions. African Americans were also appointed to higher ranks due to their educational background. During Reconstruction, Northern African American men were awarded positions of power due to their literacy. Similarly, educated African Americans in the South were appointed to higher ranks in the police force and in the local and state governments.

Formal Education

People with formal education were valued during Reconstruction. Even though the era is termed as corrupt and prone to mismanagement, in the South, many governors valued the level of education of high-ranking government officials. Generally talking, African Americans are identified as illiterates during the Reconstruction period, but some of them were educated. Others had fair education. To illustrate, in the executive office of governors, appointed African Americans were highly educated. Similarly, in judiciary positions above that of justices of the peace, elected or appointed African Americans were legally literate. Moreover, literate African Americans held positions like superintendent of education. African Americans also who held the position of secretary of state. Among police officers, African American college graduates were also employed. Furthermore, at the state level, some African Americans with college degrees were appointed to several positions. Take the case of Jonathan Wright, who was the first African American appointed to the South Carolina Supreme Court. He was admitted to practice law in Pennsylvania after passing the bar. Other African American lawyers were Robert Brown Elliott and Macon B. Allen. Elliott was trained under Sergeant Fitz Herbert of the London Bar in England. Meanwhile, Allen passed the bar in Maine and in Massachusetts. The information regarding Allen is discussed in the chapter covering judiciary duties performed by African Americans. Self-educated African Americans were also appointed as lawmen. This was the case of Benjamin Montgomery, who was appointed sheriff in Bolivar County, and who was able to read and write in English.

During the Civil War, many educated African Americans from the North were sent to the South to perform philanthropic work. After the war, these and similarly motivated African Americans devoted their time to politics in the same region. Among them were missionaries and teachers. In the same period, many white Northern men likewise migrated to the South. They established schools for the education of the newly emancipated. At this time, African Americans were involved in the education of their children without reserve. A large number were instructed and became able to write and read. In general, they had a fair education that would help them find entry-level employment in the labor market of the time.

Importantly enough, in 1866, a revolution emerged in the educational arena. African Americans witnessed the establishment of higher educational facilities for them. Desiring education, those with high ambitions were ready to seek such a path. In the same year, Fisk University in Nashville, Tennessee, was founded. During the same period, Howard University in Washington, D.C., was also established. A few years later, African American college graduates from these educational institutions made major contributions to local, state, and national politics. Many of them were appointed as federal law enforcement officers such as collector of the Internal Revenue, gauger, land patent officer, recorder of deeds, and collectors of ports. Some African Americans were promoted from one department to another. John Lynch, for example, was a former slave who was appointed justice of the peace in 1868 by Military Governor Adelbert Ames. Then, in 1873, he was elected to Congress and served for two years. During his tenure in Congress, he presided over the deliberations of the House. He was noted as an exceptional African American by Garner, and even his political skills were appreciated by his political opponents. He was an impartial man with dignity. The factors listed above were likely considered for the promotions of African American policemen.

Promotion of African American Policemen

Historically, little is known on how African Americans were promoted to higher ranks in the police. It is difficult to ascertain how the chiefs of police or mayors promoted African Americans to those high-ranking positions. From city directories of many states, records showed that African Americans held high positions in the police force. The majority of promoted African Americans were in Charleston, South Carolina, where they held the ranks of sergeants, 2nd lieutenant, 3rd lieutenants, and lieutenants. In South Carolina, during reconstruction, the title of police lieutenant was classified as 1st, 2nd, and 3rd. In North Carolina, one African American was listed as assistant police chief in Raleigh. In Louisiana, African Americans held the rank of corporal in the police force and not only that, but also an African American was appointed police captain in New Orleans. The accounts noted above are not conclusive. Perhaps, an African American was appointed chief of police in a small town where they were in the majority. In addition to high-ranking police officers, a few African Americans held the position of chief police detective in Charleston, South Carolina.

African Americans promoted to high positions were people of integrity and good moral standing in their respective towns. It seems also that they were promoted by merit because of their work ethic or their ability to promptly fulfill the responsibilities of the positions entrusted to them. This was the case of Colonel James Lewis in New Orleans, Louisiana and James Fordham in Charleston, South Carolina. These two high-ranking African American police officers served for a long period of time in the force. Fordham is, perhaps, the African American who held the title of lieutenant of police longer than any other in the United States during the period under investigation. Likewise, he was the only African American who held the ranks of 1st, 2nd, and 3rd lieutenant in Charleston, South Carolina.

Assistant Chief of Police and Captains

In Raleigh, North Carolina, Norfleet Duston, an African American, was listed in the 1875 city directory as 1st assistant chief of police. In this year, he resided at Harrington Cor. Martin.[11] As previous city directories were not accessible at the time of this writing, it is difficult to piece together when he was first employed by the police force or the background of his appointment as 1st assistant chief of police. Similarly, due to limited data, it is a challenge to stipulate his appointment to the rank of assistant chief of police.

In 1868, in New Orleans, Louisiana, Rodolphe Lucien Desdunes writes that Octave Rey was appointed police captain during the administration of Governor Warmoth and continued to serve in that capacity during the administration of Governor Stephen B. Packard. With respect to his police duties, Desdunes recorded that Rey was an excellent captain who worked under dangerous conditions. He made important arrests in the city of New Orleans. Desdunes failed to illustrate or list the important arrests made by Rey. With respect with his relations to members of the community, Desdunes noted that Rey was well liked in his community. Additionally, he was respected and appreciated in his community.[12]

In the same state, William J. Simmons and Henry McNeal Turner (1887) recorded that James Lewis was appointed police captain in New Orleans, Louisiana. Before his promotion to police captain, he served as a police sergeant. Moreover, he was elected police administrator for the period of two years. For this position, his salary was $6,000 a month. In addition to law enforcement duties, in 1870, he was appointed the second colonel of the Second Regiment of the state militia by Governor Warmouth. With respect to his police duties, he was credited as being impartial. He served with fidelity and integrity. Along with his other law enforcement duties, he was appointed as regulator at the port. He was collector of the ports and inspector of customs. During the Civil War, he assisted with the organization of a black regiment.[13]

African American Police Lieutenants

In South Carolina, African Americans acquired political skills which were peculiar to them. They organized fusion tickets with other parities for the elections of local officials. In return, they were awarded with some minor offices. Sometimes, the mayors offered them high positions in the police force. As an illustration of this, in 1872, during the administration of Mayor John A. Wagner, an African American named James Fordham was appointed 2nd lieutenant night police in Charleston.[14] In 1872, Lieutenant Fordham resided at 70 Rutledge Avenue. In 1874 through 1876, he continued to serve with the same rank in the police department. During these years, it seems that he was not a night 2nd lieutenant of police. In 1877, at the end of Reconstruction, he held the position of police lieutenant.[15] This was a high-rank position held by African Americans in the Charleston police force. Like African

Americans, their white counterparts also held the same positions. Lieutenant Fordham was a mulatto and a freeborn man. His ancestors are believed to have been free men for many generations.

In 1874, Thomas D. Smalls was another African American who held the rank of 2nd lieutenant at the Charleston Police Department. In 1874 and 1875, he continued to serve at the same rank. In 1875, 2nd Lieutenant Smalls was working at the Upper Station. In 1876, he held the same position.[16] In 1874, James A. Williams, an African American held the position of 1st lieutenant in Charleston, South Carolina. In this year, he resided at 5 Tropman.[17] In 1875 and 1876, he was also listed in the city directory as 1st lieutenant. In 1876, his address was recorded as 29 George.[18] In 1875, Lieutenant Williams resided at 61 King.[19] In the last year of Reconstruction, his name was listed in the city directory as 1st lieutenant. In this year, he resided at 29 George.[20] In addition to police lieutenants, African Americans also held the position of sergeants of police in Charleston, South Carolina.

African American Police Sergeants

In Charleston, South Carolina, mayors did not exclude African Americans from holding the rank of sergeant like their white brethren. In 1874, Mayor Cunningham appointed African Americans to the rank of sergeant. In the Charleston city directory of 1874, Julius M. Bing was listed as an African American police sergeant. In the same year, Francis Lee, an African American, held the same position.[21] In 1875, Louis G. Brown was recorded as an African American police sergeant in the city directory of Charleston for that year. Following Brown was George H. Dantzman, an African American who served as orderly police sergeant at the Upper Station. Like African Americans listed above, George Herman was a police sergeant as recorded in the city directory of 1875, where he was retained as police sergeant in 1875. It appears he accordingly performed the duties required for his rank. Moreover, Robert J. Mears was also an African American listed as police sergeant in the Charleston city directory of 1875.[22] Additionally, James Robinson was an African American recorded in the city directory of Charleston as police sergeant at the Upper Station.[23] In 1875, Mayor Cunningham had many African American police sergeants, in contrast to previous years.

In 1876, Edward Gaillard, Charles G. Simons, Lewis Brown, and Robert J. Mears were listed as African American police sergeants in Charleston.[24] In 1877, in the last year of Reconstruction, Mayor Sales of Charleston had also three African American police sergeants: Lewis G. Brown, Francis C. Desverney, and Edward Gaillard.[25] As African Americans lived also in the suburbs of Charleston, it is sound to note that the numbers of African Americans recorded in the directory are not conclusive. Perhaps, there were African Americans police sergeants who worked in Charleston but resided in the neighboring towns. In New Orleans, Louisiana, meanwhile, Colonel Lewis was appointed sergeant of the Metropolitan police. In 1870, E.H. Mess, an African American, was listed in the city directory as police sergeant at the 6th precinct.[26]

African American Police Corporals

In contrast to South Carolina, African Americans in Louisiana lived in a political environment where whites were the majority. As a result, African Americans did not have the same political bargaining power as their brethren in South Carolina. It is almost certain that, as the minority, they were not promoted in the same manner as in South Carolina. Moreover, in Louisiana, African American policemen were disliked more than in the city of Charleston where inhabitants, to some extent, tolerated their inclusion in the police force. The towns of Charleston and Beaufort were inhabited by many African Americans. They were a political asset for the local officials such as the mayor and the councilmen. Therefore, promoting them was in the interests of the Republican Party.

On the other hand, local Louisiana officials were careful in promoting the interests of the African Americans in areas where inhabitants were against the inclusion of that group in the political arena. Perhaps, for the reasons listed above, the mayor and the governor tolerated the promotion of African Americans to the rank of corporal and captain, fearing revolt from the population. Among those who served as police corporals in New Orleans were Thomas Boswold, C. Butler, and L. MaCarty.[27] Charles Hughes was also an African American police corporal at the 6th precinct police station.[28]

In relation to the recruitments of African American policemen, many factors were taken into consideration, such as the color line, loyalty to the party, and formal education. It is difficult to definitively determine which factors had more weight during the selection process. As regards recruitment and selection, they were also promoted to higher positions than has been previously thought. Some African Americans were also transferred from police positions to the detective bureau.

Notes

1. George Washington Walling, *Recollection of a New York Chief of Police.* Caxton Book Concern, Limited, 1887, pp. 40 and 54.

2. Ibid.

3. Howard O. Sprogle, *The Philadelphia Police, Past and Present*, 1887, p. 166. Sprogle notes that Mayor King kept the police entirely independent of politics and refused to allow them to take part in the election process.

4. William Archibold Dunning, *Reconstruction, Political and Economic, 1865–1877, vol.2.* Harper & Brothers, 1877, pp. 208–09.

5. Walter Lynwood Fleming, *Documentary History of Reconstruction, Political, Military, Social, Religious, Education & Industrial, 1865 to the Present Time, vol. 2.* A.H. Clark Company, 1907, p. 402.

6. Walling, 1887, p. 599.

7. F.Z. Browne, "Reconstruction in Oktibbaha County. Publications of the Mississippi Historical Society and Franklin Lafayette Riley" Mississippi Historical Society. The Society, 1912, p. 280. In New York, the Tammany officials also used violence in the election of 1866. See John Isaacs Davenport, *The Election Frauds of New York City and Their Prevention: In Two Volumes, Vol.1 Eleven Years of Fraud, 1860–70.* The Author, 1881, p. 79.

8. Davenport, 1881, pp. 29–30, and 79.

9. Walling, 1887, p. 160.

10. Journal of Proceedings, 1871.

11. *Chataigne's Raleigh City Directory*, 1875–76, p. 63.

12. Rodolphe Lucien Desdunes, *Our People and our History.* Louisiana State University Press, Baton Rouge, 1973, pp. 114–15.

13. William J. Simmons and Henry McNeal Turner, *Men of Mark: Eminent, Progressive, and Rising.* G.M. Rewell & Company, 1887, pp. 954–56.

14. See *Charleston, South Carolina, City Directory*, 1872, p. 81.

15. *Charleston, South Carolina, City Directory*, 1874, p. 124, Also, the *City Directory* of 1875, p. 128. Moreover, in the *City Directory* of 1876, pp. 39 and 229. See also *City Directory* of 1877, p. 229.

16. *Charleston, South Carolina, City Directory*, 1874, p. 252. *City Directory* of 1875, p. 266. *City Directory* of 1876, p. 39.

17. See *Charleston, South Carolina, City Directory*, 1874, p. 281.

18. *Charleston, South Carolina, City Directory*, 1876, p. 466.

19. *Charleston, South Carolina, City Directory*, 1875, p. 302.

20. *Charleston, South Carolina, City Directory*, 1877, p. 466.

21. *Charleston, South Carolina, City Directory*, 1874, pp. 61 and 178.

22. *Charleston, South Carolina, City Directory*, 1875, pp. 67, 100, 148, 178, 202, and 247.

23. Ibid., p. 247.

24. *Charleston, South Carolina, City Directory*, 1876, pp. 158, 236, 333, and 413.

25. *Charleston, South Carolina, City Directory*, 1877, pp. 158, 204, and 236.

26. *New Orleans, Louisiana, City Directory*, 1870, p. 439.

27. *New Orleans, Louisiana, City Directory*, 1870, pp. 88, 111, 307, and 399.

28. Ibid., p. 307.

Chapter 8

African Americans as Correctional Officers
during Reconstruction

L iterature on the inclusion of African Americans as officers in correctional institutions during the Reconstruction period is unexplored. It seems that little is known about the employment of African Americans as jailors, prison guards, workhouse guards, and penitentiary guards. On the contrary, there is plenty of data on the incarceration of African Americans during the period under investigation. Before the Civil War, throughout the United States, records show that African Americans were housed as convicts in jails, prisons, and penitentiaries. There are no records indicating that they served as correctional officers in any local institutions, except in Louisiana. According to Professor Marvin Dulaney, an African American held the position of jailor in New Orleans before the Civil War.[1] He noted that Ellidgea Poindextean and Douglas C. Butler were employed as turnkeys at the city jail for a number of years.[2] Professor Dulaney did not record the year when these two African Americans were employed as jailors.

In 1862, the United States witnessed the emergence of African American correctional officers in the detention camps, jails, and military prisons established by the Union. In these facilities, African Americans performed correctional duties as if they were civilian correctional officers. From the various Civil War documents consulted, data showed that African Americans served as prison guards at Lookout Prison, and at other prison camps African American troops served as guards.[3] At the time, African Americans were soldiers but not civilian law enforcement officers. In Little Rock, Arkansas, in 1865, African American troops were assigned guard duties at the military prison. Similarly, at Ship Island, Mississippi, in 1862, they were assigned as prison guards.[4]

During the Civil War, African American troops were stationed in many camps where sometimes they served as camp prison guards. After the war, when they were mustered out of the United States Army, they were no longer permitted to perform the same duties.

During Reconstruction, in 1868, African Americans were privileged to serve in correctional institutions as guards. In the city directories of a few states, records revealed that African Americans were employed in jails, houses of corrections, prisons, workhouses, and penitentiaries as guards. For a few examples, in South Carolina, Arkansas, Florida, and North Carolina, African Americans were jailors. Perhaps, in other former Confederate states, African Americans were employed in the same capacity.

Director of the Penitentiary

The appointment of an African American as a director of the penitentiary can be traced in North Carolina in 1870. From consulted documents, it appears that this only happened in North Carolina, where an African American was appointed as executive officer of the penitentiary. Historians note that Stewart Ellison, an African American carpenter by trade, was appointed director of the penitentiary in 1870.[5] According to various historians, he served in that capacity for four years.[6] In the *Journal of the North Carolina Assembly of 1873*, his name was listed among the nominated officers for that position. His nomination in this year was well received by the North Carolina State Senate. During the confirmation hearing, 26 senators approved his nomination. On the other hand, three among them were against his nomination. As a result, he was appointed director of the penitentiary in North Carolina.[7] In 1875, his nomination was rejected at the confirmation hearing of the Senate. During the confirmation, there were 26 "ayes" and "21 nays."[8] In addition to his penitentiary employment, Ellison served also as city alderman for eight years.[9] From these positions, it is plausible to conclude that Ellison was deeply involved in the city's affairs. It is unknown if his employment was subjected to the patronage system of the time. According to Frenise Logan, Ellison received night school only. It seems that his work experience substituted for his academic instruction.

Jailors

In 1868, in Memphis, Tennessee, William Cook, an African American, held the position of turnkey at the 2nd district of the police station. It appears that the jail was established at the 2nd district at the police station.[10] More than likely, Cook was entrusted with the security of detainees housed in the police jail since turnkey and jailor are synonymous titles. In 1869, in Charleston, Jonathan Clausen, an African American, served as keeper of the county jail.[11] In 1870, the number of African American jailors was increased in Memphis. Cook continued to hold his position and others were employed. As recorded in the city directory, A.K. Davis, an African American, was a jailor at the police station building. V.H.R.D. Hays, also an African American, was a jailor at the 2nd district police station in Memphis. Moreover, J.W. Hudson, another African American, worked as a jailor at the 2nd station. Berry Jeffries was night guard at the county jail. Possibly, in 1870, a large number of African Americans were jailed at the 2nd police station.[12] It is difficult to ascertain with accuracy, but it is believable that African American jailors were more than likely employed for the protection of people of their own color. During the period under examination, African Americans had a large population in Shelby County.

In 1872, in Little Rock, Arkansas, an African American named Z.W. Woler served as jail guard. In 1872, the home address of Woler was listed in the city directory as S.W. corner of Commerce and Thirteenth.[13] In Mobile, Alabama, at the jail at the guardhouse, William Taylor, an African American, was employed as turnkey (jailor) in 1874 and 1875. In 1874, Taylor resided at east Warren 2 S. Savannah.[14] The guardhouse where Taylor worked was possibly under police jurisdiction, and that is the reason a jail was established there. As in the cities listed above, during 1876 and 1877, Henry Reed was recorded in the city directory of Jacksonville, Florida, as African American assistant jailor in the county jail located at Market central east of Ashley. While Reed was assistant jailor, Caesar Jameison was jailor.[15] In the United States Federal Census of 1870, his name was recorded as Ceasar Jameson. He was born in 1840 in South Carolina. Possibly, he moved to Little Rock, Arkansas, after the war. He lived in Jackson, Duval County. In the Census, he was listed as jailor.[16] Possibly, Reed was the assistant to Jameison. It seems that when Jameson was absent from the county jail Reed performed the duties of the jailor. Jameson and Reed worked in the same county jail as noted in the Jacksonville city directory of 1876–77.

In Hanover County, North Carolina, J.C. Smith was recorded as the keeper of the jail in the city directory of 1875.[17] In the same year, in Charleston, South Carolina, John L. Fennick was recorded as jailor in the city directory.[18] Additionally, in Charleston, South Carolina, in 1869, William Dart, an African American, was recorded in the city directory as the keeper of the workhouse.[19] In 1870, in Washington, D.C., a city where the population of African Americans was large, Crusor Collins was a guard in the United States jail as recorded in the city directory.[20]

In Indianapolis, Police Archivist Patrick R. Pearsey recorded that Conrad Burley was the first African American appointed to the Indianapolis police force as a jailor (turnkey). In his book, he noted that he served only five months in that capacity.[21] Even though he was appointed to the police force, he did not serve as a patrol officer. According to his recollection, he never served on the street. From the *Indianapolis Evening News* of August 18, 1873, data showed that Concord Burley was dismissed as a jailor in August. He was succeeded by William Porter, a white man. The journal recorded that Porter was qualified to perform the jailor's duty entrusted to him.[22] Due to the nature of his duties, it is sound to note that Burley was a strong man. At one occasion, he was overpowered by a group of prisoners at the station house, but he was able to defend himself. As a result, he punished them without mercy.[23] Burley was also an influential politician among African Americans. In addition to his jailor's work, Burley attempted to seek an elective office. In 1881, he was defeated by James A. Pritchard, a white Republican for the position of councilman. After losing the nomination, Burley rendered his support to him as a fellow Republican.[24]

Keeper in the House of Correction

In 1876, in Charleston, Edward C. Tucker was listed in the city directory as keeper of the House of Correction. He continued to hold the same title in 1877. It appears that he was the only African American in Charleston, South Carolina, who held this position at the end of Reconstruction. In 1877, Tucker resided at 8 Park.[25] The House of Correction was located at that time on S.W. Cor. Mazyck and Magazine. It appears that he was the only African American who served as keeper in the House of Correction. In the city directories of various towns which I consulted no data showed that another African Americans served in that capacity. In addition to the House of Correction, African Americans also served as prison guards.

Prison Guards

In 1871, in Little Rock, Arkansas, Winfield Scott was mentioned as keeper of the city prison. His home address at the time was 12 Elm.[26] Scott was born in Missouri in 1836. His father was from Virginia. In 1871, he was listed in the city directory of Little Rock, Arkansas, as a prison guard. In 1874, William Burke, an African American, was prison keeper in Charleston according to the city directory. He resided at 59 Rutledge Ave.[27]

Penitentiary Guards

The history of the inclusion of African Americans as keepers of the penitentiary can be traced in Little Rock, Arkansas. In 1872, in the city directory, L.K. King, an African American, was noted as guard in the penitentiary at the buildings with John Jackson.[28] In the United States census of 1870, he was listed as Lewis H. King. He was 29 years old in 1870 and was born in Kentucky.[29] Like King, Jasper Newton was an African American who held the same position. In 1872, Newton lived on Victory, between Sixth and Seventh. In the city directory, he was listed as penitentiary guard.[30] He was born in 1842 in Kentucky. He was 28 years old in 1870 as noted in the United States Census in 1870.[31] In the same year, Biven Wright was also working in the penitentiary, and he was recorded in the city directory as a guard.[32] Wright was born in Virginia in 1815. He was 55 years in 1870, as recorded in the United States Census of that year. He was married to Mary Wright. In the United States Census, his name was recorded as Biven Wright.[33]

At the local level, in Southern states, data reveal that African Americans were employed as correctional officers. Records indicate they served as jailors, prison guards, and penitentiary guards. In addition, they served in the house of correction. As to their work performance in those institutions, little is known.

Notes

1. Marvin W. Dulaney, *Black Police in America*. Indiana University Press, 1996, p. 10.

2. Ibid.

3. Thomas Edward Watson, *Watson's Magazine*, vol.15. "Point Lookout Prison." Jefferson Publishing Company, 1911, p. 340. See also Janet B. Hewett, *Supplement to the Official Records of Union and Confederate Armies. Part II of Events*, vol.78. *U.S. Colored Troops*, Serial No. 90. Bradford Publishing Company, Wilmington, Inc., 1998, p. 365.

4. Janet B. Hewett, *Supplement to the Official Records of Union and Confederate Armies. Part II of Events*, vol.78. *U.S. Colored Troops*. Serial No. 90. Bradford Publishing Company, Wilmington, Inc., 1998, pp. 365, 539, 545, and 553.

5. Frenise Avedis Logan, *The Negro in North Carolina, 1876–1894*. University of North Carolina Press, 1964, p. 29.

6. William Stevens Powell, *North Carolina through Four Centuries*. University of North Carolina Press, 1989, p. 432.

7. See *Journal of the Senate of the General Assembly of the State of North Carolina at its Session of 1872–1873*, p. 500. Confirmation of Stewart Ellison for the position of director of penitentiary among other Americans.

8. See *Journal of the Senate of the General Assembly of the State of North Carolina at Its Session of 1874–75*, pp. 663–64.

9. Logan, 1964, p. 29.

10. See *Memphis, Tennessee, City Directory*, 1868, p. 68. Cook is possibly the first African American employed as jailor in the states of the Union which were not subjected to Reconstruction policy.

11. *Charleston, South Carolina, City Directory*, 1869, p. 107.

12. *Memphis, Tennessee, City Directory*, 1870, pp. 84, 92, 140, 151, and 156.

13. *Little Rock, Arkansas, City Directory*, 1872, p. 136.

14. *Mobile, Alabama, City Directory*, 1874, p. 193. See also the *City Directory* of 1875, p. 195.

15. *Webb's Jacksonville, Florida, City Directory*, 1876–77, pp. 97 and 123.

16. See 1870 *United States Federal Census* for Ceasar Jameson.

17. *Sheriff and CO's Wilmington, North Carolina Directory and General Advertiser*, 1875–76, p. 132.

18. *Charleston, South Carolina, City Directory*, 1876, p. 223.

19. *Charleston, South Carolina, City Directory*, 1869, p. 114.

20. *Washington, District of Columbia, City Directory*, 1870, p. 80.

21. Patrick R. Pearsey, *Guardians of the Avenue 2: Biographies of African American Legends of the Indianapolis Police Department*, vol.2, May 12, 2017, p. 11.

22. See *The Indianapolis Evening News*, Monday August 18, 1873, p. 3. *Hoosier State Chronicles*.

23. Pearsey, 2017, p. 11.

24. *Indianapolis Leader*, vol.2, no. 38. Indianapolis, Marion County, April 30, 1881, p. 4. *Hoosier State Chronicles*.

25. *Charleston, South Carolina, City Directory*, 1876, p. 442.

26. *Little Rock, Arkansas, City Directory*, 1871, p. 105.

27. *Charleston, South Carolina, City Directory*, 1874, p. 76.

28. *Little Rock, Arkansas, City Directory*, 1872, p. 99.

29. *United States Census*, 1870, Lewis H. King.

30. *Little Rock, Arkansas, City Directory*, 1872, p. 115.

31. *United States Census*, 1870, Jasper Newton.

32. *Little Rock, Arkansas, City Directory*, 1872, p. 143.

33. *United States Census*, 1870, Biven Wright.

Chapter 9

○═══✦═══○

Blacks as Judiciary Officers
1868–1877

From 1868 to 1877, in the states under the Reconstruction policy, African Americans were elected to minor judiciary positions such as justices of the peace, magistrates, circuit clerks, county court clerks, and public notaries. In addition, a few among them held the title of probate court judge, city judge, and associate Supreme Court Justice. In towns where the African Americans were in the majority, they always held minor judiciary titles before the end of Reconstruction. In counties or towns where the population of African Americans and whites was divided evenly, African Americans were also appointed as magistrates. Historically, during the Reconstruction period, African Americans supported the Republican political platform. As rewards, Republican governors appointed them as judiciary officers. Moreover, African Americans also elected people of their own color as law enforcement officers.

As an illustration, James Wilford Garner notes that "where the colored voters were in the majority in a county, the office was often held by a black, though more generally by a Northern white."[1] African Americans did not have any problem electing a white person who seemed concerned about their causes. Northern men were always on the same side as African Americans since the beginning of the war. Therefore, they were considered as their liberators. Moreover, they were prone to organizing African Americans politically as well as educating them about their voting and political rights. Agents of the Freedmen's Bureau were deeply involved in the social organizations of African Americans such as the Loyal League.

In the states where governors had legal power to appoint judiciary officers, African Americans were, from time to time, entrusted with the discharge of minor judiciary duties. In 1869, in Charleston, South Carolina, W.H. Mishaw, an African American, was appointed magistrate. He worked at the Fireproof Building.[2] Similarly, in Alabama, Florida, North Carolina, Georgia, and Virginia, African Americans were not appointed to the judiciary position above that of justice of the peace. It appears that, in these states, governors were not comfortable appointing people of the African race to high judiciary positions, such as circuit judges and State Supreme Court justices. On the other hand, African American law literates were elected as well as appointed to higher judiciary positions in South Carolina and Arkansas. In South Carolina, an African American was elected to the Supreme Court.[3] In the same state, at the city level, another African American was appointed as judge in inferior court of the city of Charleston.[4] In Arkansas, an African American was appointed as City Judge of Little Rock.[5] African Americans were also appointed as solicitors of the court in some states under the Reconstruction policy.

Justices of the Peace

The title of justice of the peace can be traced back to the Kingdom of England during the Norman reign. When the colonists immigrated to American colonies, justices of the peace were entrusted with the adjudications of minor causes as they had been in England. As to the appointment of African Americans, Wentworth Cheswell was the first to be elected justice of the peace in 1768.[6] In addition to him, during the American republic, there were a few African Americans in Massachusetts who served as justices of the peace. To illustrate, Macon B. Allen was a justice of the peace in Boston. In South Carolina, he was also elected as judiciary officer. Information on Judge Allen will be discussed later in this chapter.

In 1867, with the enforcement of the Congressional Reconstruction, the appointment of African Americans to the position of justice of the peace was materialized. When African Americans were enfranchised, their numbers in the ranks of the justices of the peace increased. The appointment or election of African Americans to the position of justice of the peace depended on the political platform of the time as well as the policy of governors in power. To illustrate, the policy of many Republican governors during Reconstruction favored the appointment of African Americans to minor law enforcement positions such as justices of the peace. In Mississippi, during the government of Governor Adelbert Ames, African Americans were appointed as justices of the peace. In 1869, R. Lynch, a former slave, was appointed justice of the peace by Military Governor Ames. According to Lynch, he paid a bond of $2,000 before he was sworn in as justice of the peace. He also took an oath before the execution of the work he was appointed for.[7] Garner credited Lynch as being an impartial person when he presided over his duties at the House of Representatives in Mississippi. After his retirement from politics, Lynch's political opponents also credited his work. In 1884, he was appointed paymaster in the United States Army.[8]

In addition to the policy of governors, geographical environments also had an impact on the elections of African Americans as justices of the peace. In predominantly black counties in Mississippi, Arkansas, Alabama, North and South Carolina, and Florida, African Americans served as justices of the peace more often. In North Carolina, Governor William W. Holden appointed also many African Americans to the positions of justices of the peace and magistrates.[9] In towns or counties where African Americans had a large population, one or more people of this race held the position of justice of the peace from time to time before Democrats overthrew the Republicans in 1876.

For example, in 1874, Garner writes that in Issaquena County, Mississippi, the justices of the peace were all African Americans. In this county, Garner records that in the entire county, two whites were recorded as officers. Issaquena County was made up of many plantations where African Americans resided, and it appears that few whites resided in the county.[10] Possibly, that is the reason why two whites were local officers. It is likely also in the counties where whites were in the majority, few African Americans were elected to minor positions of power. As an example, in Scott County, Mississippi, an African American named Hightower was the only justice of the peace in that county.[11]

During 1871, in Mobile, Alabama, many African Americans served as justices of the peace. In the city directory of that year, Jacob Anderson was recorded as justice of the peace.[12] In 1874, he was still serving as justice of the peace in Mobile.[13] Anderson was the only African American listed as justice of the peace in the city directories of 1871 and 1874. In 1875, in Mobile, two African Americans served as justices of the peace. William Bates, an African American, was serving as justice of the peace in Mobile, Alabama, as recorded in the city directory. In the same city and year, another African American named John L. Roberts held the same position.[14] As in Alabama, African Americans in Little Rock, Arkansas, also held the position of justice of the peace. From its city directories, few names of African Americans were recorded as justice of the peace. In 1871, T.P. Johnson was listed in the city directory as justice of the peace. While in 1871, only one African American held that title, in 1872, Johnson Ford was added to Johnson who served in 1871.[15]

In South Carolina, many African Americans held the position of justice of the peace during the administrations of Republican governors. During the administrations of Governors Scott, Moses, Chamberlain, and Hampton, African Americans were appointed as justice of the peace. In 1872, African Americans who held the title of justice of the peace included William Rollins, who was a trial justice, which is what a justice of the peace was called in Charleston, South Carolina. In the same city, E.P. Wall was also a trial justice. He worked at Fireproof building.[16] In 1874, four African Americans were appointed justices of the peace in Charleston, South Carolina: J.C. Clausen, Robert Delesline, William Grant, and Joseph P. Howard were listed as trial justices in the city directory.[17] It seems that Governor Chamberlain, a Republican, awarded African Americans many positions as minor judiciary officers. In 1877, William F. Dower, also an African American, was a trial justice in Charleston as recorded in the city directory.

In Florida, John Wallace tells us that many blacks were appointed justices of the peace in the black belt counties. Mitchell P. Chappell was an African American justice of the peace in Jacksonville in 1876 and 1877.[18] William W. Sampson was recorded as a justice of the peace in Jacksonville.[19] The appointment of African American justices of the peace was also noted by historian William Watson Davis. According to him, Governor Reed appointed many African American justices of the peace in recognition of their political support to his candidacy.[20] Even though Davis noted that Governor Reed appointed African justices of the peace, records from the city directory do not support his account. It appears that few African Americans held that position. In Florida, the Constitution of 1868 empowered the governor with the appointment of justices of the peace for four-year terms.[21]

In 1872, in Galveston, Texas, African Americans were appointed justices of peace. In the city directory, John De Brull was listed as justice of the peace.[22] He was the only African American who held that position in 1872. As in Texas, in Little Rock, Arkansas, in 1871 T.P. Johnson and Card McClelan were justices of the peace who adjudicated minor cases. In 1872, in the Little Rock, Arkansas, city directory, Johnson Ford and T.P. Johnson served as justices of the peace. In 1876, David McWhaters was a justice of the peace in Little Rock.[23] From the three years noted above, only three African Americans held the position of justice of the peace in Little Rock, Arkansas. As in other cities, African Americans were rarely appointed justices of the peace during Reconstruction in many states. The numbers of African American justices of the peace were still minimal compared to their white brethren.

In North Carolina, African Americans were also appointed justices of the peace. To illustrate, in the 1876 city directory of Wilmington County, an African American named Anthony Howe was listed as justice of the peace. Like Howe, William Moore was an African American who held the same position.[24] In Chattanooga, Tennessee, A.J. Flowers was recorded as a justice of the peace in 1871. In the same state, in 1872, in Knoxville, attorney at law W.F. Yardley was a justice of the peace.[25] As in the states listed above, in Mississippi, many African Americans held the title of justice of the peace. Garner and other Mississippi local historians have recorded the names of African Americans who served as justices of the peace in that state. In the District of Columbia, in 1871, Duke William Anderson, an African American, held the title of justice of peace in addition to his religious duties.[26]

In 1877, Sampson Keeble was recorded in the Nashville, Tennessee, city directory as a justice of the peace. At this time, he resided on the corner of Spruce and Cedar.[27] In 1878, he was listed in the city directory as barber at R. Polk. In 1879, his barbershop was located at 6 N Cherry and he resided at 119 N Spruce.[28] In 1877, his name was also among the magistrates of Davidson County.[29] In regard to his political duties, it was in 1872 that he was elected to the Tennessee General Assembly and served from 1873 to 1874, and he was the first African American to be elected to such a position in Tennessee. In the 38th Session of the General Assembly, he was appointed to the Military Affairs Committee in the House of Representatives.[30] In addition to his government employments, he was a barber. For many years, he was listed as a barber in the city directories of Nashville. Keeble was born in Rutherford County, Tennessee, and was the slave of his own father, H. P. Keeble.[31] Before the war, he was a pressman at *The Telegraph*, a newspaper in Murfreesboro. Like Keeble in Tennessee, in Washington, District of Columbia, Reverend Duke W. Anderson was a justice of the peace. His office was located at his home at 1921 I NW.[32]

As justices of the peace, they were empowered with the adjudication of minor cases. In Florida, Davis writes that African American justices of the peace issued writs and warrants. Additionally, they tried minor cases. John Wallace notes that jurisdictions of the justices of the peace of the Constitution of 1868 covered criminal and civil cases, with the right of appeal.[33] Garner notes that in Madison County, the justices of the peace had jurisdiction over civil cases amounting to $150, and to all criminal offences such as larceny, trespass, assault, and battery, etc.[34] In Mississippi, little is known about the records of black justices of the peace. Many authors indicate only that they were illiterate. In North Carolina, Fleming writes that "justices of the peace who tried cases involving misdemeanors for which the parties might be sent to jail, could not write, and had to make their mark for their signature."[35] But from the account of Garner, we found that black justices of the peace were lenient in sentencing lawbreakers. He says, "they imposed but few fines, and shortly before the meeting of the grand jury, they usually got some friendly white neighbor to write up dockets for presentation at the proper time."[36] In Alabama, blacks prosecuted by people of their own color were convicted by the African American jury members.[37] Similarly, in Mississippi, the jury that convicted suspected criminals before the black justices of the peace was composed of people of the African race.[38] It is understandable to find that the juries in the predominantly black counties reflected their majorities. In South Carolina, black justices of the peace were accused of not being impartial to the white subjects. They have been accused of abusing white people.[39] During the administration of Governor Wade Hampton, qualified and trained African Americans were appointed as justices of the peace (trial justices) in South Carolina. Governor Hampton was prone to appoint talented officers without regard to ethnicity or race.[40] Among African American trial justices appointed by Governor Hampton were Richard Howell Gleaves of Beaufort and Martin R. Delany of Charleston. As in other states, African Americans in Louisiana were elected justices of the peace. Pierre "Caliste" Landry served as justice of the peace in Donaldsonville, Ascension Parish, in Louisiana.[41] He was also an African American with a fair education.

On April 6, 1869, in Washington, D.C., an African American named Orindatus S. B. Wall was appointed justice of the peace by President Ulysses Grant.[42] According to John Mercer Langston, Wall was among the first class to graduate from Howard Law School. Langston also noted that Wall was well-instructed in his field of studies, practicing law for some years.[43] During his law practice, Wall was regarded as a diligent and honorable attorney.[44] According to George Washington Williams, an African American historian and veteran soldier, Wall held the position of quartermaster for two years in the Bureau of Refugees, Freedmen, and Abandoned Lands. At the time of his employment at that office, the headquarters were situated at Charleston, South Carolina. As quartermaster, Wall heard disputes and other cases pertaining to refugees and freedmen. In the army, O.S.B. Wall was appointed as captain in the colored regiment. He also helped with the recruitment of African American soldiers in Ohio. He was appointed as captain by the United States Secretary of War Department, Edwin M. Stanton. In the United States Army, he was entitled to receive the same emoluments as other members of the U.S. military. Prior of his military duty, he was a merchant in Oberlin, Ohio. Williams identified him as a successful boot and shoe merchant.[45] In the same district, Rev. Duke W. Anderson was listed in the city directory as a justice of the peace. His office for that position was located at his personal house.[46] Justice of the Peace and Reverend Anderson was born in Illinois around 1820. In 1871, he was 58 years old when he was a justice of the peace. In the 1870 United States Census, he was listed as a mulatto and a teacher by occupation. He was married to Eliza Anderson, and they had children.[47]

In addition to the accounts of various writers, Justice of the Peace O.S. Wall related his life history to members of the investigation of the exodus of African Americans from the South to the North. According to his own recollections, he resided in Washington, D.C., on the corner of Seventh and Boundary Street, not far from Howard University. He also recounts that he was educated at the Quaker School in Warren County, 50 miles above Cincinnati, Ohio. He also told members of the Exodus Committee that he had been appointed as captain of the army by Secretary Stanton on March 3, 1865. He served in this position for a year before the disbanding of his regiment in 1866. In 1867, he was employed by General Howard in the Freedmen's Bureau according to his recollection. Pertaining to his judiciary duties, he said that Mayor Sayles Bowen and other leading men in Washington, D.C., petitioned the United States Attorney General for his commission as a justice of the peace. According to him, he was the first black person to be appointed to such a position in the District of Columbia.[48]

Justice of the Peace Wall was born in Richmond County, North Carolina. In Washington, D.C., he was involved with the Emigrant Aid Society and served as the president of that society. The secretary of the Emigrant Aid Society was Mr. Adams. The Emigrant Aid Society was established for the assistance of African Americans who emigrated from the South to the North.[49] In the Emigrant Aid Society, he was not only the president, but he was also one of the organizers of that society, as recorded in the *Democratic Textbook*. With Wall's efforts, two other societies were organized at Greencastle, Indiana, and at Terre Haute in the same state.[50]

Like O.S.B. Wall, another African American, was appointed justice of the peace in the District of Columbia. According to historical data, John A. Moss was first appointed by President Rutherford B. Hayes and reappointed by President Cleveland. This African American was a protégé of Senator Charles Sumner of Massachusetts.[51] Contrary to the document consulted—on February 27, 2014, during the celebration of Black History Month—Chief Judge Patricia Campbell-Smith of the United States Court of Federal Claims pointed out that "John Moss was the first African American to serve as justice of the peace in the District of Columbia in 1873 after being appointed by President

Rutherford B. Hayes."[52] Records for African Americans who served in law enforcement are sometime inconsistent. Therefore, the omission of data pertaining to those who served as lawmen is prevalent. In the *Congressional Serial Set* of 1886, data showed that John A. Moss was born in Virginia. In the same journal, he was identified as justice of the peace for the District of Columbia.[53]

Justices of the peace were also empowered with issuing warrants for making an arrest. In Louisiana, the justices of the peace had jurisdiction of the Parish Court, handling all causes involving claims of $100 or less.

Civil Magistrates

Civil magistrates were judiciary officers entrusted with the adjudication of minor cases, like the justices of the peace to some extent. Records indicate that an African American was appointed as a justice of the peace in 1768 in Newmarket, New Hampshire. On the contrary, there are no records regarding the appointment of African American magistrates before the Civil War in the Southern states. During Reconstruction, many African American magistrates were elected in the former Confederate states such as in North Carolina, Virginia, South Carolina, and Tennessee.

In Edgecombe County, North Carolina, for example, there are records indicating the election of African Americans as magistrates. Joseph Kelly Turner notes that in the Lower Fishing Creek, an African American named Benjamin Johnson was elected magistrate. In the same county, in the Lower Conetoe, Henry Telfai, an African American, was a magistrate. In Tarboro Township, Chase J.H.M. Jackson, also a black man, was a magistrate.[54] It appears in 1865, in Edgecombe County, when the legislature was empowered to appoint the magistrates, African Americans were less likely to be appointed to that position. From 1868 to 1875, the county government officers such as county commissioners, magistrates, and school committees were elected by the people.[55] In Upper Fishing Creek, North Carolina, an African American was also elected as a magistrate. African Americans in Edgecombe County were privileged with minor judiciary duties. William Bunn, a former slave, was elected magistrate before his election to the legislature in 1870 and 1872, as well as in 1877.[56]

In Mississippi, Nelson Glass and J.I. Ingram were magistrates in Bolivar County.[57] As in North Carolina, black magistrates were elected in Natchez, Mississippi. Edward King, who traveled there in 1875, notes that there were many black magistrates in that city. According to him, since 1867 when African Americans came to power, they had a share fair of magistrates in the city. He went on to stipulate that there were many black magistrates in Natchez.[58]

In Beaufort, South Carolina, African Americans also served as magistrates. It is quite possible in Hilton Head and other islands where African Americans were in majority, the magistrates who served the population were people of the African race. In 1869, in Charleston, South Carolina, two African Americans served as magistrates. R.C. Delarge and W.H. Mishaw were magistrates in that city as listed in the city directory.[59] In Edgefield County, the probate judge was an African American whom John Schreiner Reynolds believed to be incompetent.[60] In his book, *Reconstruction in South Carolina*, however, Reynolds did not mention the name of the African American probate judge. In addition, he did not specify how long the African American served in that position. Moreover, Reynolds failed to record if the African American probate judge in Edgefield County had a legal education or training. Contrary to Reynolds' claims, John Abney Chapman, the author of the *History of Edgefield County*, recorded the name of the African American probate judge in that county. According to Chapman, A.N. Baney served as an African American probate judge in Edgefield County from 1875 to 1876.[61]

County Attorneys

In Edgecombe County, North Carolina, J.E. O'Hara was an attorney. He was also chairman of the county's Republican Party. O'Hara was an educated African American, having attended law school at Howard University in Washington, D.C. In the *Journal of Negro History*, records indicated that he also received an education in New York, where he was born.[62] Eric Anderson writes that before his entrance in politics, in 1868,

O'Hara worked as a clerk to the Constitutional Convention. While in Washington, D.C., he worked as a clerk in the Treasury Department. When he moved to North Carolina, he was licensed to practice law in that state.[63] Like other Northern educated African Americans, when he went to North Carolina, he was involved in politics, getting elected as a state congressman. O'Hara was also a delegate during the Constitutional Convention. Gregoire de Roulhac Hamilton writes that he introduced an amendment which would make the cohabitation between a white person and an African American a felony. After the vote by the delegates, the amendment was defeated by a vote of 46 to 9.[64] Meanwhile, in Texas, Lawrence D. Rice writes that W.A. Price was a county attorney in 1876. According to him, Price was the only African American who served as a lawyer in Texas during that period.[65]

Minor Officers of the Court in the South during Reconstruction

Throughout the South during Reconstruction, blacks were appointed as judiciary officers of the courts. In areas where the local court was under a black justice of the peace, it was common to find that minor officers of the court were other African Americans. From the account of Garner, data show that in DeSoto and Warren Counties, Mississippi, minor officers of the court were blacks. In DeSoto County, the circuit clerk was an African American, and in Warren County, the chancery clerk was too. Similarly, in Yazoo County there were both an African American chancery clerk and a circuit clerk. One of the chancery clerks in Yazoo was a former member of legislature according to Garner. Before the war, this man had been a slave.[66] Thomas W. Cardozo was a clerk of the circuit court before being elected to the position of Superintendent of Education in Mississippi.[67]

In Issaquena, Washington, Warren, Claiborne, Panola, and Yazoo Counties, clerks of the justice of the peace court were also African Americans. These counties were under the jurisdiction of black people. In Washington County, Mississippi, Allan J. Ross held the office of chancery clerk. Garner notes that Ross was an eloquent speaker and a priest who controlled politics in his county. In 1870, in Warren County, a chancery clerk and the circuit clerk were also African Americans.

Similarly, in 1875, in Claiborne County, a black man was a circuit clerk in 1875.[68] In Vicksburg, Mississippi, Davenport, a black man, was a chancery clerk.[69] In Panola County, Mississippi, two African American Democrats were elected as circuit and chancery clerks. These men were named Felix Eldridge and M.G. Littlejohn.[70] In Yazoo County, where African Americans were the majority, Robert Bowman writes that African Americans occupied the positions of chancery and circuit clerks office for many years. According to Bowman, these blacks were incompetent, being assisted by white deputies in their daily clerk duties. However, his account was not supported by any concrete evidence for that claim.[71] In a similar manner, he failed to record the name of a white person who assisted a black circuit or chancery clerk in judiciary assignments. Moreover, African Americans served as circuit and chancery clerk during the administration of the Democrats. In 1876, Felix Eldridge and M.G. Littlejohn were elected circuit and chancery clerks as Democrat candidates in Panola County. J. Ousley of Bolivar County also served as circuit clerk.[72] In Edgefield, South Carolina, Reynolds writes that the clerk of the circuit court was a black man. John Abney Chapman writes that Jesse Jones, an African American, was a clerk of court in Edgefield County from 1874 to 1876.[73] It seems that he was the only African American who held that position during the Reconstruction period. As in the states listed above, in Arkansas, Hempstead notes that blacks were clerks of the courts. In addition to clerks of courts, Governor Clayton appointed African Americans as prosecuting attorneys.

In Alabama, the notary public acted as the justice of the peace when appointed by the governor with the power to act as such. In 1866, James T. Rapier was appointed a notary public by Governor Ames of Alabama. An African American was also appointed as judge during Reconstruction in Arkansas. In Alabama, the circuit court clerk was entrusted with issuing summons, writs, subpoenas, executions, and process, under authority of the court. He was also authorized to keep the various dockets and other records of the court.

While in the listed states African Americans were appointed to minor judiciary positions, this was not the case in South Carolina. Thomas Holt, who wrote about the political leadership of African

Americans in this state, notes that in 1872 of the 31 clerks of court, none was black.[74] By 1875, however, Edward W. Lee was a clerk at the county court in Charleston, South Carolina. In addition to the minor judiciary titles listed above, during the administration of Governor Hampton in 1877 they were appointed as jury commissioners.[75]

Jury Commissioners

During Reconstruction, African Americans were entrusted with jury services like whites. In many cases, data indicate the selection of African American jury members. During the period under investigation, few African Americans were elected jury commissioners in many former Confederates states. In Charleston, South Carolina, Richard Holloway was listed as a jury commissioner in the 1876 city directory. In 1877, he continued to perform the same duties, as recorded in that year's city directory.[76] From the beginning of Reconstruction to its end, it seems that Holloway was the only African American who held the position of jury commissioner in Charleston, South Carolina. Before 1876, in the city directories, no single African American was recorded as jury commissioner. Possibly, this position was very selective, so the candidate was more than likely well equipped for the duties entrusted to him.

A Judge on the Inferior Circuit Court of Charleston, South Carolina

Throughout the history of the judiciary system in the South, there are no records indicating that an African American was elected to the Inferior Circuit Court prior to Reconstruction. On the contrary, during Reconstruction, Democrats in South Carolina accepted the election of a qualified African American for the position of circuit judge. In 1872, Macon B. Allen, an experienced lawyer, was a candidate for that position on the Democratic ticket. Allen, who was the first known black to pass the bar for practicing law in the United States, was elected judge to the Inferior Court in Charleston, South Carolina.[77] It appears that he was elected for the position of secretary of state on the Republican ticket, but he preferred being elected for the position of judge. In 1874, in the city directory of Charleston, Allen was recorded as a judge for the criminal Court.[78] It seems that he was the first African American to hold such a position in South Carolina. In the city directories of Charleston, data did not reveal any other name of an African American criminal judge. In 1875, in the city directory Allen was listed as a lawyer.[79] Perhaps, he was not elected in that year to the judgeship. In 1876, Allen was noted in the city directory as a probate court judge in Charleston, South Carolina. He continued to hold the same position in 1877.[80] His reelection to the same position indicates that he performed his duties as a judge honorably. From several documents, no complaints were mentioned about his work ethic or his character.

Before his election as the secretary of state of South Carolina, Allen was licensed to practice law in Massachusetts and Maine in 1845. Wilson Armstead notes that Judge Allen passed a successful and rigid examination before being accepted to the Massachusetts and Maine bars. Judge Allen was well respected in Massachusetts, pleading cases for many fugitive slaves who entered that state. Judge Allen's election was followed by another African American who was elected to the municipal court of Little Rock, Arkansas.

A Municipal Judge in Little Rock, Arkansas

In 1873, the Arkansas legislature made history by electing Mifflin Wister Gibbs as a municipal judge in Little Rock. Judge Gibbs was born in Philadelphia and moved to Victoria, Vancouver Island, Canada. He attended free school established for black youth. When Mr. Gibbs returned to the United States in 1869, he received a degree in law from Oberlin College, then moved to Little Rock. In 1851—while in Alto, California—Gibbs was an activist who fought against the disenfranchisement of black people. According to him, Joan P. Townsend, W. H. Newby, and other black men including himself commenced publishing a paper with the mission of protesting against injustices to which black people were subjected, such as denying the right to vote and the right of taking an oath. In addition, the paper was employed as a means to legally secure the rights and privileges of American citizens.[81] From this account, we can stipulate that, before his election to the judiciary, Judge Gibbs was devoted to the fight against injustices for all Americans, particularly African Americans. Possibly, his passion for justice was known to many governmental officials in Arkansas, and that could be why he was appointed a municipal judge in Little Rock, Arkansas.

With respect to his appointment as judge, it was the first time in the history of any state in the United States for an African American to be elected to the municipal court. In 1866, Gibbs was elected to the Common Council of the city of Victoria in Canada. In 1872, while in the United States, he and Attorney Wheeler founded the law office of Wheeler and Gibbs, which was located at Corner Center and Markam Street in Little Rock, Arkansas. Lloyd G. Wheeler, his associate, was a graduate from a law school in Chicago. He was also a well-trained lawyer and popular in the surrounding regions. In 1873, before his election to the municipal court, Gibbs was appointed as an attorney of Pulaski County. For unidentified reasons, he resigned from that office after few months of service. In the same year, he was elected to the office of municipal court judge.[82] Judge Gibbs accepted the position after a lot thought. Few black people lived in Little Rock during the judgeship of Gibbs. Therefore, race did not have any impact for his election as it did in other cities where the governors were politically supported by the blacks. It seems that Judge Gibbs was elected due to his character, legal knowledge, and experience.

In addition to his judiciary duties, Judge Gibbs was also entrusted with federal regulatory positions. In 1877, President Grant appointed him Register of the United States Land Office for the District of Little Rock in Arkansas.[83] In 1889, he was appointed by President Harrison Receiver of Public Money. In this department, he was appointed as one of the commissioners entrusted with the sale of unsold lots on the Hot Springs Reservation at auction.[84] In regards to judiciary employment, during this period, there were few African Americans who were well equipped with legal knowledge. Judge Gibbs was not the only African American who held high judiciary position in the South during Reconstruction. In South Carolina, another African American was elected to its Supreme Court.

Associate Justice to the Supreme Court of South Carolina

The election of an African American to the highest court of South Carolina did not happen in a vacuum. When Associate Justice Hodge resigned from his office, there was no qualified white man to replace him.
Therefore, Jonathan J. Wright, an African American, was elected by the
South Carolina legislature due to his legal literacy. He studied law for
two years in Montrose after finishing high school in Lancaster. After
his law studies, he was admitted to the bar in Susquehanna County,
Pennsylvania. According to Reynolds, Judge Wright was the first African American to practice law in Pennsylvania, which he did for four
years before moving to South Carolina. Once there, he was also a Reconstruction congressman from Beaufort. He served as an Associate
Justice from 1870 to 1877.[85] When the South Carolina legislature decided
to secretly impeach him for the charge of drunkenness, Judge Wright
resigned in 1877.[86] It is possible this impeachment was applied as a pre-
text to remove him from the Supreme Court. From the various documents consulted, it seems that Judge Wright did not abuse his judiciary
power while on duty. Similarly, we did not find any accusations of bias
against him. His removal from the Supreme Court might be attributed
to the political maneuvering of that era.

Supreme Magistrates of the States

In the United States, state governors are always supreme magistrates.
Since the first English colonies in North America until the post Revolution, governors were always empowered with judiciary power. During
the Colonial Era, governors also adjudicated appeal cases and had the
right to give clemency to those convicted of crimes committed against
the states. These same powers were also entrusted to the lieutenant governor of each state.

During the Reconstruction period, an African American was appointed interim governor of Louisiana. When the impeachment of
Governor William Pitt Kellogg was pending, the Senate appointed
Lieutenant Governor P. B. S. Pinchback the interim governor in accordance with the state constitution. As governor, he had the power to give

clemency to the convicted criminals. The Constitution enacted in 1868 stipulated that "the governor shall have the power to grant reprieves for all offenses against the state, and, except in cases of impeachment, shall, with the consent of the Senate, have power to grant pardons, remit fines and forfeitures, after conviction. In cases of treason, he may grant reprieves until the end of the next session of the General Assembly, in which the power of pardoning shall be vested."[87] With this power, we discovered that Richard Frazier, who was convicted by Parish of Orleans criminal court for assault and battery in 1872, received clemency from Governor Pinchback after serving six months in prison.[88]

Like Governor Pinchback, Lieutenant Governor Davis of Alabama, who assumed the office of governor when Governor Ames was on a trip, pardoned his friends who had been convicted of crimes they committed. In addition, he pardoned criminals in county jails and penitentiaries. According to Garner, in a short period beginning on June 15 and lasting until July 25, Lieutenant Governor Davis issued 23 pardons, commutations, and remissions of forfeiture. During a similar period when Governor Ames was absent from his duties, 34 pardons, six remissions of forfeiture and six commutations of sentence were granted by Lieutenant Governor Davis. According to Garner, on January 22, 1872, Governor Davis pardoned 32 convicts, releasing them from prison. In addition, he pardoned four prisoners in jail and 17 cases before they went trial. On the contrary, Governor Ames pardoned 18 cases out of the penitentiary, nine out of jail, and none before trial.[89] Like other writers, W.E.B. Du Bois and David Levering Lewis agree that Lieutenant Governor Davis offered a large number of pardons to incarcerated people.[90] Also, Satcher notes that Lieutenant Governor Davis informed the Sheriff of Lowndes County that he was issuing a pardon to Thomas Barrentine.[91]

During Reconstruction, a few African Americans were elected lieutenant governors. In Louisiana, the first elected African American Lieutenant Governor was Dunn. He was followed by Pinchback. During the administration of Governor Kellogg, C.C. Antoine was elected Lieutenant-Governor. In Alabama, and South Carolina, African Americans were also elected to the office of lieutenant governor. In South Carolina, Alonzo J. Ransier was elected lieutenant governor on the same ticket with Governor Scott in 1870. Lieutenant Governor

Ransier was a self-educated African American. He was a delegate to the state Constitutional Convention. After the convention, he was elected as a member of the South Carolina House of Representatives. In 1872, in the same state, Richard H. Gleaves, an African American, was elected lieutenant governor on the same ticket as Governor F.J. Moses. Then, in 1874, he served as lieutenant governor under Governor D.H. Chamberlin.[92] African Americans were also employed as officers of the court.

Officers of the Court

In the courtrooms of many cities in the states under Reconstruction, African Americans held minor positions as court officers. In 1870, in the city directory of New Orleans, Charles H. Hughes was listed as an officer of the court in the 4th district recorder's court. At this time, he resided at 355 St. Mary.[93] In the city directory, his duties as officer of the court were not specified. It is unknown whether he handled cases involving people of both races. In 1872, Johnson Reed served as clerk in the District Court House in Galveston, Texas. At that time, he resided on "Cor. Tremont and Avenue Q."[94] In Washington, D.C., George T. Cokely, an African American, was listed in the 1870 city directory as a bailiff. Similarly, another African American named Joshua Parker was also listed as a bailiff in D.C. during 1870. He worked in Building 1709k, as recorded in the city directory.[95] In 1871, Henry H. Lacy was recorded as an African American bailiff. He resided at H.1152 15th NW.[96] From 1875 to 1876, in the city of Wilmington, North Carolina, George W. Bourdoux, an African American, was a city register officer at the County Court. In the same year, Lewis Sampson was a deputy register.[97] In the city directory, the location of his work was not mentioned. In Charleston, South Carolina, in 1875, Edward W. Lee was listed in the city directory as a clerk at the County Court.[98] In 1870, in the city of New Orleans, Charles H. Hughes was listed as a court officer at 4th district record's court. At the time, he lived at 355 St. Mary.[99]

Notes

1. James Wilford Garner, *Reconstruction in Mississippi.* Macmillan, 1902, p. 306.

2. See *Charleston, South Carolina, City Directory,* 1869, p. 174.

3. John Schreiner Reynolds, *Reconstruction in South Carolina, 1865-1877.* State Company, 1905, p. 128.

4. Reynolds, 1905, pp. 123 and 230.

5. Mifflin Wistor Gibbs, *Shadow and Light: An Autobiography with Reminiscences of the last and present century.* M.W. Gibbs, 1902, p. 136.

6. James Hill Fitts, *History of Newfields, New Hampshire, 1638–1911.* Rumford Press, 1912, p. 103.

7. John Roy Lynch, *The Facts of Reconstruction.* Neal Publishing Company, 1913, pp. 26–27.

8. Garner, 1902, p. 295.

9. Joseph Gregoire de Rhoulhac Hamilton, *Reconstruction in North Carolina,* vol.58. Columbia University, 1914, pp. 343–44.

10. Garner, 1902, p. 308.

11. See Forrest Cooper, "Reconstruction in Scott County." Publications of the Mississippi Historical Society, 1912, p. 135.

12. *Mobile, Alabama, City Directory,* 1871, p. 3.

13. *Mobile, Alabama, City Directory,* 1874, p. 4.

14. *Mobile, Alabama, City Directory,* 1875, pp. 10 and 90.

15. *See Little Rock, Arkansas, City Directory,* 1871, p. 81, and City Directory, 1872, pp. 78 and 97.

16. *Charleston, South Carolina, City Directory,* 1872, pp. 98, 140, and 218.

17. *Charleston, South Carolina, City Directory,* 1874, pp. 88, 102, 139, and 156.

18. *Webb's Jacksonville, FL, City Directory,* 1876–77, p. 69.

19. Ibid., p. 127.

20. William Watson David, *The Civil War and Reconstruction in Florida,* vol.53, Columbia University, 1913, p. 535.

21. John Wallace, *Carpetbag Rule in Florida: The Inside Working of the Reconstruction of Civil Government in Florida after the Close of the Civil War,* 1888, p. 357.

22. *Galveston, Texas, City Directory,* 1872, p. 50.

23. See *Little Rock, Arkansas, City Directory,* 1871, p. 81. Also, see the *City Directory* of 1872, p. 78., and the *City Directory* of 1876, p. 114.

24. *Sheriff and Co's Wilmington, North Carolina, Directory and General Advertiser,* 1875–76, p. 81.

25. *Knoxville, Tennessee, City Directory,* 1872, p. 100.

26. *Washington, District of Columbia, City Directory,* 1871, p. 5.

27. *Nashville, Tennessee, City Directory*, 1877, p. 226.

28. See *Nashville, Tennessee, City Directory*, 1878, p. 284. *City Directory*, 1979, p. 247.

29. See *Nashville, Tennessee, City Directory*, 1877, p. 51.

30. Mingo Scott, Jr., *The Negro in Tennessee Politics and Governmental Affairs, 1865–1965*, 1964, pp. 28–29.

31. Ibid.

32. *Washington, District of Columbia*, 1871, p. 1.

33. Wallace, 1888, p. 357.

34. Garner, 1902, p. 308.

35. Walter Lynwood Fleming, *Documentary History of Reconstruction, Political, Military, Social, Religious, Educational & Industrial, 1865 to the present time*, vol.2, 1907, p. 43.

36. Ibid.

37. Fleming, 1905, p. 745.

38. J.S. McNeily, "War and Reconstruction in Mississippi" *The Publications of the Mississippi Historical Society*, 1918, p. 394.

39. King, 1875, p. 429.

40. George Brown Tindall, *South Carolina Negroes: 1877–1900*. Columbia University of South Carolina, 1952, pp. 21–22.

41. See Kathe Hambrick, Pierre "Caliste" Landry. "Pioneer in Ascension Parish." The document is recorded in the Donalsonville, Public Library.

42. See Charles S. Bundy "A History of the Office of Justice of the Peace in the District of Columbia." Records of the Columbia Historical Society, Washington, vol. 5. Read before the (Society December 2, 1901). Columbia Historical Society, Washington, D.C. The Society, 1902, p. 281.

43. John M. Langston, *From the Virginia Plantation to the National Capital, or, The First and Only Negro Representative in Congress from the Old Dominion*. American Publishing Company, 1894, p. 306.

44. Ibid.

45. George Washington Williams, *A History of the Negro Troops in the War of the Rebellion, 1861–1865*. Harper & Bros, 1887, p. 142.

46. *Washington, D.C., City Directory*, 1871, p. 1.

47. See *The United States Census of 1870* for Duke W. Anderson.

48. See Exodus Committee, The Negro Exodus. Reports of the Committees: 30th Congress, 1St session-48th Congress, 2nd session, Vol.7, 1880, pp. 4, 13, and 21.

49. Ibid.

50. See *The Democratic Congressional Committee*, The Negro Exodus, Democratic Textbook, 1850, pp. 372–73.

51. Anacostia Historic District Washington, D.C. "John A. Moss."

52. See The address of Chief Judge Patricia Campbell-Smith during Black History Month on Thursday, February 27, 2014.

53. See "J.A. Moss," *Congressional Serial Set*. U.S. Government printing office, 1886, p. 562.

54. Joseph Kelly Turner and Bridges, *History of Edgecombe County, North Carolina*. Edward & Broughton Company, 1920, pp. 248–50.

55. Ibid., p. 253.

56. Turner and Bridges, 1920, p. 274.

57. Satcher, 1978, p. 43.

58. Edward King, *The Southern States of North America*. Blackie & Son, 1875, p. 293.

59. *Charleston, South Carolina, City Directory*, 1869, pp. 115 and 174.

60. Reynolds, 1905, p. 304.

61. John Abney Chapman, *History of Edgefield County: From the Earlier Settlement to 1897*. Newbery, S.C., 1897, p. 417.

62. Negro Congressman A Generation After. See *The Journal of Negro History*, vol.7, United Pub. Corporation, 1922, p. 134.

63. Eric Anderson, *Race and Politics in North Carolina*. LSU Press, 1980, p. 62.

64. Joseph Gregoire de Roulhac Hamilton, *Reconstruction in North Carolina, vol.58*. Columbia University, 1914, p. 641.

65. Lawrence D. Rice, *The Negro in Texas, 1874–1900*. Louisiana State University Press, Baton Rouge, 1971, p. 91.

66. Garner, 1902, p. 309.

67. Satcher, 1978, p. 69.

68. Ibid., p. 307.

69. Ibid., p. 331.

70. John W. Kyle, "Reconstruction in Panola County," *Publications of the Mississippi Historical Society*, vol.13, The Society, 1913, p. 76.

71. Robert Bowman, "Reconstruction in Yazoo County," *Publications of the Mississippi Historical Society*, vol.7, 1803, p. 127.

72. Satcher, 1978, p. 42.

73. Chapman, 1897, p. 417.

74. Thomas Holt, *Black over White: Negro Political Leadership in South Carolina during Reconstruction*. University of Illinois Press, Jan 1, 1979, p. 98.

75. Tindall, 1952, p. 21.

76. *Charleston, South Carolina, City Directory*, 1876, p. 269. Also, see the *City Directory* of 1877, p. 269.

77. Reynolds, 1905, p. 230.

78. *Charleston, South Carolina, City Directory*, 1874, p. 49.

79. *Charleston, South Carolina, City Directory*, 1875, p. 61.

80. *Charleston, South Carolina, City Directory*, 1876, p. 126. Also, see the *City Directory* of 1877, p. 126.

81. See Mifflin Wistar Gibbs, *Shadow and Light: An Autobiography with Reminiscences of the Last and Present Century*, vol. 3, 1902, p. 47.

82. Ibid., pp. 85, 128, and 136.

83. Gibbs, 1902, p. 185.

84. Ibid., p. 222.

85. Reynolds, 1905, p. 128.

86. Tindall, 1952, p. 17.

87. See *Official Journal of the Proceedings of the Convention: for framing a Constitution for the State of Louisiana.* J. B. Roudanez & CO., Printing to the Convention, 1868, See also Art. 58 of the Constitution of 1868.

88. See *Official Journal of the Proceedings of the State of Louisiana.* Louisiana. Legislature. Senate, 1872, p. 224.

89. Garner, 1902, pp. 298–399.

90. W.E.B. Du Bois and David Levering Lewis, *Black Reconstruction in America, 1860–1880.* Simon and Schuster, 1935, p. 447.

91. Satcher, 1978, p. 67.

92. See Carter Godwin Woodson and Rayford Whittingham Logan, *The Journal of Negro History*, vol.2, 1917, pp. 96 and 99.

93. See *New Orleans, Louisiana, City Directory*, 1870, p. 307.

94. *Galveston, Texas, City Directory*, 1872, p. 108.

95. *Washington, District of Columbia, City Directory*, 1870, pp. 78 and 301.

96. *Washington, District of Columbia City Directory*, 1871, p. 195.

97. See *Wilmington, North Carolina, City Directory*, 1875–6, pp. 35 and 126.

98. *Charleston, South Carolina, City Directory*, 1875, p. 178.

99. *New Orleans, Louisiana, City Directory*, 1870, p. 307.

Chapter 10

African American Municipal
Law Enforcement Officers

L aw enforcement in the United States is decentralized. Historically, the United States is divided into local, state, and federal governments. At the local level, there are both a city and a county government. Each level of the government has its own jurisdiction as well as law enforcement officers. This system is widely observed due to its efficiency. At the city level, the executive officer is the mayor. The affairs of the city are under his control. He has executive power and works in a close relation with the city councilmen. Before the Civil War, records do not reveal the election of an African American to the position of mayor. On the other hand, during Reconstruction, African Americans were able to elect mayors from their own people in several cities in the states under federal rule. In addition to the positions listed above, African Americans served also as mayors.

Mayors

In the states under Reconstruction policy, African Americans were not excluded from holding executive offices at the local level. From authoritative documents consulted, data revealed the election of African American mayors in the states under Reconstruction. Historians such as Canter Brown, George Alexander Swell, and Vernon Wharton have recorded data on African American mayors during Reconstruction. In his research, Brown documented authoritative information of black mayors in Florida. Wharton and Sewell also recorded information about Robert H. Wood, the African American mayor of Natchez, Mississippi. With respect to African American mayors, it is essential to note that they were elected in towns where African Americans were in the majority. Likely, white Republicans also supported the candidacy of African Americans running for that position.

During Reconstruction, it appears that African Americans held the position of mayor in few states such as Mississippi, Florida, and Louisiana. During the writing of this manuscript, there was no indication that African Americans held the position of mayor in other states. In Texas, an African American named Norris Wright Cuney was a candidate for that position, but he lost to a white Republican. In Mississippi, an African American was elected mayor in Natchez only. On the contrary, in Florida, African Americans were elected mayors in more than one city. According to Brown, African Americans were elected mayors in Lavilla, Gainesville, Cedar Keys, and Pensacola. Even though African Americans were elected mayors in those towns, the office of mayor was always occupied by whites in all other towns in Florida. In Louisiana, Pierre Landry was also elected mayor of Donaldsonville during Reconstruction. The African American mayors in of Florida and Mississippi will discussed in the following paragraphs.

Before the investigation of elected African American mayors during Reconstruction, it is pertinent to give a brief history of the title of mayor. The title of mayor is of antiquity. It appears that mayors were first appointed in the Kingdom of France. The person who served as mayor in France was called maire du palais (mayor of the palace.) French and British historians note in the Kingdoms of France and Austrasia, the mayor of the palace was an important officer. Gustave Louis M. Strass and Charles (Duke of Austrasia) write that the palace of the king was superintended by the mayor of the palace. Similarly, the king's domains were under the supervision of the mayor of palace. As the most trusted officer, the mayor of the palace was second to the king with respect to jurisdictional power.[1] In Austrasia, Pepin Le Gros was the mayor of the palace. During the reign of Clotaire II, Warnochar was the mayor of the palace in Burgundy.[2] Charles Martel and his son Pepin Duracil were also mayors of the palace in the kingdom Austrasia.[3] From the work of Louis de la Vicomterie de Saint Samson, records indicate that the title of mayors began during the reign of Clotaire. According to him, "it [mayor] was no longer [consigned] to the royal household, it [spread] all over the kingdom."[4]

It appears that the title was also imported to the Kingdom of England during the Norman era. In England, the king granted the inhabitants the right to yearly election for the mayor. According to British historians, in 1118, King Richard I granted the inhabitants of London the privilege to be governed by a mayor and two bailiffs.[5] The mayor was entrusted with the power of the governor of the town. According to John Stow, Henry Fitz Alwin was the first mayor of London. He governed for many years, till his death in 1212.[6] In the compilation of Henry Thomas Riley, the name of the first mayor of London was recorded as Henry Fitz-Eylwyne. In the same book, the name was spelled as Fitz-Ekywin.[7] After his death, in 1213, Roger-Ager Fitz Alwin became the mayor of London.[8] Similarly, in Nottingham County, King Henry V granted the city the privilege to be governed by a mayor, bailiffs, and burgesses.[9] The mayors in England were thus empowered with the administration of justice, as well as with executive power.

In 1640, the title of mayor was introduced for the first time in Colonial America. American historians agree that when the city of Georgiana was chartered, a mayor, recorder, and seven aldermen were entrusted with the administration of the affairs of the corporation.[10] The town of Georgiana was governed by eight aldermen. The mayor and the aldermen were ex-officio justices. According to the *Collections of the Maine Historical Society*, Thomas Gorges, the cousin of Sir Ferdinando Gorges, was the first mayor of Georgiana.[11] Governor Winthrop credited the newly appointed mayor of Georgiana as a gentleman of the Inns of Court.[12] The Inns were academic institutions where jurists were trained in the Kingdom of England. In Georgiana, the mayor and the aldermen also performed police work. In 1643, Roger Garde was the mayor of Georgiana.[13] In this incorporated town, police duties were executed by the mayor and twelve aldermen, including 24 councilmen.[14] The mayor was also a magistrate and had his court. It appears that the first mayor's court in colonial American was held in Georgiana. At the time of this writing, records did not indicate that a mayor court existed in any other cities in colonial American than Georgiana. In the Collection of the

Massachusetts Historical Society and the work of George Alexander Emery, this town (Georgiana) was spelled Gorgeana.[15]

In 1644, when the colony of New Netherlands was ceded to the Duke of York, it was renamed the colony of New York. In the charter of 1664 by the Duke of York, the city of New York was granted the right to be governed by the mayor. In 1665, Governor Richard Nichols appointed Thomas Willet as the first mayor of New York for a one-year term, as was the custom in England. It appears that it was also the first time the English law enforcement titles were introduced in the colony of New York. Before his appointment to the position of mayor, Willet was a merchant and one of the commissioners who witnessed the transfer of the colony of New Netherlands to the English.

In addition to the colony of New York, in 1691 when the city of Philadelphia was incorporated, a mayor was elected. According to Josiah Granville Leach, Humphrey Morrey served as the first mayor of Philadelphia in 1691. Under the charter of 1701, the Honorable Edward Shippen became the first mayor to be elected, in 1702.[16] In Hartford, Connecticut, Colonel Thomas Seymour was the first mayor, and he was elected in 1784 after the city's incorporation.[17] Seymour was born on June 19, 1757, and he was the grandson of Thomas Seymour. According to James Lelland Howard, his great father was one of the original proprietors of Hartford. He served in the cavalry during Revolutionary War and remained in that force until 1778. After his military service, he studied law in Philadelphia.[18] Contrary to Northern colonies, an intendant was elected in South Carolina instead of a mayor. This position was the equivalent to a mayor. In 1783, when the city of Charleston was incorporated, Richard Hutson was its first intendant.[19]

The accounts of African American mayors during Reconstruction have been documented by many historians. In Louisiana, Frank Lincoln Mather noted the election of an African American as mayor in 1868. In Florida, Brown recorded a few names of African Americans who served as mayor in that state. In Mississippi, Vernon Wharton also mentioned the election of an African American as mayor in 1871. The elected African mayors in the cities listed above were prominent leaders in their communities.

In 1868, the folkways of the inhabitants of Donaldsonville were no longer observed as in the past. Before the Civil War, an African American would never have been elected as mayor of the city. But after the war, with the implementation of new policies under Reconstruction, African Americans were permitted to hold any local, county, and state positions. With the enforcement with such policies, Pierre Caliste Landry, an African American, was elected mayor of Donaldsonville, Louisiana. Landry was born on the plantation of his father and master, Marcelito Provost Landry. Frank Lincoln Mather notes that he received a private education under Rev. W.D. Goodman and Rev. L.G. Atkinson. As a result, he was permitted to study law in the offices of John A. Cheebers and F.B. Earhart. Possibly it was due to his legal studies that he was entrusted with such a position. In addition to his mayoral duties, he served as tax collector, president of police jury, president of the school board, and as the postmaster of his city. He was also elected to the Louisiana House of Representatives for four years, and then to the Louisiana State Senate for six more. He was also a church minister for many years.[20] From the accounts of Henry Davenport Northrop, Joseph R. Gray, and Irvine Garland Penn, data showed that Landry grew up in the house of Pierre Damas Bouziac and Zaides. They were free people of color. Additionally, they recorded that Landry attended plantation school which was reserved to free colored children. It appears that Landry under the care of a wealthy person named M.S. Bringier, an owner of a sugar plantation in Ascension. The authors listed above documented that Bringier paid $1,665 for the slavery of Landry. In the house of his new master, he was tasked with minor positions such as being the superintendent of the yard and the servants.[21]

In 1871, Robert H. Hood was elected mayor of Natchez in Mississippi. George Alexander Sewell, who recorded information on African Americans who made history in Mississippi, noted that Mayor Hood won his election for mayor with a popular vote of 707 to 525. He took his oath as mayor on January 4, 1871, before A.C. Hussey, the clerk of the circuit court. Mayor Hood was a mulatto and deeply involved in politics. In addition to his mayoral duties, he was appointed as sheriff and postmaster in Natchez.

Historians such as Buford Satcher believe that Hood was the first African American elected to the position of mayor during the Reconstruction era. Vernon Lane Wharton recorded that when Hood was major, many aldermen were also African Americans. Mayor Hood was also involved in the printing industry before and during his political career. Data confirm that, before his involvement in politics, he and John R. Lynch were working in a printing company. On April 18, 1873, when the Act to Incorporate the Mississippi Printing and Publishing Company was passed, the names of Robert H. Hood, John R. Lynch, B.K. Bruce, and A.K. Davis—all African Americans—were also listed as being a part of the company. With respect to his early life, little is known. Historians write that he was among the few free African Americans who resided in Mississippi. It appears that his father, Robert W. Hood, a white man, was a doctor and a mayor of Natchez in 1855.

In 1873, Josiah Thomas Walls, an African American, was appointed mayor of Gainesville, Florida. As the data of the city for 1871 and 1872 were not discovered by Canter Brown, it is difficult to ascertain with accuracy if Walls was the first African American elected as mayor in Florida. Mayor Walls was born in Winchester, Virginia, and he was a career politician, also serving in the United States Congress from Florida three terms. He was also elected as congressman in the state of Florida. Before his entrance into politics, he was a farmer with a limited education.[22]

In 1874, Salvador T. Ponds was elected mayor of Pensacola. In Cedar Key, John G. Williams was elected mayor in 1873. In the same year, in the town of Lavilla, Mitchell P. Chappelle was elected mayor. He served in that position until 1876. Lavilla had been incorporated as a town in 1868. It seems that from 1868 to 1874, the mayor of the city had been a white person. Then, in 1874, the office was under a mayor of African descendent till 1877. It seems that when Chappelle left the office of mayor, he was elected as justice of the peace in Jacksonville, Florida. In the city directories of 1876 and 1877, he was recorded as justice of the peace.[23] He was succeeded as mayor by Alfred Grant, who served till 1877. According to Patricia Kenney, Grant was a native of Alabama. Kenney did not record when Grant arrived in Florida or the conditions which led to his migration there.

In 1876, Mathew McFarland Lewey was elected mayor of Newnansville, Florida. Lewey performed other duties in addition to his mayor's office. He was a postmaster and justice of the peace.[24] In 1915, Frank Lincoln Mather recorded that Lewey was invited to Florida by Josiah T. Walls. It appears that they knew each other before their involvement in politics. Lewey has been credited as being an educated politician. He attended the Presbyterian Mission School in Baltimore. In addition to that, he studied law at Howard University. He also served as a guard during the Civil War and was promoted to the rank of corporal. With respect to his occupation, Lewey was a teacher in Newnansville, Florida, for three years. He also passed the Florida bar in 1876. In the same year, he was elected as mayor of Newnansville.[25] It is possible that in Floridian towns where African Americans held the office of mayor; African Americans were the majority.

Aldermen

The title of alderman also dates from antiquity. During the Saxon era in England, the aldermen were conservators of the peace. They were also judiciary officers in their county. Furthermore, they sat in the assembly with the king. This title was also imported to America by the colonists. With respect to African Americans, there are no accounts noting that any were elected to this office before the Civil War. Records regarding the appointment of African Americans as aldermen can be traced to the military governorships during Reconstruction. Accordingly, after the constitutional enfranchisement of African Americans in 1870, the numbers of African American aldermen increased. In the cities or counties where African Americans were in the majority, sometimes many of them were elected. This was the case in Charleston, South Carolina. In the city directory of 1874, African Americans were listed as aldermen. It appears that in the second, fifth, sixth, seventh, and eight wards, African Americans were among the elected aldermen.[26]

In Knoxville, Tennessee, Isaac Gamman was the first African American alderman in 1869. In 1871, Calvin Sanders was an alderman in Little Rock, Arkansas. He was the only person of African descent elected to this position in that city. In Mississippian counties where African Americans had many voters, their numbers among the aldermen were sometimes higher than those of white counterparts. In Yalobusha County, Mississippi, African Americans were elected aldermen in Coffeeville where the population of African Americans was 400. According to Julia C. Brown, there were two African American aldermen in Coffeeville, John Scurlock and Sidney Hoskins. Brown also recorded that at one period, five African Americans were on the board of aldermen of Coffeeville.[27] Scurlock had been born in slavery but had some education. He has been credited as the leader of African Americans in his county. Because of both his popularity and his political leadership of African Americans, many whites associated with him for their political gain.[28]

Constables and City Marshals

In the United States, constables had the same duties as they did in England. There, constables were empowered with police duties by the Statute of Winchester of 1285. According to Patrick Coloquhon and John Reeve, the Statute of Winchester entrusted the constable with arrest power and detention of suspects. As in England, in colonial American as well as in the United States, the constables had the arrest power. They patrolled the cities and maintained law and order. When modern police departments were organized in many cities, the constables were still active. Similarly, the city constables performed the same law enforcement duties as the constables in the Southern cities during Reconstruction.

In South Carolina, according to the Constitution of 1868, the deputy constables appointed by the chief constable were entrusted with the preservation of the public peace and the execution of the laws throughout the state. They were also empowered to maintain peace and order as well as to prevent crime.[29] African Americans appointed as deputy constables performed the same duties as their white counterparts, since all were ordered to do so by the Constitution of 1868.

With respect to African Americans, records indicate that they held the positions of constables and city marshals during Reconstruction. Military and civilian governors appointed African American constables. In towns where African Americans were in the majority, some of them were elected constables or city marshals. In towns such as Charleston,

Jacksonville, Memphis, Little Rock, Arkansas, Wilmington, and Mobile, from time to time during Reconstruction, African Americans were elected to the position of constables. In 1869, J. Osburn and Frank Oliver, both African Americans, were listed as constables in the city directory in Charleston, South Carolina.[30] In Little Rock, Arkansas, Henry Clay served as deputy constable as noted in the city directory of 1872. In the following year, Samuel Garrett was also recorded as constable in the Little Rock, Arkansas, city directory. In the same city and state, in 1873, James W. Andrews was a deputy constable. Garrett continued to serve in the same capacity in 1873.[31] In Knoxville, Tennessee, in the 1872 city directory, William L. Brooks was listed as a constable.[32] Across the state, in Memphis, George S. Hayden was listed as African American constable in 1868.[33] African American constables had arrest power and took suspects to jail, as recorded by William Watson David.[34] Just like those who were constables, African Americans were recorded as city marshals in some city directories. For an example of this, in 1871 W.A. Rector was a city marshal in Little Rock, Arkansas.[35] In 1875, George W. Price, Jr., was a deputy city marshal in Wilmington, North Carolina, as was recorded in the city directory.[36] In addition to African American police constables and marshals, they were also appointed as city regulators during Reconstruction.

City Regulators

Anglo-Americans have observed the regulatory folkways of their forefathers in England. At each level of the government, regulatory agents are entrusted with the collections of taxes. Additionally, law enforcement officers are appointed for the regulation of government institutions at each level. At the local level, city regulators collect taxes, issue licenses, and control the operations of private business, as well as city government institutions. In each city, various regulators are appointed for this purpose. It is common to find in each city tax collectors, city appraisers, city clerks, health officers, street commissioners, weights and measures officers, veterinarians, light inspectors, and so on. These officers also have the power to fine law violators in the areas of their jurisdictions. Even though regulators are law enforcement officers, they do not have the same powers as police officers in the maintenance of public order and safety. Sanitary agents maintain public safety, but they can only do so in the framework of their limited duties regarding sanitation.

In the history of the United States, African Americans were always excluded from performing regulatory duties before the Civil War. In 1867, in the cities under Reconstruction, new political designs were introduced by military governors. The inclusive political policy became the norm of the time. African Americans, who were once excluded from the city politics, were for the first time a part of that body. They were entrusted with regulatory positions at the local level as well as state. In many cities, African Americans were appointed as election registrars. In a similar manner, some of them were appointed tax collectors. In 1870, after the ratification of the 15th Amendment, African Americans were fully part of the American body politic and allowed employment at each level of the government.

In the city directories of the 1870s in the former Confederate states, African Americans were listed as city regulators. Even though the numbers of those who served in that capacity were small, it is worth recording the names of African Americans who served. In 1869, in the city directory of Charleston, South Carolina, M.G. Camplin, an African American, was listed as assistant city assessor. He lived at 54 Morris.[37] In 1869, he was the only African American listed as a city assessor. If there were others, their names were not mentioned in the city directory. In 1874, T.H. Jones was another African American who served as assistant city assessor in Charleston, South Carolina.[38] From the numbers of African American assessors appointed in Charleston, South Carolina, records indicate that they were less likely to be appointed to that position. The assessors were paid according to tax collected and properties assessed, but African Americans were denied such privileges. During Reconstruction, assessors were as well paid as the sheriff. As tax collectors, they received a percentage of the money they collected. In the District of Columbia, William P. Ryder, an African American, was listed as the assistant assessor in its 1870 city directory.[39] As in Washington, D.C., in Norfolk, Virginia, an African American named P.G. Morgan was recorded in the 1872 city directory as assistant assessor at large.[40] It appears that he was the only black person to hold a municipal office in that year. Possibly, he had some education and that was the reason why he was appointed to such duties. As an assistant assessor, he was obligated to deal with taxes and the assessment of properties in Norfolk in coordination with his superior, the assessor.

In addition to assessors, African Americans held various regulatory positions as noted in the beginning. In 1870, in Mobile, Alabama, James Bragg was a street commissioner.[41] He was also a regulator who had a control over the management of that city's streets. In 1874, in Charleston, South Carolina, Robert Gordon, an African American, also held the position of superintendent of streets.[42] Possibly, this title was an equivalent of commissioner of streets in Mobile, Alabama. In addition to street regulators, African Americans were also appointed to the position of city inspector. In 1874, James L. Walker was listed as a city inspector in the directory in Charleston, South Carolina. In 1875, Edward Walker was also recorded as city inspector in Charleston, South Carolina.[43]

Like street commissioners, African Americans were also employed as sanitary inspectors. In 1876, Alexander Artope was a sanitary inspector in Charleston, South Carolina. In the same year, F. Lancelot Wall was also a sanitary inspector in the same city. It appears that in 1877 there were only two African American sanitary inspectors in Charleston, South Carolina, as recorded in the city directory.[44] As sanitary officers, there was doubt that their jurisdictional power covered black communities in the city of Charleston and the surrounding suburbs. Likewise, in 1875 and 1876, in Wilmington, North Carolina, Allen J. Denton held the position of health officer. He resided on Queen between 10th and 11th.[45]

In 1875, African Americans were also appointed as city appraisers in South Carolina. According to the city directory of Charleston, South Carolina, John N. Gregg, an African American, was a city appraiser. In the same year, Thomas H. Jones was an assistant city appraiser.[46] It seems that Jones was an assistant to Gregg. In the city directory of that year, there were no other names holding the same positions. In 1876 and 1877, Thomas H. Jones was promoted to the position of city appraiser.[47] In 1875, he was an assistant. It seems that Jones was the most qualified African American among the others. His promotion to city appraiser indicates that he performed the duties entrusted to him accordingly.

In cities where ports were established, African Americans were sometimes appointed as administrators of those ports. In Charleston, a coastal town, a few African Americans held the title of port warden. In the city directory of 1869, J.C. Holloway, an African American, was listed as port warden in Charleston, South Carolina. In the following years, they also held such positions. As an illustration, in 1874, three African Americans held the position of port warden in Charleston, South Carolina. These men were J.B. Wright, H.G. Thomas, and B. Moncrief. Wright was also listed as port warden in 1875. Thomas Henry continued to serve in the same position till the end of Reconstruction. In 1877, James J. Young, another African American, was port warden.[48] Because of their position, these African Americans had jurisdiction over tax collections at the ports where they were assigned. In 1870, an African American named James H. Ingraham was listed in the New Orleans city directory as port warden.[49] Like port warden, African Americans also held the position of city tax collector.

In 1875, in Wilmington, North Carolina, George H. Jackson was a deputy tax collector. He resided at that time on 2nd Cor. Walnut.[50] Similarly, William K. Price was a deputy city collector and treasurer in the same city and year.[51] It appears that he was the only African American in Wilmington, North Carolina, who performed duties in two separate jurisdictions. In 1870, in the District of Columbia, John F. Cook, an African American, held the position of city regulator. This African American was more than likely educated. Possibly, the position he held in the national capital was entrusted to educated people or those who had some education. In 1870, he resided at 1005 16th NW.[52] African Americans also served as guards in the building or government facilities.

In Charleston, South Carolina, W.T. Oliver was inspector of naval stores.[53] It seems that he was a trusted, moral, and loyal person because his duties were of a sensitive nature. In the naval store, navy equipment was more than likely kept there. If Oliver had not been trusted by the officers at the naval store, he would not have been allowed to work there. It seems also that he had some education and was able to read and write. As inspector, he had to write reports on his inspections. In addition to city regulators noted above, African Americans were assigned clerk duties at the municipal level. In 1870, in the District of Columbia, Daniel Chew was recorded in the city directory as clerk in the city hall. In the same year, Henry O. Johnson was assistant clerk in the Centre Market. Likewise,

Alfred Parry was a clerk at E. Market.[54] In 1874, in Charleston, South Carolina, African Americans also served officers of the market. In the city directory, Hore H. Stephen was a clerk in the Centre Market, and Simons James was a clerk in the Upper Market.[55] These African American officers more than likely enforced rules and regulations enacted for the administration of the markets. Chew continued to save as clerk in the city council in 1871, and in that year, he resided at 1718 K. NW.[56]

School Regulators

African Americans were also appointed municipal regulators in colored schools. During Reconstruction, many schools were built for the instruction of African Americans. In most the cases, those schools were regulated by African Americans. In 1869, George F.T. Cook was appointed superintendent of colored schools in Washington, D.C. He continued to serve in the same position for many years. In the city directory of 1873, his name was recorded as superintendent of the public schools. In 1875, in Galveston, Texas, Joshin Jones was the superintendent of the colored school. In Tennessee, Mingo Scott, Jr., recorded that Edward Richman, an African American, held the position of School Commissioner from 1874 to 1876. He was elected in the Thirteenth District in Davidson County. Richman was an educated African American who, according to Scott, Jr., had graduated from Oberlin College. After his education, he was a teacher in a private school where he instructed free persons of color before the Civil War.[57] The African Americans illustrated above were entrusted with the enforcement of the school regulations.

Clerks in Regulatory Agencies

During the period under examination, African Americans were also employed as clerks in various regulatory agencies. In many states under the Reconstruction policy, the names of African Americans occasionally appear in city directories as clerks in municipal regulatory departments. In 1870, in New Orleans, Louisiana, J.O. Lainez and other African Americans served as clerks at the auditor's office. Like Lainez, F.G. Llorens held the same position at the auditor's office.[58] E.R. Longpre, also an African American, served as a clerk in the New Orleans auditor's office.[59] In 1872, John A. Washington, an African American, was serving in the sheriff's office as a clerk. During Reconstruction, the sheriff was a regulatory agent, also functioning as a county tax collector. As at the local level, African Americans served as clerk in the office of state representatives. As clerks, it is sound to note that the African Americans listed above handled various legal documents, such as filing, and mailing correspondence related to their regulatory offices.

Watchmen and Guards

In many cities under Reconstruction policy and in the District of Columbia, African Americans were employed as watchmen guarding private and government institutions. In addition to that service, others acted as guards. In Washington, D.C., for example, Perry Carson, an African American, served as watchman at the City Hall in 1870. It is unknown whether he was a city employee or if he was employed in a private security company. In the same year, John N. Hunt was recorded in the city directory as night watchman at Howard University. It looks like many African Americans held the position of watchman in Washington, D.C. In Mississippi, when the Democrats overthrew Republicans, a number of local African American officers were appointed watchmen in the government building.[60] In 1870, Henry Piper was a watchman at the United States Treasury Department in the nation's capital.[61] Watchmen are law enforcement officers entrusted with the protection of properties and persons. In 1870, the Department of Treasury employed its own watchmen.[62] In this case, it is credible to note that Piper was an employee of the Treasury.

In 1869, J. Walker was listed as the keeper of the Military Hall in Charleston, South Carolina. In 1872, he continued to serve in the same position. In fact, he was the only African American who held this position in Charleston between 1869 and 1872.[63] In 1874, Chas Simons was listed in the Charleston city directory as keeper of the Court House. The court was located at W5 Court House Square.[64] While Simons held the position of keeper of the Military Hall, George H. Dantzman was the keeper of the city magazine in 1876.[65] In Mobile, Alabama, Ebenezer

Nicholas, an African American, served as a watchman at the powder magazine.[66] It seems that he worked for the government.

In 1876, in Little Rock, Arkansas, Oliver L. Gordon was a guard at Building Cross, located at SE Cor[ner] 12th.[67] In 1875, in Raleigh North Carolina, Robert Fort and Washington Jones also served as guards.[68] The location where they worked was not recorded in that year's city directory. These two African Americans also held the same position in 1876. These guards were more than likely employed by the authority of the municipal government. In Mobile, Alabama, Claiborne Thomas worked as warehouse keeper at Vass Fosdick & Co.[69] In this capacity he was likely responsible for the protections of people as well as goods in the warehouse.

Notes

1. Gustave Louis M. Straus and Charles (Duke of Austria), *Moslem and Frank; Or, Charles Martel and the rescue of Europe*, 1854, p. 108.

2. Ibid.

3. *Thesaurus Geographicus: A New Body of Geography*. Swall, 1695. See also, Louis de la Cicomterie de Saint-Samson, *The Crimes of the Kings of France: From Clovis to Lewis XVI*, translated from the French by J. Trapp, A.M. James Ridway, 1791, pp. 12, 16, 19. Pepin Le Gros was also mayor of the palace under King Thieri. Pepin was the grandson of Pipin L'Ancient, who was the mayor of palace to Dagobert, king of Austrasia. The information was recorded by Charles Claude Hamilton, *An Epitome of Universal Chronology, history and biography, forming a companion to Irving's Stream of history, from the German of F. Strass, and continued to the year 1826*. G.B. Whittaker, 1826, p. 33.

4. *The Crimes of the Kings of France: From Clovis to Lewis XIV*. Translated from the French by J. Trapp. A.M., James Ridway, 1791, p. 12.

5. John Stow, *Survey of London, Written in the year 1698*. A New Edition Edited by William J. Thmos, Esq. London: Whittaker and CO., 1842, p. 185.

6. Ibid.

7. Henry Thomas Riley, *Chronicles of the Mayors and Sheriffs of London, A.D. 1188 to A.D. 1274*. Trubner & Company, 1863, vol. 3.

8. Stow, 1842, p. 186.

9. James Orange, *History and Antiquities of Nottingham*, 1840, p. 373.

10. George Alexander Emery, *Ancient City of Gorgeana and Modern Town of York (Maine) from its Earlier Settlement to the present Time: Also Its Beaches and Summer Resorts*. G.A. Emery, 1874, p. 40.

11. See Collections of the Maine Historical Society. [1st Ser., vol.2.] Maine Historical Society, 1847, p. 57.

12. Ibid.

13. Emery, 1874, p. 42.

14. Ibid.

15. Ibid., p. 41.

16. Josiah Granville Leach, "Humphrey Morrey, First Mayor, 1691–1692". The Pennsylvania Magazine of History and Biography. Historical Society of Pennsylvania, 1894, pp. 419–20, and 423.

17. See James Leland Howard, *The Origin and Fortunes of Troop B: 1788, Governor's Independent Volunteer Troop of Horse Guards Case.* Lockwood & Brainard Company, 1821, p. 18.

18. Ibid.

19. *Ordinances of the City Council of Charleston, in the State of South Carolina: Passed Since Incorporation of the City. Collected and Revise of to a Resolution. Charleston (S.C.)* W.P. Young, 1802, p. 22.

20. Frank Lincoln Mather, *Who's Who of the Colored Race: General Biography Dictionary of Men and Women of African Descent, vol.1,* 1915, p. 170.

21. See Joseph Davenport Northrop, Joseph R. Gray, and Irvine Garland Penn, *The College of Life; Or, Practical Self-educator: A Manual of Self-Improvement for the Colored Race. Giving Example and Achievements of Successful Men and Women of the Race, Including Afro-American Progress,* 1896, p. 45.

22. See *The Journal of Negro History,* vol.vii – April, 1922 –No.2, "Negro Congressmen a Generation After," p. 159.

23. *Jacksonville, Florida, City Directories,* 1876–77, p. 69.

24. Ibid.

25. Mather, 1915, p. 176.

26. *Charleston, South Carolina, City Directory,* 1874, p. 13. W.J. Mckinley was alderman in ward 2. S.B. Garrett and A.B. Michelle were in ward 3. W.G. Fields represented ward 4 as an African American alderman.

27. Julia C. Brown, "Reconstruction in Yalobusha and Grenada." Publication of the Mississippi Historical Society, 1912, p. 269.

28. Ibid., p. 227.

29. Acts of the General Assembly of South Carolina. State Printers, 1868, p. 14.

30. *Charleston, South Carolina, City Directory,* 1869 pp. 180 and 183.

31. See *Little Rock, Arkansas, City Directory,* 1871, p. 51. *City Directory,* 1872, p. 38. *City Directory,* 1873, pp. 22 and 59.

32. *Knoxville, Tennessee, City Directory,* 1872, p. 38.

33. *Memphis, Tennessee, City Directory,* 1868, p. 109.

34. William Watson David, *The Civil War and Reconstruction in Florida*, vol. 53. Columbia University, 1913, p. 588.

35. *Little Rock, Arkansas, City Directory*, 1871, p. 102.

36. *Sheriff and Co's Wilmington, NC Directory and General Advertiser*, 1875–76, p. 119.

37. *Charleston, South Carolina, City Directory*, 1869, p. 103.

38. *Charleston, South Carolina, City Directory*, 1874, p. 168.

39. *Washington, District of Columbia, City Directory*, 1870, p. 333.

40. See *Norfolk, Virginia, City Directory*, 1872, p. 124.

41. *Mobile, Alabama, City Directory*, 1870, p. 17.

42. *Charleston, South Carolina, City Directory*, 1874, p. 137.

43. Ibid., p. 13, See also, *City Directory, 1875*, p. 290.

44. *Charleston, South Carolina, City Directory*, 1876, pp. 180 and 450.

45. *Sheriff and Co's Wilmington, NC, Directory and General Advertiser*, 1875–76, p. 53.

46. *Charleston, South Carolina, City Directory*, 1875, pp. 137, 165.

47. *Charleston, South Carolina, City Directory*, 1876, p. 289. See also *City Directory*, 1877, p. 289.

48. *Charleston, South Carolina, City Directory*, 1869, p. 140. *City Directory*, 1874, 14. *Charleston, South Carolina, City Directory*, 1875, pp. 279, 307. *City Directory*, 1877, p. 436.

49. *New Orleans, Louisiana, City Directory*, 1870, p. 311.

50. *Sheriff and Co's Wilmington, NC, and General Advertiser*, 1875–76, p. 82.

51. Ibid., p. 119.

52. *Washington, District of Columbia, City Directory*, 1870, p. 84.

53. *Charleston, South Carolina, City Directory*, 1874, p. 215.

54. *Washington, District of Columbia, City Directory*, 1870, pp. 69 and 206.

55. *Charleston, South Carolina, City Directory*, 1874, p. 14.

56. *Washington, District of Columbia, City Directory*, 1871, p. 61.

57. Scott, Jr., 1964, p. 30.

58. See *New Orleans, Louisiana. City Directory*, 1870, pp. 354 and 377.

59. Ibid., p. 379.

60. Garner, 1902, p. 414.

61. *Washington, District of Columbia, City Directory*, 1870, pp. 65, 195, and 310.

62. See Richard Peters, ed., *The Public Statutes at Large of the United States of America*, vol. 16. Little, Brown, 1871, p. 9.

63. See *Charleston, South Carolina, City Directory*, 1869, p. 214. Also *City Directory* of 1872, p. 218.

64. See *Charleston, South Carolina, City Directory*, 1874, p. 248.

65. *Charleston, South Carolina, City Directory*, 1877, p. 198.
66. *Mobile, Alabama, City Directory*, 1870, p. 133.
67. *Rock, Arkansas, City Directory Little*, 1876, p. 86.
68. *Raleigh, North Carolina, City Directory*, 1875–76.
69. *Mobile, Alabama, City Directory*, 1871, p. 196.

Chapter 11

African American State and County Officers

The ratification of the 15th Amendment to the Constitution of the United States shaped the political culture of the country. After the passage of this amendment, African Americans were included in the American political body. They were enfranchised and eligible to hold political positions at each level of the government. At the state and county levels, they held elective and appointive positions such as regulators or any other law enforcement capacities in the states under Reconstruction. On the contrary, in other states of the Union, African Americans were always excluded from holding state and county offices. The exclusion of African Americans in those states was not completed by any explicit law, but through the policies and political folkways observed in those states for many years preceding the enactment of the 15th Amendment.

Politically, African Americans were lawmakers and state executive officers in the United States. Throughout the states subjected to Reconstruction, they were elected to the State House of Representatives as well as to the State Senate. In a like manner, a great number of them held executive positions at the state and county levels. At the state level, records show that African Americans were elected lieutenant governors, secretaries of state, superintendents of public instruction, secretaries of the treasury, and superintendents of public works. Additionally, one of them was appointed Superintendent of Immigration in Arkansas. Moreover, some African Americans were employed as clerks in the Treasury Department, as happened in Louisiana. Data on African Americans who held such positions will be discussed below.

To illustrate, in Louisiana, Oscar J. Dunn was lieutenant governor to Governor Henry Clay Warmoth.[1] As a lieutenant governor, he was the president of the Louisiana State Senate and president of the police board. Dunn has been credited with being a principled person. On one occasion, someone attempted to bribe him, hoping that he could use his influence for a bill which that person had interest in; Dunn "responded to him that his conscience was not for sale." In the same state, P.B.S. Pinchback was also lieutenant governor and acting governor. Like the two African Americans listed above, C.C. Antoine was also a lieutenant governor in Louisiana. In South Carolina, R. H. Gleaves and Alonzo J. Ransier were also lieutenant governors.

Gleaves was first elected as lieutenant governor in 1872 under T.J. Moses. In 1872, he defeated R.H. Cain of Charleston and E.J. Adams of Columbia, both African Americans. Gleaves was a native of Beaufort and member of the Constitutional Convention of the Republican Party in 1867.[2] In 1874, he was elected lieutenant governor on the same ticket with Governor Chamberlin. During the reelection of Governor Chamberlin in 1876, he was also reelected as lieutenant governor, but he withdrew after Democrats pressured him.[3] After the election of 1876, African Americans were no longer active in the political arena of the state.

Ransier did not have any formal education in a school. Historians believe that he was a self-educated man. In 1868, he was selected as a delegate member of the State Constitutional Convention. In 1869, he made his first appearance in South Carolinian politics as a member of the State House of Representatives. In 1870, he was elected lieutenant governor of that state.[4] Ransier, as noted by John Schreiner Reynolds, advocated for equal rights, both politically and socially, between the races. When he was elected, the constitutional term of office was two years, with the eligibility for reelection.[5] The salary of a lieutenant governor in South Carolina was set at $2,500 per year. Another $1,000 was paid to him while acting as president of the senate, which brought the total amount of the salary as lieutenant governor to $3,500 per year.[6]

Likewise, in Mississippi, Alexander K. Davis was elected lieutenant governor. Even though Davis was elected lieutenant governor, before his nomination to that position, his party members were concerned about whether he was fit for that executive office.[7] Lieutenant Governor Davis also acted as governor when Governor Albert Ames traveled to a different state. While acting as governor, he was accused of abusing his power. In 1876, he was charged with accepting a bribe and pardoning a murderer, Thomas H. Borrentine. The latter had been charged with the killing of Ann Thomas in Lowndes County. For his misconduct, Lieutenant Governor Davis was brought before the judge, and he was found guilty. As a result, he was discharged from office as well as restricted from holding power and trust.[8]

With respect to the office of Secretary of State, Francis L. Cardoza was appointed to this position in South Carolina for a term of four years. In addition, he served as clerk in the Treasury Department in Washington, D.C. He was a native of South Carolina and attended the University of Glasgow in Scotland for four years. Afterwards, while in London, he received his religious instruction at the Presbyterian Seminaries. It seems that he also took religious education at Edinburgh.[9] The nomination of Cardozo for secretary of state was objected to by a few delegates, but he finished by defeating his competitors by 77 to 30.[10]

In 1872, Jonathan C. Gibbs was appointed Secretary of State in Florida under the administration of Governor Harrison Reed. Secretary Gibbs was a college-educated African American, graduating from Dartmouth College in Hanover, New Hampshire. He was also a Presbyterian minister, and he was appointed the Superintendent of Education by Governor O.B. Hart. He has been credited by many historians as being a knowledgeable African American. It appears that he was the only African American who served in the state executive office during Reconstruction. His appointment was well received by people of color who believed that Governor Reed was obligated to appoint an African American to the executive office. John Wallace, writing during the time when Gibbs was Secretary of State and Superintendent of Public Instruction, credited him for his intelligence and political acumen. Wallace said that "Gibbs was the best educated delegate during the Constitutional Convention as well the most conservative and public speaker."[11]

In 1873, in Mississippi, an educated African American named James Hill was also appointed secretary of state. According to John Roy Lynch, Hill was an intelligent man, fit for the position entrusted to him. His nomination for that office was not questioned. Party members believed that he was a suitable person for the position. It was believed if elected, he would perform his duties accordingly and would satisfy the public's needs. Lynch described him as being young and aggressive at the time. Hill was also an educated African American.[12] Like Lynch, historian James Wilford Garner described Hill as a competent officer who succeeded in escaping the impeachment orchestrated by the Democrats against him in 1876.[13] From the views of Lynch and Garner, it is sound to note that Hill performed his duties very well. In South Carolina, during the administration of Governor Daniel H. Chamberlain, Henry E. Hayne was Secretary of State. In 1873, when he enlisted in the school of medicine in Charleston, some professors resigned. But he continued his studies at the university. Hayne started his political endeavors in Marion County. According to William W. Sellers, in 1868, he was elected state senator representing his county. It was in 1872 that he was elected state treasurer.[14] During his nomination to secretary of state, Hayne had to compete against his fellow African Americans. He defeated F.H. Frost, a native of Williamsburg and an African American.[15]

In addition to executive state titles listed above, African Americans were appointed as superintendent of instruction. In some states, this position was identified as superintendent of education such as in Mississippi. In Florida, Jonathan Gibbs served as State Superintendent of Education. In 1873, in Mississippi, Thomas W. Cardozo was the State Superintendent of Education. He was a confidential and an influential advisor of Governor Ames.[16] Before his appointment to the state executive office, he was a circuit clerk in Warrant County. Garner says that he was under impeachment at the time when he was appointed to serve as superintendent of education. Charles Nordhoff, who visited Cardozo during his impeachment process, recorded that he was not indicted. In 1876, when the Democrats were in control of the state and local governments, Cardozo was charged with misconduct after an investigation ordered by the new government. As a result, he agreed to resign in exchange for the dismissal of his charges. His approach was approved by the State Speaker of the House, H.M. Street. As he hoped, the charges against him were dropped, and he resigned from his position as superintendent of education.[17]

In Arkansas, J.C. Corbin, also an African American college graduate, served as Superintendent of Schools. He attended Oberlin College and migrated to Arkansas when he joined the United States Army.[18] Corbin was born to enslaved parents from Richmond, Virginia. In 1872 upon his arrival in Little Rock, Arkansas, he served as chief clerk in the city's post office.[19] It appears that when he started working in the post office, he became familiarized with African American town leaders. Possibly, it was also during this period that he joined politics. In Louisiana, William G. Brown, an African American, was appointed State Superintendent of Instruction.[20]

In North Carolina, James W. Hood was appointed State Assistant Superintendent of Public Instruction. Before his appointment, he was a magistrate during the provisional government of Governor Holden. Hood was an educated African American and a religious minister. During the Constitutional Convention, he was selected as a member among the delegates of North Carolina. With respect to his religious affiliation, he was a minister of the African Methodist Episcopal Zion Church, which was organized in Philadelphia in 1812. As a native of Chester County in Pennsylvania, he was sent to the South during the Civil War. In addition to his ministerial duties, he also served as a bishop in the A.M.E. Church.[21] In 1871, in Alabama, Pyton Finley, an African American, was a member of the State Board of Education. He has been credited by Walter Lynwood Fleming for introducing resolutions requesting the establishment of a university for African Americans. Possibly due to this and other resolutions, in 1873, the Lincoln School at Marion County became a colored university. In addition to this, a normal school (teacher-training institution) was also established for his people.[22] These African Americans worked hard for the establishment of free schools in their perspective states for the interests of their brethren.

Like other executive offices, African Americans held positions in the state treasuries in Louisiana, Florida, and South Carolina. In Florida, Jonathan Gibbs, who has been listed already, was appointed secretary of treasury in 1872 by Governor Harrison Reed. In Louisiana, in 1872, Antoine Dubuclet was listed as state treasurer.[23] This African American served in this position for many years. In 1876, his occupation appeared in the city directory as state treasurer. In 1876, his office was located at the State House, and his home address was listed as 268 Canal Street.[24] The work performed by Dubuclet while state treasurer was commended by members of the commission who conducted an investigation verifying whether or not he should be impeached. Chief Justice Edward D. White of the United States Supreme Court, at the end of the investigation, concluded that he accomplished his duties honorably, even though some irregularities were discovered.[25] In South Carolina, Francis L. Cardozo also served as state treasurer in addition to his executive position as Secretary of State. He was state treasurer during the administration of Governor Daniel H. Chamberlain and Lieutenant Governor Richard H. Gleaves, who was also an African American.[26]

Regulators at the State Level

Generally, a small number of African Americans were appointed as law enforcement officers at the state level. From the records found during the investigation of this topic, data in Arkansas indicated that William H. Grey, an African American, held the position of Commissioner of Immigration and state land officer from 1872 to 1874.[27] In Mississippi, an African American also served as immigration commissioner. James Wilford Garner notes that when the Democrats overthrew Republicans during Reconstruction, the salary of an African American commissioner of immigration in Mississippi was reduced from $2,000 yearly to $100. He was also ordered to fund the expenses of that office.[28] Like the Department of Immigration, other departments were also affected during the transition from Republican to Democrat rule. Furthermore, an African American served also as assistant adjutant-general of the state in South Carolina.

In Arkansas, the governor appointed Reverend J.T. White to the position of State Commissioner of Public Works.[29] He served also as a senator in the same state and was a member of the Constitutional Convention in 1868. On the sixth day of the convention, he was asked to offer a prayer, to which he agreed.[30] In South Carolina, Henry W. Purvis of Richland County was elected an adjutant-general in 1872. During his nomination, he was not opposed by any other candidate.[31] In 1877, he was 31 years old and resided in Columbia, South Carolina.[32] As the adjutant-general, he was responsible for the overseeing the state's militia, as well as furnishing military equipment to these organizations. During his interview on the history of Hamburg militia, Purvis noted that military equipment used by that group had been given to them by his predecessor.[33] From his account, it is plausible to note that one of the responsibilities of the adjutant-general was administering the state military equipment. In the same state, on March 25, 1869, the governor appointed Robert Elliott as assistant adjutant-general of the state. This Massachusetts-born African American was educated; he pursued his studies in Jamaica and in England, attending Eton College at the University of London. Additionally, he studied the law at the office of Sergeant Fitz Herbert, of the London Bar. In South Carolina, he was elected to the lower legislature in Barnwell County. In 1868, he was again elected to the state legislature. He also served as sheriff in his county.[34]

In Mobile, Alabama, in the city directory of 1872, an African American named Spencer Terrell was a state lottery agent. He resided near the corner of Claiborne and St. Louis.[35] In Louisiana, in 1870, F. Dubuclet was a chief clerk in the office of the treasurer of the state. Similarly, A.D. Dubuclet was also a clerk in the same office. It seems that these African Americans were related to Dubuclet, the state treasurer of Louisiana. In addition to the clerks listed above, Phillip Pardone, an African American in New Orleans, was also recorded in the city directory as clerk in the office of the state treasurer.[36] In addition to the positions listed above, in each state under the Reconstruction policy, many African Americans were elected as house and senate members at the state level. To illustrate this, in New Orleans, Louisiana, William Merill was a member of legislature.[37] In Richmond, Virginia, in 1870, Ballard T. Edwards was listed in the city directory as a member of the legislature. On the other hand, Frank Moss was recorded as a colored state senator.[38] Robert C. Delarge, an African American, was appointed state land commissioner in South Carolina. In addition to this position, he was also a member of the 42nd Congress.[39]

County Level

The county is the most important government jurisdiction in the United States. This jurisdictional division is governed by the shire reeve (sheriff). This title of antiquity comes from the Saxon kings in England. Then as now, the sheriff is an executive officer of the county. He has jurisdictional power over county jails. He also appoints his deputies and other officers in the county. During the Reconstruction, the sheriff was also a tax collector. In addition to the sheriff, members of county boards of supervisors were also law enforcement in that level, being entrusted with regulating county affairs. Moreover, county commissioners and superintendents of schools were regulators who enforced laws related to the jurisdictional power entrusted to them. In the county courts, African Americans also held minor positions such as clerks.

County Board of Supervisors

This board of supervisors administered the affairs of the county. It was sometimes called county commissioners, or the board, or the county board. The power of the board of supervisors in the South was noted by Garner, a historian of Mississippi. In the South, Garner writes, the county board was a legislative and administrative body of great responsibility.[40] This office was found throughout many states in the South. In Mississippi, Alabama, North Carolina, Virginia, Arkansas, and South Carolina, members of the board of supervisors were entrusted with many local responsibilities. In addition to the legislative and administrative power, they were law enforcement agents with regulatory power. With such power, they were entrusted with building or repairing public buildings and bridges. Also, the county board was empowered to assess and disburse taxes. Similarly, supervising the construction and maintenance of roads and highways, selecting juries, awarding county contracts, examining as well as determining the loan process were under the jurisdiction of the board of supervisors.[41] On this board, African Americans had the same power and jurisdictions as their white counterparts. In Mississippi, South Carolina, Arkansas, North Carolina, Virginia, and Alabama, African Americans were elected as members of the board of supervisors. As in the states listed above, in Florida many African Americans held positions on the Board of Supervisors.

In 1869, in Charleston, South Carolina, E.P. Wall was county commissioner. It appears that he was the only African American appointed to that position in that year. In 1872, the name of Wall was not listed as county commissioner in Charleston. Instead, R.M. Gregory, also an

African American, was recorded as county commissioner in the city directory of 1872. In addition to his county duties, Gregory was a farmer. It is possible that he was elected to that position because he was an owner of land and well respected by other African Americans. Two years later, W.H. Thompson was county commissioner in Charleston, South Carolina. In 1876, Thompson was reappointed to the position of county commissioner and continued to serve in the same capacity in 1877. Thompson was the longest-serving African American on the county board. It seems that he performed well the duties entrusted to him. From the account of the Charleston city directories, it looks like one African American was permitted to serve as county commissioner each year.[42] In Marion County, three African Americans were elected county commissioners. According to William W. Sellers, Jonas Deas, Lawrence Mills, and Enos Reeves were elected county commissioners in Marion County. Sellers recorded that these African Americans were ignorant and were not knowledgeable about the duties entrusted to them.[43] In Edgefield County, South Carolina, three African Americans were elected as county commissioners. Ned Tennant was among the African American county commissioners in Edgefield County. John Schreiner Reynolds notes that African American county commissioners in Edgefield County were illiterate and could not even read their own names.[44]

In North Carolina, however, multiple African Americans served on the boards of county commissioners in areas with high percentages of black people. Joseph Gregoire de Rhoulhac recorded that in Jones County, North Carolina, a great number of commissioners were poor African Americans and whites. He went on to note that in Halifax County, the board of commissioners was under the control of African Americans. According to him, the county was governed by a five-member board of commissioners, elected by popular vote.[45] In the same state, Joseph Kelly Turner and John Luther Bridgers recorded that Henry C. Cherry, an African American, was county commissioner for several years. These two authors credited Cherry as being a good man. The position of board of county commissioners was established by the Reconstruction Constitution of 1868. Before this Constitution, the duties entrusted to the county board of commissioners were under the jurisdiction of the county court.

In 1869, in Mississippi, General Ames appointed Sam West, an African American, as a member of the board of supervisors to represent beat three. West was a preacher and resided in the Windham plantation in Scott County. Forrest Cooper noted West was illiterate. West was a victim of the political turmoil of that time. He was killed during a confrontation between African Americans and whites.[46] In 1874, in Marshall County, in northern Mississippi, three African Americans members were elected to the board of supervisors. There was only one white person on the board. In Madison County, Mississippi, every member of the board was an African American.[47] John Wilson, an ex-slave who resided close to Como, was a member of the board of supervisors in 1872 and 1873.[48] Similarly, Lang Hunt, an ex-slave, also served as a member of the board of supervisors in Como from 1872 till 1875. Jerry Hilblew was the only African American in Como from beat three on the board of supervisors in 1874 and 1875. Peter Shegog, an African American from beat three in Panola County, served on the board during the 1874–1875 term.[49] As it was in other counties, in 1874 two African Americans were members of the board of supervisors in Carroll County.[50] In Bolivar County, where African Americans were a majority, Louis Stubblefield and James J. Joor served on the board between 1869 and 1890.[51]

In Mississippi, after the Constitution of 1869, the board of police was called the board of supervisors. Possibly, the regulations and management of the police force was under the jurisdiction of the board. When the board of police became the board of supervisors in Mississippi, Price Hogan and Spencer Watkins, both African Americans of Monroe County, were members of the board. Watkins became a member of the board in 1870 and resigned in 1871. In 1872, there were two African Americans along with three white members of the board in Monroe County. Geo Strong and Price Hogan were African Americans on the board in that year. In the same year, Wm. Watson was elected as the replacement for W.L. Walton, a white person. At this time, there were three African Americans on the board and two whites. As there were three blacks, they had the possibility to elect one of them as president of the board. Consequently, Price Hogan was elected president of the board of supervisors of Monroe County, Mississippi. Similarly, in

Oktibbeha County, Caesar Hyde, John Gamble, and Jupiter Yates were members of the board of supervisors.[52] In 1874, there were still three blacks on the board of supervisors in Monroe County.[53] Price Hogan has been credited as an educated African American preacher. When he was elected in 1870, he conducted various projects throughout the county. Under his leadership, many building projects were constructed. The Tombigbee River Bridge at Aberdeen was also built when he was a member of the board.[54] In Virginia, Robert Witting was a member of Board of the Supervisors of Henrico County from 1875 to 1877.[55]

Sheriffs

Sheriffs in the South were one of the most important county officials with much political influence and much power. In Mississippi, under the Reconstruction Constitution, the sheriff controlled the selection of the trial juries and appointed one of three registrars. He was also a tax collector for the state and the county.[56] With the inclusive Republican political system, many African Americans were elected sheriffs in the black counties in some states. From the work of Walter Lynwood Fleming, data indicated that in Sumter County, an African American was elected as sheriff. According to him, the African American sheriff could not read.[57] Contrary to Sumner County, in the city directories of Mobile, Alabama, no single African American was recorded as sheriff.

In Mississippi, many African Americans were elected sheriffs. In South Carolina, they were always appointed as deputy sheriff. In Florida, records show African Americans were elected sheriffs. Reconstruction writers such as Garner, King, and Nordoff documented that African Americans elected many of their own people to that position. To illustrate, in Mississippi, in DeSoto County, Issaquena County, Jefferson County, and Bolivar County, African Americans were always elected to the office of sheriff during the Reconstruction. Blanche K. Bruce was one of the African Americans who was elected sheriff in Bolivar County in 1871 during the administration of Governor Alcorn. He also served as sergeant-at-arms during the administration of Governor Alcorn. He was also appointed to the rank of colonel. As sheriff, he was also tax collector for the state and his county. Sheriff Bruce was born into slavery in Prince Edward County, Virginia. According to Booker T. Washington, Bruce had been instructed in the same area where his master's son received a formal education.[58] Before his appointment to the position of sheriff, Bruce was the superintendent of education in Bolivar County. He was also the first African American United States senator. After his senatorial term, he was appointed to the United States Internal Revenue Service.

From the account of Garner, records indicate that during the administrations of Governors Alcorn and Powers, African Americans held the position of sheriff in many counties in Mississippi. In 1873, a black sheriff was elected in Issaquena County. In DeSoto County for years at one time or other an African American was elected to the position of sheriff. In 1876, a black sheriff was serving his fourth term. This sheriff was more than likely elected in 1870.[59] From Satcher's account, we discovered that twelve African Americans were elected sheriffs during Reconstruction.[60] Satcher tells us that in counties such as Adams, Hinds, Coahora, Monroe, Jefferson, Holmes, Issaquena, and Washington, African Americans served as sheriffs. For the names of those who served in the listed counties, refer to the work of Satcher.[61]

In Mississippi, sometimes the appointment of an African American as sheriff was disapproved by the Democrats. When Governor Ames appointed Peter Crosby sheriff and tax collector in Warrant County, members of the Democratic Party forced his resignation. As a result, Crosby sought help from Governor Ames who called the United States Army to reinstate Crosby to his office. The event of Crosby led to violent exchanges between whites and African Americans.[62] Crosby also had the problem for paying bond like other African Americans elected or appointed to the local or county offices. During the Reconstruction period, candidates elected for the office of sheriff were required to pay the bond. This requirement was not based on race or ethnicity. Even though the case of Crosby led to violence, in Hinds County, Harney, an African American sheriff, used his position to unite the two races. During his term of office, he avoided violence between African Americans and whites by requesting a meeting with Captain Frank Johnston, the commander of the Jackson Company of militia. Due to his approach, a peace term was convened between the two races. His action was appreciated by the people.[63]

In Virginia, Luther Porter Jackson notes that R.D. Ruffin was a sheriff in Alexandria County from 1873 to 1874. Ruffin was born a slave in 1837 and was appointed to the rank of sergeant in the Civil War. After the war, he attended Howard University where he studied law and graduated in 1874.[64] Ruffin was more than likely among the literate black sheriffs during Reconstruction. In Arkansas, Edward King notes that in black counties, many African Americans elected as sheriffs.[65] In Lee County, Furburch, an African American who was murdered due to violence, was a sheriff of that county.[66] In Alabama, African Americans also served as sheriff. From the account of Walter Lynwood Fleming, records indicate the black sheriff of Sumter County was illiterate.[67]

In South Carolina, Florida, and North Carolina, African Americans also held the position of deputy sheriff. An example of this is John A. Mushington who, in 1869, was a deputy county sheriff in Charleston. In 1874, two African Americans were listed as deputy sheriff in the Charleston city directory. C.F. Burke and John Burnham were African American sheriffs in Charleston, South Carolina, in 1874. Then, in 1875, another African American was also listed in the city directory as deputy sheriff.[68] It appears that in South Carolina, precisely in Charleston, African Americans were rarely appointed to the position of deputy sheriff. If the records in the city directory are correct, African Americans did not hold the position of sheriff. The highest position they were appointed to was deputy sheriff.

In Jacksonville, Florida, Professor Canter Brown recorded a few names of African Americans who served as sheriff in Florida. His research shows that from 1868 to 1877 African Americans, at one time or another, served as sheriff in Franklin, Hamilton, Jefferson, Lean, Madison, and Monroe Counties. In Franklin County, Henry Hutchinson served as sheriff from 1874 to 1877. He was the only African American whom Professor Brown listed as being a sheriff. As in Franklin County, in Hamilton County, Benjamin F. Collier was the only African American who held the position of sheriff during Reconstruction, serving in this position from 1874 to 1877. Contrary to the counties listed above, in Jefferson County, Lafayette N.B. McCray and George W. Monroe were African Americans who were elected as sheriff.[69] In Jacksonville, in 1876 and 1877, John H. Brown, an African American, held the position of deputy sheriff.[70] It appears that the population of African Americans was large in the Floridian counties where they were elected sheriffs.

The sheriffs were well paid because they received their salary from the taxes they collected. It appears that sheriffs who collected a high amount of taxes were well paid. In Washington County, Mississippi, for example, the annual salary of the sheriff was $15,000.[71] Garner also notes that the salary of a sheriff ranged as high as $20,000 per year in some counties, with the average not falling below $5,000.[72] Contrary to the estimate of Garner noted above, we discovered that in Issaquena County in 1876, an African American sheriff who was serving his fourth term as a sheriff only earned $3,000 per year.[73] It is unknown why he received less money. Possibly, he did not collect enough taxes in that year.

In Virginia, an educated African American served as sheriff from 1873 to 1874. R.D. Ruffin was born in 1837 and was educated at Howard University, graduating in 1874. It appears that while he was sheriff of Alexander County, he was still pursuing his education. Before he began his law enforcement duties, Sheriff Ruffin had fought in the Civil War, holding the rank of sergeant.[74] Black sheriffs were also elected in Louisiana, Florida, and South Carolina. In Florida, Canter Brown lists that David Montgomery was sheriff from 1868 to 1873. In addition, he was also a tax collector from 1868 to 1869. He was reelected from 1872 to 1877. In the South, the sheriff also was a tax collector. In the same state, George W. Monroe was sheriff of Jefferson County.[75]

At the county level, African Americans also held minor positions. In addition to sheriff and deputy sheriff, African Americans also worked in the sheriff's office as clerks. According to the Charleston city directory of 1872, John A. Mushington, an African American, held the position of clerk in the office of the sheriff, located in Columbus.[76] The African American sheriffs listed above are not complete because data were not collected from all the counties in states under Reconstruction. In addition to the position of sheriff, they were also elected as the coroner.

Coroners

During the Reconstruction period, a few African Americans held the title of coroner, like their white counterparts. In Charleston, South Carolina, Little Rock, Arkansas, and Wilmington, North Carolina, African Americans were appointed as coroners and deputy coroners. In 1874, William E. Burke was listed in the Charleston city directory as an African American deputy coroner. In Edgefield County, South Carolina, an African American named Carroll was a corner. When a white coroner by the name of Hardy Walls resigned, Carroll was appointed instead.[77] In addition to South Carolina, in Arkansas and Mississippi, a few African Americans served as coroner. In Wilmington, North Carolina, data also revealed that African Americans held the same position. In Wayne County, Michigan, a state which was not subjected to Reconstruction policy, an African American was appointed county coroner in 1876. According to the data collected from the *Michigan Manual of Freedmen's Progress*, John Wilson, an African American, was elected coroner of Wayne County as a Democrat in 1876. He was the first person of that race to be elected to public office in Michigan. Like Wilson, Thomas D. Owens was elected coroner in the same county. He was a barber in Detroit, and one of the oldest African Americans in the town of Detroit.[78] Throughout the history of the United States, Wentworth Cheswell was the first person of that race to hold the title of coroner in Newmarket, New Hampshire, from 1785 to 1787 in Rockingham County.[79] At the time of the writing of this book, no evidence was found of any African Americans being elected or appointed coroner before him.

County School Officers

In 1868, in the states under the Reconstruction policy, new regulations and laws were enacted for the administration of public instruction. At the county level, the superintendent of public instruction was entrusted with the regulatory power for the management of county schools. Like the county superintendent, county school board members were also empowered to control the administration of the schools. In North Carolina, school committees also exercised regulatory powers. Additionally, county school examiners also had regulatory powers and were charged with issuing teaching certificates, as well as making sure that teachers followed the curricula. County examiners were appointed by the county commissioners.[80]

Among African Americans, William P. Mabson was a school examiner in Edgecombe County, North Carolina. This African American was a teacher by profession. He attended Lincoln College in Chester County, Pennsylvania. His entered politics in 1872 when he was elected to the Pennsylvania State House, and in 1874 he was elected to the State Senate. It seems that after his education, Mabson returned to North Carolina, his native state. He was born in 1846 in Wilmington, North Carolina.[81] During his years of service as county examiner, 200 teachers were certified. Because Mabson believed in children receiving a quality education, he held the teacher certification process to a high standard.[82]

In the township of Tarboro in Edgecombe County, North Carolina, an African American named Davis Harris was elected as member of the school committee. In Deep Fisher Creek in the same county, Israel Merritt held that position. In the township of Upper Fisher Creek, also in Edgecombe County, L. Garrett, Carter Bellamy, and N. Bellamy were African Americans on school committees.[83] It appears that in this township, African Americans were in the majority. As members of the school committees, these African Americans were entrusted with the hiring, management, and dismissal of teachers. The provisions for the school buildings and furniture were also under the jurisdiction of the school committee. Moreover, they enforced the regulation about teachers only using the text assigned by the school boards. Gathering school reports and statistics was also among the mandates entrusted to them.[84]

In South Carolina and Florida, African Americans were also appointed as school regulators. Professor Canter Brown, Jr., recorded names of African Americans who held such positions during Reconstruction. According to his data, George W. Lindsley served as superintendent of schools in Escambia County from 1873 to 1875. In Leon County, Charles H. Pearce was superintendent of schools from 1868 to 1872. Similarly, in Marion County, Isaac Black, also an African American, held the same title.[85]

In Mississippi, African Americans were appointed as county superintendents of education. James Wilford Garner recorded pertinent data on African American superintendents of public instruction. According to him, in counties such as Bolivar, Wilkinson, Washington, Issaquena, and counties located along the river, African Americans held the position of county superintendent of education. He notes that B.K. Bruce was superintendent of public instruction in Bolivar County before his appointment as sheriff in the same county.[86] In Wilkinson County, Garner says that the African American superintendent of public instruction was schooled at Oberlin College in Ohio.[87]

Minor Officers at the County Level

At the county level, African Americans were also appointed auditors, assessors, and school superintendents. The audits and assessments of county properties were under the jurisdictions of county auditors and assessors. In a like manner, county schools were under the control of county superintendents of schools. In the states under Reconstruction, records showed that few African Americans were appointed to the positions listed above. In 1869, in Charleston, South Carolina, T.S. Denny was recorded as a county assessor. He resided at 33 Market, as noted in the city directory. Like Denny, Chas Secba, also an African American, was a county assessor in the same city during 1869. In 1869, A.J. Ransier was county auditor. He lived at 8 Sires, as recorded in the city directory. In the same city, in 1972, S.L. Bennett served also as county auditor at Fireproof Building. He resided at 13 Wall. In the 4th district of Charleston, J.M.F. Dereef was also an African American county assessor in 1872.

African Americans were also appointed as county school superintendents and school commissioners in many counties in Mississippi, Alabama, and South Carolina. In 1876, in Reverend J.E. Hayne was recorded in the Charleston city directory of that year as county school commissioner. His office was located at Fireproof.[88] In fact, in the predominantly black counties, the county superintendent of education was always an African American. It is likely, then, that other African Americans were appointed to the county school committee. African

Americans also held the position of county school examiner. To illustrate, William P. Mabson held that position in Edgecombe County. He was born in Wilmington, North Carolina, on November 1, 1846. And as a graduate of Lincoln College in Chester County, Pennsylvania, he was well educated. It appears that Mabson returned home along with other African Americans after the Civil War to assist his people. As to his governmental duties, in 1872, he was elected to the State House, and then in 1874 he was elected to the State Senate.[89]

In Oktibbeha County, Jim McNichols held the position of county treasurer. While most of those who held this position were wealthy, McNichols was poor. It appears that he was an honest African American who performed his duties accordingly. F.Z. Browne notes that the opportunities to generate money while working as a treasurer were immense.[90] The emolument for this work was high. As McNichols was not criticized by the author, it is an indication that he was a good county servant. Unfortunately, African Americans who held positions as such were always termed as ignorant or illiterate.

Notes

1. Ella Lonn, *Reconstruction in Louisiana after 1868*. G.P. Putnam's Sons, 1918, p. 6.

2. John Schreiner Reynolds, *Reconstruction in South Carolina, 1865–1877*. State Company, 1905, pp. 59 and 224.

3. See *The Journal of Negro History, Some Negro Members of the Reconstruction, Conventions, and Legislatures and Congress*, 1920, p. 99.

4. James Jefferson Pipkin, *The Negro in Revelation, in History, and in Citizenship: What the Race had done and is doing*, 1902, p. 63.

5. Reynolds, 1905, pp. 81 and 143.

6. Ibid., p. 159.

7. John Roy Lynch, *The Facts of Reconstruction*. Neal Publishing Company, 1913, p. 73.

8. Ibid., p. 406.

9. William J. Simmons and Henry McNeal Turner, *Men of Mark: Eminent, Progressive, and Rising*. G.M. Rewell & Company, 1887, pp. 429–30.

10. Reynolds, 1905, p. 224. Reynolds writes that he had five competitors.

11. John Wallace, *Carpetbag Rule in Florida: The Inside Working of the Reconstruction of Civil Government in Florida*, 1888, p. 55.

12. Lynch, 1913, p. 75. Lynch wrote, "The nomination of Hill was favorably received, because it was believed that, if elected, he would discharge the duties of the office in a way that would reflect credit upon himself and give satisfaction to the public," p. 75.

13. James Wilford Garner, *Reconstruction in Mississippi*, 1902, pp. 293–94.

14. William W. Sellers, *A History of Marion County, South Carolina, from Its Earliest Times to the Present*, 1901, pp. 95–97.

15. Reynolds, 1905, p. 224.

16. Charles Nordhoff, *The Cotton States in the Spring and Summer of 1875*. 1876, p. 74.

17. See *A History of Mississippi: From the Discovering of the Great River by Hernando Desoto, including the Earliest Settlement made by the French under Iberville, to the Death of Jefferson Davis*, 1891, p. 406.

18. Edgar Wallace Knight, *Public Education in the South*. Ginn, 1922, p. 362. See also Carter Godwin Woodson, *The Negro in Our History*. Associated Publishers, 1922, p. 252.

19. Simmons and Turner, 1887, p. 829.

20. See John Wesley Cromwell, *The Negro in American History: Men and Women Eminent in the Evolution of the American of African Descent*, 1914, p. 26.

21. See *The Mississippi Valley Historical Review*, 1915, pp. 529 and 559. See also Simmons and Turner, 1887, p. 133.

22. See Walter Lynwood Fleming, *Civil War and Reconstruction in Alabama*, 1905, p. 617

23. See *New Orleans, Louisiana, City Directory*, 1872, p. 132.

24. See *New Orleans, Louisiana, City Directory*, 1876, p. 251.

25. See *The Journal of Negro History*, vol. 2 on Antoine Dubuclet, 1917, p. 77.

26. See *The World Almanac & Book of Facts*, 1875, p. 54.

27. See Town and County: Race Relations and Urban Development in Arkansas, 1865–1905. University of Arkansas, 1878, p. 29.

28. Garner, 1902, p. 410.

29. Ibid., p. 591.

30. See *Debates and Proceedings of the Convention Which Assembled at Little Rock, January 7th, 1868*. Arkansas Constitutional Convention, 1868, p. 77.

31. Reynolds, 1905, p. 224.

32. See Congressional Set, on the interview of Adjutant General Henry W. Purvis of January 5, 1877, p. 401.

33. Ibid., pp. 401–03.

34. James Jefferson Pipkin, *The Negro in Revelation, in History, and in Citizenship: What the race has done and is doing*, 1902, p. 63.

35. *Mobile, Alabama, City Directory*, 1872, p. 215.

36. See *New Orleans, Louisiana, City Directory*, 1870, pp. 188 and 468.

37. Ibid., p. 364.

38. See *Richmond, Virginia, City Directory*, 1870, pp. 100, 169.

39. Pipkin, 1902, p. 63.

40. Garner, 1902, p. 307.

41. Ibid.

42. *Charleston, South Carolina, City Directory*, 1869, p. 214. See also, *Charleston, South Carolina, City Directory*, 1874, p. 264. *Charleston, South Carolina, City Directory*, 1876, p. 438. *City Directory*, 1877, p. 438.

43. William W. Sellers, *A History of Mario County, South Carolina: From Its Earliest Times to the Present, 1901, 1902*, pp. 90–98.

44. Reynolds, 1905, p. 304. John Abney Chapman wrote also that Ned Tennant, an African American, was rewarded the office of County Commissioner. 1897, p. 260.

45. Joseph Gregoire de Rhoulhac Hamilton, *Reconstruction in North Carolina*, vol. 58. Columbia University, 1914, p. 648.

46. See Forrest Cooper, "Reconstruction in Scott County." *Publications of the Mississippi Historical Society*, 1913, pp. 112 and 130.

47. Ibid., p. 308.

48. See John Kyle, "Reconstruction in Panola County." *Publications of the Mississippi Historical Society*, vol. 13, The Society, p. 25.

49. Ibid. For more information, see Lang Hunt, Jerry Hibbler, and Peter Shegog, *African American Members of the Board in Panola County*, p. 25.

50. Fred M. Witty, "Reconstruction in Carroll and Montgomery Counties" *Publications of the Mississippi Historical Society*. The Society, 1909, p. 119.

51. Satcher, 1978, p. 39. In 1890, African Americans were disfranchised and prevented from holding local positions, but in Bolivar County, they were still part of the local government.

52. See F.Z. Browne, "Reconstruction in Oktibbeha County." *Publications of the Mississippi Historical Society*, 1913, p. 273.

53. George J. Leffwich, "Reconstruction in Monroe County." *Publications of the Mississippi Historical Society*, vol.9, 1906, pp. 53, 58, and 61.

54. Satcher, 1978, p. 39.

55. Jackson, 1945, p. 43.

56. Garner, 1902, p. 305.

57. Fleming, 1905, p. 743.

58. See George Washington Williams, *History of the Negro Race in America, 1619–1880*, vol.2, 1883, p. 444. The information can also been found in Booker T. Washington's *The Story of the Negro*, vol 2. Association Press, 1909, p. 23.

59. Garner, 1902, pp. 306 and 308.

60. Satcher, 1978, p. 39.

61. Ibid.

62. Nordhoff, p. 79.

63. See *A History of Mississippi: From the Discovery of the Great River by Hernando Desoto, Including the Earliest Settlement made by the French under Iberville, to the Death of Jefferson Davis*, 2891, p. 402.

64. Jackson, 1945, p. 36.

65. Edward King, *The Great South*. American Publishing Company, 1875, p. 228.

66. Nordhoff, 1876, p. 33.

67. Fleming, 1905, p. 743.

68. *Charleston, South Carolina, City Directory*, 1869, p. 177, City Directory of 1874, p. 76, City Directory of 1875, p. 108.

69. Canter Brown, Jr., *Florida's: Black Public Officials*, 1998, pp. 159, 160, 164–65, 169, and 172.

70. *Webb's Jacksonville, FL, City Directory*, 1876–1877, p. 66.

71. Garner, 1902, p. 305–06.

72. Ibid.

73. Ibid.

74. Jackson, 1945, p. 36.

75. Brown, 1998, p. 112.

76. *Charleston, South Carolina, City Directory*, 1872, p. 156.

77. Chapman, 1897, p. 417. John Schreiner Reynolds writes also that African Americans held the position of corner in Edgefield, South Carolina. See *Reconstruction in South Carolina*, 1905, p. 304.

78. See Michigan Freedmen's Progress Commission, *Michigan Manual of Freedmen's Progress*. J.M. Green, 1915, p. 35.

79. James Hill Fitts, *History of Newfields, New Hampshire, 1638–1911, 1912*, p. 103. See also *The New Hampshire Provincial and State Papers*, vol. 20, 1891, p. 558.

80. Edgard Wallace Knight, *Public Education in North Carolina*, Houghton Mifflin Company, 1916, p. 235.

81. Turner and Bridgers, 1920, p. 274.

82. William Harvey Quick, *Negro Stars in All Ages of the World*. S.B. Adkins & Company Printers, 1898, p. 257.

83. Ibid., p. 249–50.

84. Knight, 1916, p. 235.

85. Brown, Jr., 1998, pp. 157, 165, and 171.

86. Garner, 1802, p. 307.

87. Ibid., p. 309.

88. *Charleston, South Carolina*, 1876, p. 261.

89. Turner and Bridgers, 1920, pp. 270 and 274.

90. Browne, 1913, p. 279.

Chapter 12

African Americans as Federal Law Enforcement Officers

Historically, from the Civil War to the end of Reconstruction, Union officials established strong relationships with African Americans. Some of the generals advocated the employment of African Americans in the ranks of the Union soldiers. General Ulysses Grant was among those who supported President Lincoln on his policy to enlist African American men in the Union Army.[1]

Additionally, during Reconstruction, Grant was an enforcer of the policy championed by the radical Republicans in the American Congress for the inclusion of African Americans in the American body politic. Likely, he supported generals such as Sheridan who fiercely objected to the policy of President Andrew Johnson toward African Americans. In 1869, when General Grant was elected president of the United States, African Americans from various states in the South were appointed as agents to the federal level.

It is also important to stress that the relationship was born between high-ranking military officers and African Americans. Among these generals, some were elected to the State House and State Senate. In such positions, the elected military officers were grateful for the services African Americans furnished to the Union; and, as a result, they were from time to time encouraged to recommend them for law enforcement positions. Moreover, lawmakers who believed in the causes of the Union established mutual relationships with African American leaders such as Frederick Douglass and John Langston. Lawmakers understood the impacts African Americans made during the Civil War. Similarly, they were eager to advocate for the causes of African

Americans and enacted impartial laws, which would be beneficial to the entire country.

African Americans contributed unconditionally and voluntarily for the security of the United States. As a reward, Union lawmakers instituted legislations for the security of the newly freedmen. In a like manner, they were included as law enforcement agents at the federal level. From the city directories consulted, records indicate African Americans held the positions of collector of internal revenue, auditor, assessor, register of deeds, United States Marshal, clerk of the custom house, and inspector of the House. Before the appointment of African Americans listed above, they were employed as agents of the Freedmen's Bureau.

The Employment of African Americans in the Freedmen's Bureau

The Freedmen's Bureau became law on March 3, 1865, after the experiment which started in Sea Island, South Carolina. In the same year, the Bureau was extended to other insurrection states. As a federal agency, it was under the Department of War and was termed the Bureau of Refugee, Freedmen, and Abandoned Lands.[2] The Freedmen's Bureau had various mandates. It was a social and a regulatory agency. In this study, we are concerned about the regulatory aspects of this agency. As the relationship between the emancipated slaves and their former masters deteriorated, it was difficult for the two groups to reconcile easily. Likely, the mistrust existed between the former masters and African Americans. Therefore, the Freedmen's Bureau became a mediator for the two groups. Due to the mistrust, it was difficult for the African Americans to sign a reasonable contract with their former masters who still had an economic monopoly. Generals such as Howard understood that former masters would punish their former slaves due to their support to the Union. With this reasoning, General Howard began to enforce the contract regulations between the freedmen and their former masters. The regulation of contracts became a legal mandate of the Freedmen's Bureau. In addition to the enforcement of contracts, judicial cases regarding the newly freed men were under the jurisdiction of the agents of the Freedmen's Bureau. To improve communication between whites and blacks, some African Americans were employed as agents of this agency.

As early as 1865, many African Americans were engaged in assisting the Freedmen's Bureau commissioners. Honorable John Mercer Langston was appointed general inspector of the Bureau of Refugees, Freedmen, and Abandoned Lands.[3] In 1864, Rev. Hiram R. Revel was assisting the provost marshal with the management of the affairs of the Freedmen's Bureau in Vicksburg, Mississippi. Before his appointment to the Freedmen's Bureau, Rev. Revel assisted with the recruitment of African Americans in the first black regiment of Maryland. In addition to the formation of that regiment, he helped with the raising of the second black regiment in Missouri. When Rev. Revel settled in Natchez, Mississippi, he was appointed alderman of the city under the administration of General Adelbert Ames, the Military Governor.[4] Rev. Revel was a native of Fayetteville, North Carolina, where he was born. According to Booker T. Washington, he was born on September 1, 1822, to free parents. Possibly due to the status of his parents, he was accepted to attend the Quaker seminary in Union County, Indiana. After this school, he was also admitted to Knox College in Galesburg, Illinois, where he finished his education about 1847. After his education, he served as a preacher and lecturer in Indiana, Illinois, Ohio, and Missouri. As a preacher, he served as pastor of the Methodist Church in Baltimore.[5] He was also elected United States Senator.

R.G. Delarge was also an agent of the Freedmen's Bureau from 1867 to 1868. The previously mentioned African Americans, among others, assisted the commissioners and assistant commissioners of the Freedmen's Bureau with the regulation of land and other contracts. There were also those who helped with the superintending of schools. Delarge was born in Aiken, South Carolina, on March 15, 1842. In addition to his service to the Freedmen's Bureau in 1867 to 1868, he was active in local and state politics where he held some positions such as justice of the peace and State Commissioner of the Sinking Fund. He was also elected land commissioner.[6] As an educated African American, there is reason to believe that he held many positions because he performed his duties professionally and faithfully.

African American Law Enforcement Agents
of the Federal Government

African Americans were included as federal law enforcement officers during the administrations of President Abraham Lincoln, Andrew Johnson, and Ulysses Grant, including for a short period of time before the end of the Reconstruction by President Rutherford Hayes. During the administration of President Lincoln, the facts on African Americans who served as agents of the federal level are limited. During the administration of the successors to Lincoln, the policy observed by them impacted the inclusion of African Americans as agents at the federal level. During Grant's presidency, the patronage approach was frequently observed in the employment process at the federal level. It appears that many African Americans were assigned regulatory duties in many states during President Grant's administration. Even though the president supported the employment of African Americans at the federal level, obstacles were still present in the towns where they were assigned such duties. To illustrate this, in 1869, Rev. Henry McNeal Turner was appointed by President Grant postmaster of Macon, Georgia, but he was forced to resign because of political persecution. Afterwards, he was appointed coast inspector of customs by President Grant. In addition to his employment as inspector, he was appointed a United States Government Detective.[7] He was the only African American appointed as detective at the federal level in Georgia as data indicate. As a detective, it is more than likely that he was assigned with investigative duties at the custom office. It appears that the president was aware that Rev. Turner's life would be in danger while dealing with angry clients who did not want his presence at that location. The post office being a public place, the possibilities for his harassment were numerous.

With respect to the varying policies of different presidents, during the administration of Andrew Johnson, African Americans were not privileged in joining national politics. As a result, few people of the African race were appointed as federal law enforcement officers. On the other hand, President Grant continued with positive believe for the inclusion of African Americans in the political arena of the county. It seems that he followed his military approach toward African Americans during his presidency. From 1869 to 1877 when he was president, African Americans were appointed to the federal level as regulators.

In 1864, under President Lincoln, Reverend John Hudson Riddick, an African American, worked at the custom house of Norfolk, Virginia, when Major J.H. Hudson was a special collector. Major Hudson was appointed by Lincoln to serve in that city. The duties performed by Reverend Hudson were not mentioned by William J. Simmons and Henry McNeal Turner. As to their descriptive data, he was born close to Sunbury, Gates County, in 1848. It seems that when he was around nine years old, he was sold to Reverend Isaac Hunter of Virginia.[8] Possibly, while in the house of Reverend Hunter, Riddick learned how to read and write. Because of his literacy, Major Hudson had no problems hiring him.

During the administration of President Grant, William Pitt Kellogg appointed P.B.S. Pinchback as collector at the custom house in New Orleans. However, according to William J. Simmons and Henry McNeal Turner, Pinchback declined this offer from the collector of port.[9] In the same year, Oscar J. Dunn, also an African American, held the position of intelligence officer at the customs house. In 1867, Dunn lived at 333 Custom House. In 1868, in the same state, Louis Harris, also an African American, served as gauger. In this year, he resided at 68 Prieur.[10]

Under the Grant administration in 1869, African Americans were included in federal law enforcement agencies. They were appointed to the Internal Revenue Service and the Customs House. Moreover, they were also employed as clerks in the Treasury Department. In Washington, D.C., in 1869, John F. Cook, an African American, was recorded in the city directory as deputy collector in the Internal Revenue Service. He resided that year at 384 16th W.[11] In 1870 and '71, he held the position of city register in the D.C. municipal government.[12] He continued to serve in Internal Revenue Service for many years during the administration of President Grant. In 1873, his name was listed in the city directory as 4th Auditor Clerk, and he resided at 913 22nd NW. Before his appointment as a collector to the Department of Internal Revenue, in 1867 John F. Cook was a teacher in Washington, D.C. In the city directory of that year, his address was listed as 384 16th West.[13] According to John Wesley Cromwell, Cook was born in Washington, D.C., on September 21,

1833, where he was educated. From the account of William J. Simmons and Henry McNeal Turner, John F. Cook attended the school his father, also named John F. Cook, founded.[14] In 1868, he was appointed register. With regards to his Internal Revenue duties, he served under Presidents Grant, Hayes, Garfield, and Arthur. He resigned during the administration of President Cleveland.[15]

In Tennessee, James Carroll Napier was among African Americans appointed as a clerk to the Department of Treasury. He was employed by the Treasury while he was a student at Howard University in Washington, D.C. In 1868, he was appointed county claims commissioner of Davidson County by Governor William G. Brownlow. His duty was to investigate the claims of Tennesseans against Confederate and Union soldiers during the Civil War. He served in this capacity from 1868 to 1870, before his departure to Washington, D.C., to attend Howard University. Mingo Scott notes that he was encouraged by John Langston, a family friend. As a reminder, Langston was a professor and the dean of the law school.[16] In 1871, his name appeared in the city directory as clerk at the office of 6th Auditor. He continued to work in the same capacity till 1874. At Howard University, he studied law and graduated in 1872. After his studies, he was accepted to the bar in Washington, D.C. In 1875, when he returned to Nashville, he also passed the Tennessee bar. As he did in D.C., he continued to work for the Department of Treasury in Nashville, but he did so in a different capacity. In the Nashville city directory of 1876, his occupations were recorded as gauger and an attorney. In 1878, he worked as the United States storekeeper. In the following year, he was transferred to the Treasury Department again. It appears that even in 1880 and 1881, he was still serving as a gauger.[17]

Like Napier, Thomas A. Sykes was also an African American who served for many years as a regulatory agent at the Department of the Treasury. Sykes was a native of North Carolina. There, he served in the legislature and he also worked in the Treasury Department. When he moved to Nashville, Tennessee, he was reemployed in the same department. In 1877, he was recorded in the city directory of Nashville as a United States Gauger. He continued to hold the same position in 1878 and thereafter. In the city directories of 1880 and 1881, his name appeared in the city directories as a United States Gauger.[18] In the same state, William H. Gibson, a free African American from Baltimore, Maryland, was appointed by President Grant as a mail agent at the L. & N.R.R. branch in Knoxville. Four years later, he was appointed as a gauger in the United States Department of the Internal Revenue.[19]

In South Carolina, data also showed that African Americans were included as federal regulatory agents. From the Charleston city directory of 1869, a few of them were listed as clerks at the Customs House. One of them was recorded as a night inspector at the Customs House. Additionally, an African American was listed in the city directory as an officer at the Customs House. As an illustration, William H. Berney served as a clerk at the Custom House. At that time, he resided on Morrison near Rutledge Ave. In the same year and city, H. Larcomb was an officer at the Customs House and resided at 85 Calhoun.[20] L.F. Wall was inspector at the Custom House. His address was recorded as Calhoun near Anson.[21] He continued to serve in the same capacity in 1872. Like Wall, S.H. Maxwell was an African American who served as an inspector at the Charleston Customs House.[22]

In Washington, D.C., John Brown was recorded in the 1870 city directory as an African American clerk in the Treasury department. Like Brown, Solomon Johnson was also a clerk in the Department of Treasury. His address in the city directory was listed as 1153 17th N.W. In the same city as Brown and Johnson, Charles H. Lemos, a person of African descent also, was recorded in the city directory as a clerk of the Third Auditor Office.[23] In 1870, three African Americans held minor positions at the federal level in Washington, D.C. African Americans were also employed at the Texas Customs House as federal agents.

In the 1870 city directory of Galveston, Texas, G.T. Ruby, an African American worked at the Customs House. In the same year, the city directory of New Orleans, Louisiana, recorded the names of African American federal agents. According to the city directory of 1870, Luengo Penn was an officer at the Customs House in New Orleans. He resided at 340 Bourbon Street. In the same city, Alfred Perrin, also an African American, was a deputy inspector.[24]

In addition, African Americans were appointed to the United States marshals, deputy united marshals, as well as to the D.C. sanitation agency. In the Internal Revenue Service, they were appointed as collectors, agents of the United States Customs House, Special Collectors, auditors, assessors, and inspectors of the ports. In addition to the presidents noted previously, senators and congressmen recommended the names of African Americans for federal employment.

African Americans on the Board of Health

The first African American to be appointed to the board of health in the District of Columbia was Hon. John Mercer Langston. This African American was born a slave on a plantation in Louisa County, Virginia, on December 14, 1829. His father, also master was Captain Ralph Quarles, a plantation and slave owner. Langston was the slave of his own father according to the system of the time. Even though Quarles was a slave owner, he believed that the institution needed to be abolished. He also supported the abolition by the owners themselves.[25] From his father's views, we can speculate that Langston was well cared for.

After the death of his father, Langston moved to Ohio where he attended Oberlin College. He studied law at the office of a lawyer. His political life started in the little city of Brownhelm, where he worked in the local government as noted in the previous chapter. In 1863, he was employed by George L. Stearns as a military recruiter for the 54th and 55th Massachusetts black regiments. In addition to those duties, he assisted with the recruitment of the Ohio and Illinois black regiments. Langston also helped with the recruitments of black soldiers for the Union upon the request of Stearns, an old friend of John Brown and an influential wealthy merchant.[26]

Possibly due to his education and connection with the United States officials, on March 15, 1871, he was appointed a member of the Board of the National Capital by President Grant. The board was established in accordance with the law passed by Congress on February 21, 1871.[27] He was the first person of this race to be included on such board. As a board member, possibly he joined other members in regulating sanitary problems in the capital and the District of Columbia. He was also appointed Minister Resident and Consul General to Haiti. He was the first black person to be elected to the Congress of the Old Dominion. Langston has been credited for establishing the law school at Howard University. In addition to his scholarly and governmental work, he was a defender of the rights of African Americans.

United States Marshals and Deputy Marshals

From the records of various documents, data show that African Americans held the position of United States marshal and deputy marshal. Among the most noted African Americans was Frederick Douglass. As one of the black leaders, he made many sacrifices for the wellbeing of his people as well as for the security of the United States. During the Civil War, he was among African Americans assigned the recruitment of African men for the ranks of the Union. He was the advocate of equal pay in the army and requested by President Lincoln to work on the protections of African American prisoners of war under the Confederate jurisdiction. In addition to his duties as recruiter, he lectured against the enslavement of African Americans. Likely, he was politically involved during the campaigns of Republican presidents. As to the recruitment assignment, he assisted with the enlistment of African American soldiers for the 54th and the 55th regiments of Massachusetts. Charles and Lewis, the sons of Douglass, were enlisted in the Massachusetts regiments listed above.

With respect to his employment to the federal government, in 1871, he was appointed by President Grant to serve in the Territorial Legislature of the District of Columbia. In the following year, the president selected him as one the presidential electors-at-large for New York. His appointments were not limited to those listed above. In 1877, he became a member of the Washington police commissioners by the appointment of President Grant. During the administration of President Rutherford B. Hayes, Douglass was appointed marshal for the District of Columbia. During the administration of President James A. Garfield, he was appointed to the office of Recorder of Deeds of the District of Columbia.[28] He became associated with the most prominent American men of the time such as Governor Andrew of Massachusetts, Senator Charles Sumner, Senator Henry Wilson, Hon. Hamilton Fish, and Secretary of State Samuel Pomeroy. Due to his relationship with some of the people listed above, he was able to meet President Lincoln during the Civil War to discuss the policy regarding the security and equal payment of black soldiers.[29]

In addition to Marshal Douglass, African Americans were appointed as deputy marshals to various towns and territories. From the Oklahoma Historical Society and D.C. Gideon, we discovered that in 1875, Bass Reeves, an African American, was appointed deputy marshal by Judge Isaac C. Parker, who administered the federal court at Fort Smith, Arkansas, in the Indian Territory.[30] Deputy Marshal Reeves was born a slave in the Arkansas Territory in 1838. Little is known about his childhood. During his enslavement, he belonged to Colonel George R. Reeves, the former Speaker of the Texas House of Representatives. According to the Oklahoma Historical Society, Deputy Marshall Reeves was brought up in Lamar and Grayson Counties. Even though he grew up in Texas, it was in Arkansas where he was involved with federal lawmen. When he lived in Van Buren, Arkansas, most of the time he was employed as guide to United States marshals who maintained law and order at Fort Smith, Arkansas, in the Indian Territory.[31] He also served as scout and tracker. Possibly, due to his courage and loyalty to the federal officers, Judge Parker decided to employ him as a lawman. As a deputy marshal, he assisted with the arrests of many reputed criminals, including Native Americans. Gideon notes the arrests of men for horse theft. In addition, he had two wagon loads of prisoners. From the account of Art T. Burton, we learn that in addition to Deputy Marshal Reeves, there were other African Americans who served as deputy marshals in Native American territories. According to Burton, African American deputy marshals who served in the Native American Territory included Grant Johnson, Rufus Cannon, Crowder Nix, Ike Rogers, and Bynum Colbert.[32] These African American deputy marshals, who were familiar with the Native Americans' land, assisted with the arrests and the deterrence of criminals.

In Charleston, South Carolina, an African American also held the position of United States Deputy Marshal. In the city directories of 1874, Alex F. Farras was listed as United States marshal. In 1876, he was listed as Special Department United States Marshal. He held the same position in 1877 as noted in the city directory.[33] It seems that Farras was the only African American appointed to that position in the city of Charleston. In Virginia, Rev. John Hudson, a former slave, was appointed deputy marshal in Norfolk in 1872. Rev. Riddick served also as agent of the customs house in Norfolk in 1864. He was a native of North Carolina. He was born in Gate County on April 1, 1848. He moved to Norfolk, Virginia, in 1857, where he became the slave of Rev. Isaac Hunter. He was appointed special collector of President Lincoln, until he was excluded from his duties by President Johnson.[34]

Postmasters

Like other federal law enforcement agencies, in the United States Postal Service, African Americans were granted some positions of power. To illustrate, in Macon, Georgia, Rev. Turner was appointed postmaster by President Grant. During the administration of President Grant, we discovered that many African Americans were appointed to federal positions. Many historians credited Grant for protecting blacks during the Civil War. When General Halleck denied access to blacks hoping to enter the Union army, General Grant at that time defied that order. He showed his appreciation by valuing their services. In addition to the Internal Revenue positions, President Grant appointed Rev. McDuffe Wilder and Dr. B.A. Boseman as postmasters. Dr. Boseman was appointed postmaster to the port of Charleston and Rev. Wilder was postmaster at the port of Columbus, South Carolina. The term of service for these two men was extended by President Rutherford B. Hayes in 1877.[35] In Mississippi, an educated African American named Ben Booth was a postmaster in Water Valley for almost three years. This African American was portrayed as a polite and accommodating by Julia C. Brown. Even though he was a wonderful person, when the Post Office was robbed during his administration, he was removed from his assignments.[36] In the city of Tarboro, in Edgecombe County, North Carolina, two African Americans served as postmasters. Like the African Americans listed above, Francis L. Cardozo was appointed to the office of the auditor of the Postal Service in 1876.[37]

Notes

1. F.N. Thorpe, *The Civil War. The National View*, 1906, p. 344. Thorpe notes that "General Grant favored the use of Negro soldiers." He went on to note that "General Grant gave vigorous support to the president's policy of arming the negroes." According to him, on August 26, 1863, General Grant wrote to the president that "there is no objection, however, to my expressing an honest conviction; that by arming the negro we have added a powerful ally. They will make good soldiers and taking them from the enemy weakens him in the same proportion they strengthen us."

2. Laura Josephine Webster, *The Operation of the Freedmen's Bureau in South Carolina*, vol.1, issue 2. Department of History of Smith College, 1916, pp. 84–85.

3. See John Mercer Langston, *From Virginia Plantation to the National Capital: or, the First and only Negro Representative in Congress from the Old Dominion*. American Publishing Company, 1894, p. 249.

4. Booker T. Washington, *The Story of the Negro*. Doubleday, Page, & Company, 1909, pp. 11–12.

5. Ibid.

6. George Washington Williams, *History of the Negro Race in America from 1619 to 1880*. G.P. Putnam's Sons, 1883, p. 581.

7. William J. Simmons and Henry McNeal Turner, *Men of Mark: Eminent, Progressive, and Rising*. 1887, p. 815

8. Ibid., p. 752.

9. Ibid., pp. 761–63. Pinchback was born a free man from a white father, Major William Pinchback. His mother was a mulatto and a slave of his father. During the Civil War, Pinchback assisted with recruiting free men of color for the causes of the Union by General Benjamin F. Butler. On October 12, when he finished recruiting men for the Second Regiment of Louisiana Native Guards, he was appointed captain and commended Company A.

10. *New Orleans, Louisiana, City Directory*, 1868, p. 207.

11. See *Washington, District of Columbia, City Directory*, p. 199.

12. See *Washington, District of Columbia, City Directory*, 1870, p. 84.

13. *Washington, District of Columbia*, 1867, p. 205. See also the *City Directory*, 1873, p. 137.

14. Simmons and Turner, 1887, p. 120.

15. John Wesley Cromwell, *The Negro in American History: Men and Women Eminent to the Evolution of the American of African Descent*, 1914, pp. 230.

16. Mingo Scott, Jr., *The Negro in Tennessee Politics and Governmental Affairs*. Nashville: Rich Printing Company, 1964, p. 30.

17. See *Nashville, Tennessee, City Directory*, 1876, p. 217. Also, *Nashville, Tennessee, City Directory*, 1878, p. 346. *Nashville, Tennessee, City Directory*, 1880, p. 362. *Nashville, City Directory*, 1881, p. 374.

18. See *Nashville, Tennessee, City Directory,* 1877, p. 347. Also, *Nashville, City Directory*, 1881, p. 462.

19. Simmons and Turner, 1887, p. 547.

20. *Charleston, South Carolina, City Directory*, 1869, pp. 90, 94, 104, 143, 156, 168, and 213. In the city directory, F.H. Carman, T.M. Holmes, S.J. Maxwell, and Joseph Quash were recorded as clerks at the custom house.

21. *Charleston, South Carolina, City Directory*, 1869, p. 213.

22. *Charleston, South Carolina, City Directory*, 1872, pp. 144 and 218.

23. *Washington, District of Columbia, City Directory*, 1870, p. 50, 208, and 234.

24. See *New Orleans, Louisiana, City Directory*, 1870, pp. 474 and 476.

25. Ibid., p. 11.

26. Langston, 1894, p. 198.

27. Ibid., p. 318.

28. See Frederick Douglass, *The Life and Times of Frederick Douglass : From 1817–1882.* Christian Age office, 1882, pp. 291, 298, 305, and 359.

29. Douglass, 1882, p. 421.

30. See Oklahoma Historical Society, Reeves, Bass (1838–1910).

31. Ibid.

32. Art. T. Burton, Black Gun, Silver Star: *The Life and Legend of Frontier Marshal Bass Reeves.* University of Nebraska Press, Apr 1, 2008, p. 4. Burton listed many names of African American deputy marshals. See p. 4.

33. See *Charleston, South Carolina, City Directory*, 1874, p. 117., *City Directory*, 1876, p. 222. See also *City Directory* of 1877, p. 222.

34. Simmons and Turner, 1877, pp. 752–53.

35. George Brown Tindall, *South Carolina Negroes, 1877–1900.* University of South Carolina Press, 1952, p. 65.

36. Julia C. Brown, "Reconstruction in Yalobusha and Grenada Counties," *Publications of the Mississippi Historical Society*, vol.12, 1912, p. 228.

37. Carter Godwin Woodson and Rayford Whittingham Logan. *The Journal of Negro History*, 1920, p. 98.

Chapter 13

Conclusion and Summary

African Americans have been employed in law enforcement earlier than many historians and law enforcement experts have recorded. As this study indicates, in Newmarket, New Hampshire, an African American held various law enforcement positions such as justice of the peace and coroner during the Colonial era. Before the Civil war, in the North as well as in the South, African Americans were among those who maintained law and order. Regarding Southern states, it was in Louisiana where we found that African Americans performed police work in addition to the militia duties. But during the wars, African Americans were included in the militia of many states for the preservation of peace and security against the enemies of the United States. This was the case in the War of 1812. In 1840s Florida, African Americans were among militiamen who served the interests of the United States.

In the beginning of the military Reconstruction, African Americans, by the order of the generals, were included in law enforcement agencies in many states in the South. As early as 1867, African Americans were appointed justices of the peace, police officers, magistrates, and registrar officers. After the framing of the Reconstruction constitutions of many former Confederate states, African Americans were fully included in various agencies of law enforcement such as the police, courts, prisons, and other regulatory agencies at the local, state, and federal levels. Throughout Southern states, except Georgia, African Americans were able to hold many positions in the local level where they were the majority. This was true in Mississippi during the Republican administration. In Edgecombe County, North Carolina, African Americans were also dominant politically in some wards.

Bibliography

Primary Sources

Data on African American law enforcement officers during the Reconstruction period were collected from the city directories of various towns in the states under Reconstruction policy.

Similarly, from the city directories facts on African American policemen and regulators in Washington, D.C., Indianapolis, Indiana, and Memphis, Knoxville, and Nashville, Tennessee, were collected from the city directories in addition to secondary sources.

Ancestry Com. U.S. City Directory, 1822–1995 [Database on–line] Provo, UT, USA: Ancestry.Com Operations, Inc., 2011. Original Data: Original sources vary according to directory. The title of the specific directory being viewed is listed at the top of the image page.

The United States Census of 1870 for the selected names of African American law enforcement officers.

Secondary Sources

Anderson, Eric. *Race and Politics in North Carolina, 1872–1901: The Black Second.* Baton Rouge: LSU Press, 1981.

Armistead, Wilson. *A Tribute for the Negro.* Negro University Press, 1848.

Bradford, Sarah O. *Scenes in the Life of Harriet Tubman.* W.J. Moses, Printers, 1869.

Brown, Carter. *Florida's Black Public Officials, 1867–1924.* University of Alabama Press, 1998.

Brown, William W. *The Negro in the American Rebellion: His Heroism and His Fidelity.* Lee & Shepard, 1867.

Burges, John W. *The Civil War and the Constitution, 1859–1865,* vol. 2. C. Scribner's Sons, 1901.

Coffin, Charles C. *Four Years of Fighting.* Ticknor and Fields, 1866.

Cox, Samuel S. *Union-Disunion-Reunion. Three Decades of Federal Legislation.* Punan Knoccuk, 1904.

Danning, William A. *Reconstruction, Political and Economic, 1865–1877*, vol.22. Harper & Brothers, 1877.

Du Bois, W.E.B. *Black Reconstruction in America 1860–1880.* Simon and Schuster, 1935.

Dulaney, Marvin W. *Black Police in America.* Indiana University Press, 1996.

Duncan, Russell. *Freedom's Shore: Tunis Campbell and the Georgia Freedmen.* University of Georgia Press, 1986.

Emilio, Luis F. *History of the Fifty-Fourth Regiment of Massachusetts Volunteer Infantry, 1863- 1865.* Boston Book Company, 1894.

Fertig, James W. *The Secession and the Reconstruction of Tennessee.* The University of Chicago Press, 1898.

Ficklen, John R., and Pierce Butler. *History of Reconstruction in Louisiana (Through 1868).* Johns Hopkins, 1911

Fleming, Walter L. *Civil War and Reconstruction in Alabama.* Columbia University Press, 1905.

Fleming, Walter L. *Documentary History of Reconstruction, Political, Military, Social, Religious, Educational & Industrial, 1865 to the Present Time*, vol.2. A.H. Clark Company, 1907.

Foner, Eric. *Freedom's Lawmakers: A Directory of Black Officeholders during Reconstruction.* New York: Oxford University Press, 1993.

Garner, James W. *Reconstruction in Mississippi.* Macmillan, 1902.

Gibbs, Mifflin W. *Shadow and Light: An Autobiography with Reminiscences of the Last and Present Century*, vol.3. N.W. Gibbs, 1902.

Gillett, James B. *Six Years with the Texas Rangers, 1875 to 1881.* Von Boeckmann. Jones Company, 1921.

Greeley, Horace. *The American Conflict: A History of the Great Rebellion in the United States of America, 1860–65.* O.D. Case, 1867.

Hamilton, Joseph Gregoire de R. *Reconstruction in North Carolina.* Columbia University, 1914.

Harden, William. *A History of Savannah and South Georgia*, vol. 2. Lewis Publishing Company, 1913.

Hazelton, Joseph P. *Scouts, Spies, and Heroes of the Great Civil War.* Providence, R.I. W.W. Thompson & Co., 1893.

Higginson, Thomas W. *Army Life in a Black Regiment.* Boston: Field, Osgood, & Co., 1870.

Holt, Thomas C. *Black over White: Negro Political Leadership in South Carolina during Reconstruction.* University of Illinois Press, 1977.

Hurd, John C. *The Law of Freedom and Bondage in the United States*, vol.2. Little, Brown, 1862.

Jackson, Luther P. *Negro Office Holders in Virginia, 1865–1895.* Norfolk, Guide Press, 1945.

James, A.R., Standard History of Memphis, Tennessee: From a Study of the Original Sources. H.W. Crew, 1912.

Jervery, Theodore D. *The Slave Trade. Slavery and Color.* Columbia, S.C. The State Company, 1925.

Johnson, Edward A. *History of Negro Soldiers in the Spanish American War: And other Items of Interest.* Capital Printing Company, 1899.

Keating, John M. and O.F. Veeder. *History of the City of Memphis and Shelby County, Tennessee: With Illustrations and Biographical Sketches of some of its Prominent Citizens*, vol.1, D. Mason & Company, 1888.

King, Edward. *The Great South.* American Publishing Company, 1875.

King, Grace E. *New Orleans: The Place and the People.* Macmillan, 1896.

Langston, John M., *From the Virginia Plantation to the National Capital, Or, The Only Negro Representative in Congress, from the Old Dominion.* American Publishing, 1894.

Lonn, Ella, *Reconstruction in Louisiana.* G.P. Putnam's Sons, 1918.

Lynch, John R. *The Facts of the Reconstruction.* Neale Publishing Company, 1913.

Scott, Mingo. *The Negro in Tennessee Politics and Governmental Affairs.* Nashville: Rich Printing Company, 1964.

Nordhoff, Charles. *The Cotton States in the Spring and Summer of 1875.* B. Franklin, 1876.

Phillips, Ulrich B. *American Slavery: A Survey of the Supply, Employment and Control of Negro Labor as Determined by the Plantation Regime.* 1918; Baton Rouge, 1966.

Reynolds, John S. *Reconstruction in South Carolina, 1865–1877.* Columbia, S.C.: The State Co., 1905.

Robinowitz, Howard N., "The Conflict between Blacks and the Police in the Urban South, 1865 1900." *The Historian*, 39 (November, 1976): 64–66.

Rousey, Dennis C. *Policing the Southern City, New Orleans 1805–1889.* Baton Rouge: Louisiana State University Press, 1996.

Rousey, Dennis C. "Black Policemen in New Orleans during Reconstruction." *The Historian*, 49 (February, 1987): 223-243.

Rowland, Dunbar. *Official Letter Books of W.C.C. Claiborne 1801–1816*, vol.2. State Archives and History, 1917.

Satcher, Buford. *Blacks in Mississippi Politics 1865–1900*. University Press of America, 1978.

Sewell, George A. *Mississippi Black History Makers*. Jackson: University Press of Mississippi, 1977.

Vincent, Charles. *Black Legislators in Louisiana during Reconstruction*. Louisiana State University Press, Baton Rouge, 1976.

Wallace, John. *Carpetbag Rule in Florida*. Da Costa Printing and Publishing House, 1888.

Washington, Booker T. *The Story of the Negro: The Rise of the Race from Slavery*, vol. 2. Association Press, 1908.

Wharton, Vernon L., *The Negro in Mississippi, 1865–1890*. The James Sprunt Studies in History and Political Science. Chapel Hill: University of North Carolina Press, 1947.

Wooter, Dudley G. *A Complete History of Texas for Schools, Colleges, and General Use*. The Texas History Company, 1899.

Index

CPSIA information can be obtained
at www.ICGtesting.com
Printed in the USA
LVHW091524210121
677111LV00016B/562/J

9 780998 971667